M.

For the third time since World

W   onal

C

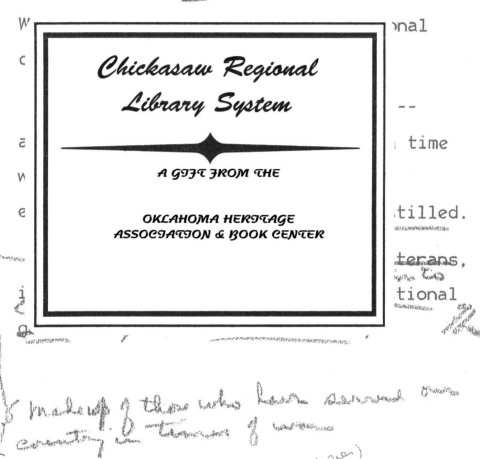

Chickasaw Regional Library System

A GIFT FROM THE

OKLAHOMA HERITAGE
ASSOCIATION & BOOK CENTER

--

time

tilled.

terans,

tional

BRYCE HARLOW

BRYCE HARLOW

MR. INTEGRITY

BY BOB BURKE AND RALPH G. THOMPSON

FOREWORD BY DR. HENRY KISSINGER

KENNY A. FRANKS **SERIES EDITOR**
GINI MOORE CAMPBELL **ASSOCIATE EDITOR**

OKLAHOMA HERITAGE ASSOCIATION

OKLAHOMA **TRACKMAKER** SERIES

OTHER BOOKS

BY BOB BURKE:

Lyle Boren: Rebel Congressman
3,500 Years of Burkes
These Be Thine Arms Forever
The Stories and Speeches of Lyle H. Boren
Corn, Cattle, and Moonshine:
    A History of Hochatown, Oklahoma
Like a Prairie Fire
Push Back the Darkness
The Irish Connection
Lyle H. Boren: The Eloquent Congressman
Dewey F. Bartlett: The Bartlett Legacy
Glen D. Johnson, Sr.: The Road to Washington
An American Jurist:
    The Life of Judge Alfred P. Murrah
Mike Monroney: Oklahoma Liberal
Roscoe Dunjee: Champion of Civil Rights
From Oklahoma to Eternity:
    The Life of Wiley Post and the Winnie Mae
Out From the Shadows: The Life of John J. Harden
Glory Days of Summer: The History of Baseball
    in Oklahoma
Abe Lemons: Court Magician
Alice Robertson: Congresswoman from Oklahoma
Victor Wickersham: Your Best Friend
Historic Oklahoma
A Passion for Equality: The Life of Jimmy Stewart

Printed in the United States of America

ISBN 1-885596-15-4

LC Number 99-69684

Designed by Carol Haralson

OKLAHOMA HERITAGE ASSOCIATION
201 NORTHWEST FOURTEENTH STREET
OKLAHOMA CITY, OKLAHOMA 73103

Photographs:
Harlow addresses the Bryce Harlow Foundation
dinner following remarks by Vice President
George Bush in 1983. Courtesy Emmett W.
Hines, Jr.

After Harlow presented a final draft of a speech
or statement to President Dwight D. Eisenhower,
he personally approved it for final typing. The
President wrote on this proposed D-Day
statement in 1954, "OK, Type and give to Jim
H. [Press Secretary James Hagerty], DE."
Courtesy Dwight D. Eisenhower Library.

THIS BOOK IS DEDICATED TO INTEGRITY IN
PUBLIC AFFAIRS AND TO THE MEMORY OF
BRYCE HARLOW WHO WAS UNSURPASSED IN
EXEMPLIFYING THAT PRICELESS QUALITY.

OUR GREATEST REWARD WILL BE IF HIS
EXAMPLE, AS REPORTED HERE, SERVES AS AN
INSPIRATION TO OTHERS OF GENERATIONS TO
COME.

CONTENTS

PROPOSED D-DAY STATEMENT

This day is the tenth anniversary of the landing of the Allied

Expeditionary Force in Normandy. That combined land-sea-air operation

was made possible by the joint labors of cooperating nations. It

depended for its success upon the skill, determination and self-

sacrifice of men from several lands. It set in motion a chain of

events which affected the history of the entire world.

Despite the losses and suffering involved in that human effort,

and in the epic conflict of which it was a part, we today find in those

experiences reasons for hope and inspiration. They remind us particularly

of the accomplishments attainable through close cooperation and friendship

among free peoples striving toward a common goal. Some of my most

cherished memories of that campaign are those of friendly cooperation

with such distinguished military leaders of foreign nations as Field

Marshal Montgomery, Admiral Ramsay, Marshal of the Royal Air

Force Tedder, Marshal DeLattre de Tassigny, Marshal Juin and General

LeClerc. I recall my pleasant association with the outstanding Soviet

soldier, Marshal Zhukov, and the victorious meeting at the Elbe of the

Armies of the West and of the East.

Writing the biography of a great American patriot like Bryce Harlow is a challenging undertaking. His influence permeated the administrations of several United States Presidents. Because Harlow vowed to never write a book about his experiences in government, we were left to weave the story of his life and contributions to our democracy from mountains of information in his files in two presidential libraries and from personal interviews with dozens of important figures in American history with whom he worked.

The willingness of people to participate in the writing of Harlow's biography was heartwarming. Time and again, the famous, and not so famous, went beyond our expectations to recall Harlowisms, dig deep into their archives for proof of Harlow's imprint upon history, or recommend still another name of someone whose life was impacted by Harlow.

We are indeed grateful to many people who helped make this book possible.

Harlow's widow, Sally, and his children, Peggy, Trudy, and Larry were gracious with information, photos, and encouragement. Procter & Gamble Vice President Jane Fawcett-Hoover and corporative archivist Edward M. Rider provided photos and historical documents from Harlow's time with the company.

Some of America's most important public servants and captains of industry in the second half of the 20th century allowed us interviews. Without their information, the Harlow story could not adequately be written. Those who granted interviews and provided information were President Gerald R. Ford; President George Bush; Chief Justice William H. Rehnquist; Robert Dole; Dr. Henry Kissinger; George P. Shultz; James A. Baker, III; Donald Rumsfeld; Melvin R. Laird; Lamar Alexander; Howard H.

Baker, Jr.; John J. Rhodes; General Andrew J. Goodpaster; Brigadier General John S. D. Eisenhower; Henry Bellmon; David L. Boren; Robert Bennett; Robert H. Michel; Patrick J. Buchanan; Corinne C. Lindy Boggs; Hugh Sidey; William B. Ewald, Jr.; Stephen H. Hess; Martin Anderson; Lyn Nofziger; William Safire; Clyde A. Wheeler, Jr.; Don V. Cogman; Jonathan Rose; Emmett W. Hines, Jr.; Edward A. McCabe; Allan Cromley; Claude E. Hobbs; William H. Darden; James D. "Mike" McKevitt; Charles Colson; Tom C. Korologos; J. R. Morris; David J. Elliott; Mrs. John R. Gomien; William B. Prendergast; William G. Whyte; Don Goodall; Henry Roemer McPhee; Gary Hymel; Victor Gold; and W. DeVier Pierson.

Gems of information came from Chris LaRocco, Executive Director of the Bryce Harlow Foundation; Archivists Herbert L. Pankratz, David Haight, and Dwight Strandberry at the Dwight D. Eisenhower Library at Abilene, Kansas; Kevin Lynch and staff at the Bryce Harlow Institute on Business and Government Affairs at Georgetown University at Washington, D.C.; the staff of the Gerald R. Ford Library at Ann Arbor, Michigan; the staff at the Richard M. Nixon Library at Yorba Linda, California; the Columbia University Oral History Collection; and archivists Gregory Goodell and Pat Anderson at the National Archives, College Park, Maryland.

In Oklahoma, Eric Dabney and Debi Engles assisted us in research and transcription of interviews. Sharon Henshall ably handled correspondence and coordination of interviews. Carol Campbell, Mary Phillips, Robin Davison, Billie Harry, and Melissa Hayer at the Oklahoma Publishing Company library provided valuable photos, as did Chester Cowen at the Oklahoma Historical Society.

Mary Hardin, Kitty Pittman, Steve Beleu, Adrienne Abrams, Melecia Caruthers, Carol Guilliams, and Marilyn Miller always make research at the Oklahoma Department of Libraries enjoyable and fruitful.

Bill Welge, Rodger Harris, and Judith Michener at the Oklahoma Historical Society pointed us in the right direction many times during the massive research.

We are grateful to have the artistic talent of Carol Haralson in the design and layout of the book. She is the best in the business. Dr. Kenny Franks and Gini Moore Campbell are expert editors who guided our progress as the work took shape.

Thanks to Oklahoma Heritage Association Chairman of the Board Lee Allan Smith and President Paul Lambert for totally supporting the preservation of Oklahoma's great heritage.

BOB BURKE

RALPH G. THOMPSON

MARCH, 2000

In his classic book of advice to young rulers, Machiavelli cautioned that "the great majority of mankind are often more influenced by things that seem than by those that are." Today's rulers have most of the problems Machiavelli wrote about, but in particular, they can ill afford any confusion between appearances and reality.

To guard against such confusion, every great leader requires the services of a few trusted advisors. When we wish to be unkind, we refer to them as Machiavellis. When we wish to be generous, they are known as Elder Statesmen. No matter... it is all the same. Such individuals must possess a special gift to find reality among conflicting points of view and a special kind of relationship to the leader they serve.

One of the most revealing things about Bryce Harlow is that he served an amazing number of leaders of our nation: Two Presidents officially and four Presidents unofficially, two great military leaders, and Congressional leaders too numerous to mention. His eleven years of service in the White House as a key presidential advisor are matched by few others in the history of that institution.

This book details the life and times of Bryce, whom I came to know and admire when I first joined the Nixon White House as National Security advisor. At every stage of my career, and especially in times of crisis, I turned to Bryce for advice and counsel, as I have repeatedly illustrated in my memoirs.

Bryce's beginnings are not unlike those of many others. However, when you start reading about his staff work for General George C. Marshall, his work as a War Department liaison with Congress, his role as assistant librarian for the House of Representatives, his responsibilities as an aide to an Oklahoma congressman, his leadership as Chief of Staff of the House Committee on

Armed Services, and ultimately his major role as counselor and senior advisor to Presidents, you soon discover that you have something very special here. Bryce Harlow, you see, did all of these things and then virtually single-handedly created the entire modern advocacy industry.

During his 24 years of federal service, Bryce Harlow was in and out of the White House, in and out of congressional offices, and in and out of the private sector so often that it was almost difficult to keep track. The problem was that Presidents, Congressmen, industrial giants, and anybody who was anybody in the business of government in Washington sought and "required" his advice and counsel. And Bryce heard the call and responded.

During his federal service Bryce Harlow was the most respected expert of unquestioned ability and integrity in every aspect of life in Washington, D.C. His every act brought credit to his country and to those institutions he served, whether the military services, the legislative branch, various administrations, or the business community.

The names of national leaders he served have become legendary in the history of the Republic. If each were able to pen a foreword for this history they would write that those legends were created in part by the sturdy fabric of reality woven day by day by Bryce Harlow.

DR. HENRY A. KISSINGER

BRYCE HARLOW

Bryce Harlow as a high school sophomore in January, 1930. Courtesy *The Daily Oklahoman.*

President Lyndon B. Johnson (LBJ) was on the telephone. Suddenly, a wide-eyed secretary whispered, "Mr. Harlow, President Eisenhower is calling." Harlow put his hand over the receiver and said, "Tell him I'll call right back, or put him on hold." Harlow continued to listen to the Texas drawl of LBJ as the phone blinked with President Dwight D. Eisenhower on hold. In ran another aide with a frightful look on his face. "Mr. Harlow, Mr. Harlow. The president-elect wants you in his office immediately."

Just how important was one man whose counsel was demanded simultaneously by a former president, a sitting president, and a future president?

The scene was November, 1968, at New York City's Pierre Hotel, the transition headquarters of newly-elected President Richard Nixon. Harlow, whose influence within the power circles in the nation's capital was legendary, had been called in by Nixon to piece together a transition team that would take over the White House and the leadership of the free world in two short months.

✦

The Harlow name was important in Oklahoma long before Bryce Nathaniel Harlow was even a glimmer in the eye of his father.

Victor Emmanuel Harlow (1876-1958) was born in Chantilly, Missouri. His mother, Mary Adeline (Davis) Harlow, was the daughter of one of the early settlers of Missouri. His father, James Harlow, was a country doctor. His ancestors, primarily Scottish and English-American, were philosophers, poets, writers, physicians, ministers, and lawyers. One ancestor, Matthew Thornton, even signed the Declaration of Independence.

Victor Harlow was something of a child prodigy, learning to read at age two and writing for the local newspaper at age eight. When he was 10, a book of his poetry was published and at 15 he taught in a county school. By the time Harlow was 20, he had earned degrees from colleges in La Grange, Missouri, and Alton, Illinois, and had become a college professor of Latin and Greek. At age 22, he was chosen president of Webb City College, in Webb City, Missouri, making him the youngest college president in America of his time.

Victor Harlow read everything from the classics to murder mysteries, and he absorbed all he read. Impelled by a student's instinct, he explored the fields of literature, music, science, art, economics, and religion.[1] While at Webb City, Harlow married May Van Hooser in 1900 and fathered two children, Victor and William. After May died in 1903, Harlow questioned his religious beliefs and rejected teachings of the orthodox church in which he had claimed membership. He turned to philosophy for answers, gave up teaching, and became editor of a newspaper in Alton, Illinois. However, Harlow's love of teaching returned him to Webb City within a few months.[2]

May Harlow's older sister, Emma, helped Harlow care for his small children. Emma was a gifted teacher of music and drama. She and Harlow, an accomplished violinist, formed a sought-after musical team that often traveled to the newly-opened Cherokee Strip, later Oklahoma, to play in orchestras. Harlow admired great music so much that he sacrificed to save money to finance weekly trips to Enid to play his violin with other talented musicians.

In 1904 Professor Harlow made a permanent move to what would become Oklahoma. He was named Principal of Northwestern Academy, a school established at the town of Carrier, ten miles northwest of Enid, in 1898 by the Congregational Home Missionary Society of Boston, Massachusetts. The institution was an educational, religious, and cultural center of the Cherokee Strip and

Victor Harlow was a philosopher, an adorer of truth. He never was too busy or too preoccupied with his own life to miss an opportunity to propound his views of religion to other persons in difficulty. He died October 6, 1958. Courtesy *The Daily Oklahoman.*

Rex Harlow joined his brothers Victor and Jonathan in establishing Harlow Publishing Company, the only general publishing house in the Southwest in the years immediately following World War I. Courtesy *The Daily Oklahoman.*

was considered a feeder school for Kingfisher College, established at Kingfisher, Oklahoma Territory, in 1895. Northwestern Academy consisted of three frame buildings located on a ten-acre tract donated by local citizens. Among its early students was Lizzie Pharies, the mother of Dr. Paul Sharp, who later became president of the University of Oklahoma.[3]

Harlow accepted the Northwestern Academy position on one condition, that his sister-in-law Emma Van Hooser be hired as drama and music professor.[4] School officials complied with the request.

Within weeks of his arrival in Carrier, Harlow founded the town's first newspaper. He wanted to become a full-time publisher and writer so in 1906 he left his job at Northwestern Academy and established a newspaper in Enid, Oklahoma.

At Oklahoma statehood, he became campaign manager for Charles West, an Enid attorney and friend of Harlow who became Oklahoma's first attorney general. With a whirlwind campaign win under his belt, Harlow's stock was on the rise. His brother, Rex, later wrote, "Henceforth he was recognized as one of the political leaders of Oklahoma. His keen, analytical mind, energy, and resourcefulness made him very valuable to the Democratic party, and he was received with open arms into the inner circle of its leaders."[5]

When the new state government was formed, Harlow was appointed secretary of the new Board of Public Affairs, which he largely organized. A few months later, Harlow bought a newspaper in Shawnee, Oklahoma, the *Shawnee Daily Herald.* The community was in the middle of a boom, a boom that burst, along with Harlow's paper, within a year. Harlow bought the paper back from a court-appointed receiver, and made it profitable again.

In 1911 Harlow married Gertrude Gindling and entered the printing business, as the Harlow-Ratliff Printing Company, in Oklahoma City. The following year he founded a new and unique newspaper, a weekly publication called *Harlow's Weekly.* For the next three decades *Harlow's Weekly* was a mother lode of information on Oklahoma political, social, and economic developments. Harlow had an uncanny sense of what was going on at the State Capitol and often scooped larger newspapers with predictions of major political events and decisions. His reporting on political races and the behind-the-scenes maneuvering in state government was accurate and thought-provoking.

In 1915 Harlow founded the Harlow Publishing Company in Oklahoma City. Assisted by his brothers, Rex and Jonathan, Harlow used his contacts with politicians to land printing contracts with state government agencies. He housed his presses and editors in a building at 531 Northwest Second Street (later Couch Drive) in downtown Oklahoma City. The first book to bear the Harlow imprint was *Skinkah,* a book of poetry. Harlow Publishing won a lucrative contract in 1917 to publish *Oklahoma Reports,* the official version of cases decided by the Oklahoma Supreme Court and Court of Criminal Appeals. Until the 1960s Harlow Publishing was a leading textbook and historical publisher in Oklahoma. Harlow's *Oklahoma Leaders* and *Oklahoma's Young Leaders* continue to serve as major sources of biographical information about many of Oklahoma's pioneers.

Harlow published several of his own writings. In 1924, his *Jesus, the Man* was called by the *New York Times* one of the four most significant books ever published about Christ. The book was a result of 30 years of study and Harlow's devotion to the Unitarian Church. A decade later Harlow published a history of Oklahoma. His brother Rex became a well-known and successful author of childrens' books.[6]

Harlow's marriage to Gertrude Gindling produced four children. Harlow taught them well. He, and his wife, who opened a school for gifted children in their home, instilled their children with a love for the classics. Harlow expounded on philosophy and taught his offspring to think. For each child he set the pattern for inquisitiveness and mental trail-blazing.[7]

Their firstborn, James G. Harlow, was the youngest graduate in the history of Oklahoma City's Central High School. He was president of Harlow Publishing Company, executive director of the Oklahoma Frontiers of Science Foundation, dean of the University of Oklahoma College of Education, and president of West

Victor Harlow, Jr. also entered the printing business with his father in Oklahoma City. Courtesy *The Daily Oklahoman.*

Below: Gerturde Harlow, left, was named Oklahoma Mother of the Year in 1959. Here she receives her citation from Judge Tom Brett. Courtesy *The Daily Oklahoman.*

Gertrude Harlow, right, and daughter Dorothea.

Virginia University. His son, James G. Harlow, Jr., rose through the ranks to become president, chief executive officer, and chairman of the board of Oklahoma Gas and Electric Company and was considered a giant among Oklahoma's civic and industrial leaders. As chairman of the board of the Edison Electric Institute, a trade association of American utilities, he became known worldwide for his leadership in the field of electric utilities. Four Harlows, Bryce; James G.; James G., Junior; and his wife, Jane, an Oklahoma City civic leader and distinguished Oklahoman, have been inducted into the Oklahoma Hall of Fame. No other family in state history has such representation in the Hall of Fame.

Victor and Gertrude Harlow had two other children, John and Dorothea, over the next three years. Then on August 11, 1916, a bouncing baby boy named Bryce Nathaniel Harlow was born in Oklahoma City.

Like his siblings, Bryce was extremely intelligent. By the age of three, his mother had taught him to read numerous juvenile books. He developed a love of history by talking to his father about historical figures and events and reading Harlow Publishing

Company books. Bryce started school at age six but was placed in the third grade. Even though he was by far the youngest in his class, Bryce still had more reading ability than any of his classmates. By age nine he was in junior high school and graduated from Central High School at age 16. He loved airplanes and openly expressed to his family that he might want to be an airplane mechanic or a college president. Bryce believed he was equipped for either job.

Bryce's quest for knowledge was almost unquenchable. He began his studies at the University of Oklahoma in earnest and completed his bachelor's degree program in three and a half years. He graduated from OU in 1936, at age 19, with numerous honors, including Phi Beta Kappa. He was also captain of the varsity tennis team. On the day Bryce graduated from OU, he told his mother, "I wish I could spend four more years here—there's so much more to learn."[8]

James G. Harlow, Jr., and his wife Jane promoted Oklahoma and its heritage by participating in numerous civic and charitable causes. Courtesy *The Daily Oklahoman.*

Dr. James G. Harlow was named West Virginian of the Year in 1975 for his leadership as president of West Virginia University. Courtesy *The Daily Oklahoman.*

Even though Bryce spent most of his college time studying, he did have an occasion to meet a special girl, Betty Larimore. Bryce met Betty through her sister, Phoebe. The Larimore girls were prominent in the OU Kappa Alpha Theta sorority. Bryce and Betty dated infrequently as Bryce worked long hours for his father at Harlow Publishing in the summers. By age 20, Bryce reached his adult height of only five feet four inches.

During the summer after college graduation Bryce considered his options. His father wanted him to remain in the publishing business. However, Bryce opted to continue his education and enrolled at the University of Texas at Austin to pursue a master's degree in government.

Bryce entered, and won, a model-plane flying contest in Oklahoma City in 1929. Courtesy *The Daily Oklahoman.*

After a year in Texas, Bryce moved back to Oklahoma City and was admitted to the master's program in government at OU. He attended classes in the mornings and worked at Harlow Publishing in the afternoons. On many evenings one could find Bryce with Betty, either studying or taking in a movie on campus corner.

In 1938 Bryce decided to write his master's thesis on the workings of the Ways and Means Committee of the United States House of Representatives. To get firsthand knowledge of the actual operation of the Committee, Bryce looked for a legislative position that would place him in the middle of congressional action. His father's influence with the Oklahoma congressional delegation en-

Betty Larimore was a junior at the University of Oklahoma in 1937. Courtesy *The Daily Oklahoman*.

abled Bryce to be appointed as a member of the House library staff. As an assistant librarian, Bryce's authority level was just below that of the doorman.

Bryce arrived in Washington, D.C., in September, 1938, on the evening train at Union Station. He thought of his future as he stepped off the train, walked briskly through the mass of people, and headed for a hotel. He intended to stay in Washington only long enough to complete the research for his dissertation. He planned to return to Oklahoma within a year and teach in the public schools. Luckily for America, his stay in the nation's capital would be much longer.

ON-THE-JOB TRAINING

HARLOW WAS A PERSON WHO WAS NEVER INVOLVED IN BUMPS
IN RELATIONSHIPS. WHEN HE WAS IN A ROOM, THE GEARS
TENDED TO MESH SMOOTHLY RATHER THAN GRIND.

DONALD RUMSFELD

The Ways and Means Committee was first established by
House rules in 1802 as one of five standing committees in the
United States House of Representatives. Many congressional observers believe it is among the most powerful committees in Congress. Its members, elected by the majority party caucus, serve as a
committee to select members of other important House committees. During the session, Ways and Means Committee members
exercise the important function of devising means of raising revenue to run the massive federal government.

Bryce Harlow chose the Ways and Means Committee as the
subject of his master's thesis after reading everything he could find
about the internal workings of Congress and talking with Oklahoma Congressman Wesley E. Disney, a close friend of Victor
Harlow.

Harlow was genuinely unqualified to serve as an assistant librarian in the House. That did not matter because Harlow soon
found out that "under the patronage system, the House librarian
had nothing at all to do. He did that with a high order of skill."[1]

Harlow went about his task as House assistant librarian with a
passion. He arrived early and stayed late. He worked on his mas-

ter's thesis in the mornings. But when the House went into session at noon, he spent every minute he could observing the congressional process, listening to every whisper and shout of debate. He had total access to the floor of the House and memorized names of congressmen and the districts they represented. Harlow worked for the staff librarian of the House, "a man with a fourth-grade education who loved cruelty, the meanest man who ever lived, worse than Dracula, Nero, and Herod."[2]

In a speech much later in his career, Harlow described the House librarian, "He weighed some 240 pounds and looked as fiercely indomitable and as distinguished as Charles Evans Hughes. He had ridden with the posses out west—in Oklahoma Territory, the days of the real New Frontier. He had served two terms in the state legislature when the members still toted guns right up to the chamber door. He was tough and mean, unlettered and grandly primitive."[3]

A sad experience for Harlow came during his first six months on the House staff. A fellow assistant librarian, despondent over losing his job because of the death of his congressional sponsor, hanged himself with a rope strung between bookshelves in a room adjacent to where Harlow worked on his master's thesis.

Harlow thought the suicide such a pity that he railed about the patronage system in a letter to columnist Drew Pearson. Harlow's point was that while Congress was "self-righteously enacting the Hatch Act to keep the Executive Branch employees politically undefiled, there skulking beneath the Congressional halo was the character-eroding, sleazy patronage system."[4] Pearson never acknowledged Harlow's letter.

From his post as assistant librarian, Harlow was able to observe firsthand the complex dealings of the Ways and Means Committee. He interviewed all its members and reviewed the legion of bills and proposals that came before the body. He used the information gleaned from long hours of work to write a weekly column for his father's *Harlow's Weekly.* The column, entitled "Oklahoma News in Washington," was a detailed description of the activities of Oklahoma's congressional delegation and a progress report on legislation of interest to Oklahoma. Harlow also was laying the foundation for a long career in the federal government. In his future years at the very seat of power, every position he held was linked to the lessons he learned on the House floor.[5]

Harlow's library experience was a superb political science laboratory. He discovered that each congressman had at least one exceptional quality, whether it be an imposing physical appearance, debating prowess, intellectual competence, expertise in a given area, or even just a story-telling skill. As he watched party leaders at work, from Speaker John Bankhead to Majority Leader Sam Rayburn and Majority Whip John McCormack, and observed committee chairmen "adroitly pilot their bills around parliamentary shoals," Harlow's "faculty-implanted sneer" of contempt for Congress began to fade away. He developed a profound respect for the legislative process.

Harlow revered Speaker Bankhead, "The towering prestige of the Speaker came to life as day after day, an arm's length away, I watched him in action. Never again would he be a shadowy figure with a dry-as-dust list of meaningless duties which one commits to memory in beginning civics. When on critical legislative occasions he would leave the Speaker's chair to address the House, the hush that would fall upon the chamber, the deference accorded him, the party unity thus engendered, profoundly impressed this wide-eyed youngster from out West."[6]

Harlow observed Majority Whip McCormack's happy fencing across the political aisle with Republican Whip Charles Halleck and Everett Dirksen; the surprising mastery of legislative detail by senior committee members; the frenzy of Democratic and Republican whips as they rallied their troops for critical votes; the hubbub of lobbyists at every entrance of the House; the unending logrolling among the members; the parliamentary trickery of veteran congressmen; the quiet but pervasive influence of the House parliamentarian; and the pyramiding frustrations and futile flailings of freshmen congressmen.[7]

The United States House of Representatives was far different in the 1930s than the House portrayed to the American people at the close of the 20th century. Staffs were small, there was less strain on congressmen and their staff. Most congressmen had only two staff members. Congressman Jacob Javits, Republican from New York, represented the largest district in the country with a staff of four people.

At the end of the congressional session in 1939, Harlow put his observations of personnel, organization, and procedure of the Ways and Means Committee into his master's thesis, which won immediate acclaim from leaders of the House. Veteran Committee members praised Harlow for capturing the true spirit of the congressional process and suggested that the thesis be issued as a public document. Harlow submitted his thesis for consideration of his major advisers at the University of Oklahoma, Dr. Royden J. Dangerfield and Dr. Oliver Benson. The thesis sailed through the approval process but Harlow's masters in government would not be officially awarded until 1942.

Congressman Disney, a member of the Ways and Means Committee, was so impressed with the work of his fellow Oklahoman that he offered Harlow a job on his staff. Harlow faced a crossroads in his life. Should he return to Oklahoma and marry Betty and follow his father's footsteps in the teaching profession? Should he continue his education at Harvard where he once intended to pursue a doctoral program? Or should he use the incredible wealth of knowledge he had obtained from thousands of hours of research for his thesis and stay on Capitol Hill? After several sleepless nights, he chose to stay in Washington and join Disney's staff for $40 a month more, "a major advance in salary in 1940."[8] Betty wholeheartedly agreed with the decision and told Harlow she would marry him within a year.

Disney, a Democrat, barely made it to Congress by upsetting Republican incumbent Charles O'Connor in the 1930 general election in Oklahoma's First Congressional District. Disney was re-elected for six more terms and served in the House until he retired at the end of the 1944 session.

Harlow joined a small staff of two other so-called congressional secretaries, a term that has evolved to what we now call legislative or administrative assistants. The secretaries were expected to work twelve hours a day at least three times a week, all day Saturdays, and usually Sunday mornings while Congress was in session. Days off were rare while lawmakers were in town. The work was hard but Harlow loved every minute of it. His spirit thrived on the back room negotiations, the analysis of bills before Disney's committees, and the rubbing of shoulders with the power brokers on Capitol Hill. Harlow was diminutive in size, but large in knowledge. He was only 23 years old but commanded respect from Democrats and Republican House members alike who recognized his grasp of the legislative process.

Harlow had learned the technical side of Congress from his job in the House librarian's office. His work with Congressman Disney introduced him to the other side of public service, the constituent. In a speech years after his service on Disney's staff, Harlow still recalled his recognition of who members of Congress were working for:

> It meant the old man in a shanty in the across-the-tracks area of Tulsa, Oklahoma, who once a month would pencil us letters. It meant the bank president, the chairman of a corporate board, the teachers, the doctors, the veterans. It meant the politicians, the farmers, the women, the school kids, the ministers and the Boy Scouts. It meant the interventionists, the isolationists, the Republicans, as well as the Democrats.[9]

Harlow played the part of congressional secretary with a passion. He never refused to talk to or answer a request from any of Disney's constituents. He listened to the pleas of a songwriter who indignantly demanded Disney compose the music for cowboy ballads he penned. When a patriotic society asked Disney for soil from the grounds of Mount Vernon, the Washington Monument, the Lincoln Memorial, and other hallowed spots around Washington, to put at the base of a brave, little cherry tree, Harlow "earned everlasting gratitude and doubtless scores of votes by sending neatly-labeled bottles of dirt of various colors and textures collected from an unpaved parking lot behind the Congressional Office Building."[10]

Harlow, a registered Democrat since he turned 21, was a bi-partisan early in his experience in Washington, D.C. He understood the partisan battles, but thought it silly for members to vote against legislation that would help their constituents back home just because a leader told them to vote no.

Harlow's service on Disney's congressional staff was during a critical period of American history. Europe was at war and America was slowly but surely being drawn into the conflict. Harlow shared his boss's convictions that the United States should financially support England and France against Adolph Hitler's armies but should avoid direct intervention in the war in Europe.

War clouds cast ever-lengthening shadows and Harlow often went sleepless, working and re-working legislation for Disney to take to the Ways and Means Committee which was searching for the right revenue measures to shore up America's defense.

As the country's military forces expanded, Harlow wondered if he should join the Reserve Officers Training Command (ROTC). He was deeply patriotic and thought more than once he should be serving in uniform. Finally Harlow joined the Army Reserve.

On September 25, 1940, Harlow and Betty were married in Oklahoma City. Now Harlow had two people to worry about as world conflict caused uncertainty about the future. He later kiddingly told friends he married Betty so he could eliminate the costly trips back and forth to Oklahoma to see her.

Harlow moved his bride to Washington and continued his work with Congressman Disney. Meanwhile, Betty took a job as a secretary on Capitol Hill to supplement the family income and give her an outlet to use her degree in journalism she had earned at the University of Oklahoma.

Even though Congressman Disney represented primarily Tulsans in Congress, he and other members of the Oklahoma delegation were deeply involved in having a military depot built somewhere in the Oklahoma City area. Harlow, through his family and business connections in Oklahoma, was helpful in pointing Oklahoma City leaders such as Chamber of Commerce Manager Stanley Draper and *The Daily Oklahoman* publisher E.K. Gaylord in the right direction at the War Department.

Congress approved a military appropriations bill in March, 1941, that provided funds for the construction of three military depots. The Secretary of War was empowered to select the sites for the depots. Oklahoma City went into action. Draper, Gaylord, and auto magnate Fred Jones called upon Harlow for recommendations of how to approach Army Air Corps officials who were looking at possible depot sites with their eyes on the availability of labor, housing, utility services, rail connections, and highway transportation needed to service a large military base. Harlow, who intimately knew the workings of the War Department, set up meetings between Oklahoma City leaders and decision-makers in the military and Department of War.[11]

Within a year, Oklahoma City was chosen as the site of a military depot. For nine months the facility was called Midwest Air Depot but was renamed Tinker Field, for Brigadier General Clarence Tinker of Pawhuska, Oklahoma, a part Osage, who was lost near Midway in the Pacific on a bombing mission.[12]

In July, 1941, five months before the United States would enter World War II after the bombing at Pearl Harbor, Harlow was placed on active duty as an officer in the public information office of Army Chief of Staff General George C. Marshall. Harlow wrote speeches for generals and crafted news releases for senior War Department personnel.

Harlow's secretarial skills won him an early place of importance in the eyes of Marshall. Harlow, whose shorthand was flawless, could be relied upon to take complete, accurate notes of highly confidential meetings involving America's military leaders.

In early 1942, Marshall formed a congressional relations division. Marshall, a tall, lean, vigorous man with blue eyes, and one of President Franklin D. Roosevelt's principal advisers on war strategy, recognized the importance of the military maintaining excellent relations with Congress. He was a long-time advocate of military readiness, a goal that could only be accomplished if the

Congress appropriated sufficient funds to expand America's armed forces. Marshall's job was difficult because many members of Congress rejected calls for the United States to actively involve itself in the fracas in Europe.[13]

Marshall appointed Brigadier General Wilton B. "Jerry" Persons to head the new office of congressional relations. Persons, a Harvard Business School graduate, had more than a decade of experience on Capitol Hill. As a junior officer stationed in Washington, D.C., Persons first met another junior officer, Dwight D. Eisenhower. Persons represented the War Department as liaison officer to Congress from 1933 to 1937. After two years of service outside Washington, Persons returned in 1939 as liaison between the Deputy Army Chief of Staff and Congress. When General Marshall created a comprehensive unit to handle relations with Congress, Persons was his choice to head the operation.

Persons' first move was to convince Harlow to join his staff because of Harlow's familiarity with many members of Congress and his knowledge of the legislative process.

Persons and Harlow were plowing new ground. It was the first time the American military establishment maintained an office with the specific responsibility to improve relations with Congress and keep the pipeline of communication open between the War Department and Capitol Hill.

Harlow enjoyed his assignment in the congressional relations office. He was in the middle of the war action on the home front. Across his desk came requests from battlefield commanders for more support from Congress. Inquiries from members of Congress directed to either President Roosevelt or the War Department ended up in Harlow's care. Many of the requests from legislators concerned assignment and promotion of soldiers.

In the wartime years, Harlow discovered, Congressional influence and power was "very real indeed."[14] Some members of Congress got "downright mean" over denials of promotions and assignments.

Harlow became the focal point for all significant Congressional mail on Army matters. The volume of mail engulfed him, but the plan worked like a charm. Harlow later described how the system worked, "Congressmen would telephone a request to me. I would likely have to say no. Then by phone or letter, with heightening frustration, they would start up the hierarchical line. Regardless of its addressee, each communication would come automatically to me to prepare the reply. Ever sweetly, but ever firmly, and ever over the other person's signature, back would go my initial no."[15]

As the war dragged on, contact between the Pentagon and Congress intensified. Pressure from the National Association for the Advancement of Colored People (NAACP) resulted in black soldiers fighting alongside their white counterparts, despite opposition from certain vocal congressmen. New York Democratic Congressman Hamilton Fish, who had commanded black troops in World War I, bitterly complained when Army commanders assigned black soldiers to work battalions and purposely held blacks from combat.[16]

Harlow was inundated with complaints from congressmen whose constituent soldiers were in active combat zones for long periods without relief. Harlow and other members of the congressional relations staff worked double shifts to answer the hundreds of letters and phone calls received each day. Letters were drafted for the signature of President Roosevelt, General Marshall, other commanders, the Secretary of War, and policy makers in the War Department.

Harlow was assigned the sensitive task of answering criticism of the Army's system of giving deferments to farmers and professional athletes. Deferment was a touchy issue at best. Congressmen and Senators from rural areas of the nation were afraid that too many young men would be drafted, leaving old folks to look after the farms. The same pressures for deferments came from urban legislators who were afraid skilled workers in plants would be forced to enlist, leaving war production lagging.

When columnist Drew Pearson and newscaster Walter Winchell accused the Army of taking better care of German prisoners-of-war than America's own fighting men, Harlow orchestrated a series of appearances by Secretary of War Henry L. Stimson and General Marshall before congressional committees investigating the allegations.[17]

General Marshall and General Persons leaned heavily upon Harlow to draft the proper diplomatic reply to all the Army's political correspondence. Harlow's unique writing ability also served Marshall in other areas. Each year at Christmas, Marshall asked Harlow to draft a different "Merry Christmas" letter to each of the 50 members of the military appropriations committees in both houses of Congress. Harlow enjoyed working for Marshall, of whom he spoke almost reverently, "He was almost Christ-like. His awesome self-discipline, poise, stern demeanor, and obvious selflessness made him a living symbol of the professional military code of honor."[18]

Most of Harlow's assignments during the war were serious in nature. But Harlow's ghost-writing role among the great figures of the war had its amusing moments. Once, Navy Secretary Frank Knox suggested to President Roosevelt that it would be a smart move to make New York City Mayor Fiorello LaGuardia a military governor in his native Italy.

Roosevelt passed the letter to Secretary of War Stimson who turned to Harlow for an answer. Harlow nosed around among War Department thinkers and then drafted for Stimson a tortured answer which rejected the Knox idea as inoffensively as possible. Stimson could not resist writing across the bottom of the letter, "Mr. President, please tell Frank I have no objection at all if he wants to make Fiorello an admiral of the Navy."[19]

With only a few years under his belt in the nation's capitol, in the midst of the fracas of power and influence, Harlow had already developed assets always welcome in government. He was smart, a hard worker, and unselfish. But his unshakable integrity overshadowed his other good qualities in making him a man that Washington never wanted to lose.

The Harlow family grew during the war. On January 11, 1943, Betty gave birth to Margery Gindling Harlow, the first of the couple's three children, nicknamed "Peggy" early in life. The baby's middle name was given in honor of her maternal grandmother.

A second baby girl was added to Harlow clan June 18, 1945, when Trudy Paxton Harlow was born at Columbia Hospital for Women in Washington. Her middle name Paxton was Harlow's mother's maiden name.

In January, 1946, Harlow left his Pentagon assignment and moved Betty, Peggy, and Trudy back to Oklahoma, to civilian life. Harlow became vice president of Harlow Publishing Company which prospered in textbook publishing, not only in Oklahoma, but across the region.

Back to Washington

What Will Rogers did for our ability to laugh at our problems, Harlow did for our ability to believe that we can solve our problems.

CLYDE A. WHEELER, JR.

Harlow's entry into the private business world in Oklahoma was short-lived. He and Betty enjoyed living in Oklahoma City near relatives and friends from college. He was challenged by his position as vice president of Harlow Publishing Company, which had become the largest textbook-publishing firm west of the Mississippi River. However, Harlow missed the hustle and bustle of Capitol Hill. In spirit, Harlow had never left Washington, D.C. His father had instilled in him a deep love and appreciation for the processes of government and public service. As Harlow managed the family's business, he read and absorbed stacks of newspaper and magazine accounts of the continuing saga of government in post-war America.

In 1946 Congress began a reorganization of its oversight and control of the United States military establishment. In the Congressional Reorganization Act of 1946, the House of Representatives combined its Naval Affairs and Military committees into one huge Armed Services Committee. As expected, there was a power struggle between committee chairmen, a struggle exacerbated by the 1946 general election in which Republicans won control of the House.

Congressman Walter G. "Ham" Andrews, Republican from New York, was chosen chairman of the new House Armed Services Committee. His Democratic colleague at the top of the seniority list was Carl Vinson from Georgia. One of the infant committee's first tasks was to hire an efficient and knowledgeable staff to guide members through hundreds of bills and thousands of amendments concerning America's military effort, that even in peace time, was eating up larger and larger chunks of the national budget.

Vinson, a veteran congressman, was for a decade chairman of the House Naval Affairs Committee and was considered a "long, loud, and lonely advocate of a big Navy."[1] Vinson's call for building up the United States Navy sufficiently to defend American possessions in the Atlantic and Pacific generally went unheeded until the country was cast into war by events at Pearl Harbor.

Brigadier General Wilton Persons, for whom Harlow had worked at the Pentagon, was a key adviser to the House Armed Services Committee on the matter of staffing. One of the first names Persons suggested to Chairman Andrews was that of Harlow. Persons told Andrews that Harlow knew everyone in the House and was known throughout Capitol Hill for his absolute honesty and straightforward approach of convincing members of Congress to swing to his position on pending legislation.

Harlow accepted Andrews' offer to join the Armed Services Committee staff. Harlow and Betty moved back to Washington in 1947 and found an apartment near the Capitol. As was his life-long *modus operandi,* Harlow jumped feet-first into his new responsibilities, reading everything possible to prepare him for the long hours and delicate conversations with Pentagon generals and congressional leaders.

America was at peace, but threats of uprisings in several pockets of instability in the world made strong defense a major priority of the administration of President Harry Truman and the 80th Congress. Harlow's primary job was to dissect proposed legislation and explain its provisions and implications to Armed Services Committee members who did not have sufficient time to study long and complicated bills.[2]

As a staff member of the Armed Services Committee, Harlow gained the respect of many leaders, both Democrat and Republican. He won the respect of House Speaker Sam Rayburn, Harlow's neighbor from north Texas. Harlow later described Rayburn as

> . . . tough and rough, and he scared people. He was a little man, and he daunted big men—came right up to their belt buckle, you know. He was tougher than any of them, an absolute leader. He humbled Lyndon Johnson—and that's pretty good. He did it through sheer personality, though he was able, too, and smart. You knew that you either worked with him or he'd kill you. And if you earned his enmity, you'd rue it.[3]

Harlow's judgment on the meaning and import of military legislation was generally accepted by members of the committee. One exception was an early run-in with rookie Congressman Lyndon B. Johnson of Texas, better known as LBJ. Johnson, who served as secretary to a Texas congressman before being elected to the House himself in 1946, had very little power and was prone to humiliate those around him who had even less power.

During a closed door session of the Armed Services Committee in 1947, Johnson asked Harlow if a minor item in a bill had been checked out with the federal agency that was affected by the provision. Harlow, with his unusually vast knowledge of the process and the agency, said Johnson need not worry about it. Johnson was furious, accusing Harlow of "acting like a congressman." LBJ ordered the bill be tabled "until the staff member finishes the job he was supposed to do."[4]

Harlow's compliance with Johnson's request did not placate the tall Texan. At the next staff meeting Johnson continued his tirade against Harlow who was infuriated and threatened to quit. Harlow told one committee member that he had had enough of Johnson's bullying and was going home to Oklahoma.

Congressman Vinson was told of Harlow's impending resignation and went to Harlow's office to persuade him to stay. When Harlow reiterated his intent to leave the committee staff, Vinson took him by the arm and headed to Speaker Rayburn's office. He sat Harlow down in the Speaker's Lobby, and summoned Johnson from the House floor. Vinson sat down between the two men and said, "Now Lyndon, you put on quite a show this morning. And now Bryce is going to quit... We can't have that. So you're going to tell him you're not going to do that anymore."[5] Johnson quickly apologized in a rare moment in American history when a future vice president and president was humbled before a staff assistant. Later when LBJ was elected to the Senate, and was looking for someone to head the Democrat Senate Policy Committee, he offered the position to Harlow. Harlow declined.

Harlow's close association with Vinson continued as Democrats reclaimed the majority in the House in 1948. As Vinson was elevated to the chairmanship of the House Armed Services Committee, Harlow was promoted to head the committee's growing staff. As staff director and majority counsel of the committee, Harlow's role in shaping national military affairs was enlarged because of his smooth working relationship with House members from both sides of the aisle.

Vinson became Harlow's mentor as the young Oklahoman immersed himself in the activities of the House Armed Services Committee. Vinson, who served in the House longer than anyone else in history, taught Harlow that real power is personal, not official, and is a force that comes from within and is married to intelligence and hard work. Vinson lived out his principles in guiding the Armed Services Committee with its 37 tough members, "If he couldn't bull his way to a desired end, he would wheedle his way. If he couldn't do either, he would flash change course and triumphantly lead his mutinous associates in the direction they were demanding to go. He dominated the witness interrogation. He simply ignored the fledgling members. He made decisions for the entire Committee with the whim of steel."[6]

Harlow and Vinson had the same work ethic. Vinson arrived at his office at 6:30 A.M., opened his mail himself, read and absorbed newspapers from his Georgia district, allocated staff assignments, and by 7:30 A.M. was ready for breakfast, "a half day's work already parceled out."[7]

Harlow appreciated the power of a congressional committee with the clout to "harass, humiliate and investigate at the drop of a whim."[2] He found committees could be amiable and cooperative one day and "devilishly irascible the next." Harlow's observations gave him a lasting impression of how sensible legislation was created from a series of events that seemed calculated to failure. He surmised, "Ordinarily the end product of such interplays between a variety of interests is a compromise meticulously contrived by legislative sculptors. Sooner or later the legislators chisel out a masterpiece called 'the art of the possible.' The object d'art may well have three legs, one eye and a badly curved spine, but usually the darn thing will stand upright and take fearful punishment. Ungainly but sturdy, you might say, is the ordinary output of the legislative studio."[9]

Harlow was always kind and considerate of junior staffers who looked to him as a role model. William H. "Bill" Darden began his career in Washington working under Harlow's tutelage. Not only did Darden learn immeasurably from Harlow's words and actions, he sought Harlow's counsel long after their service together on the House Armed Services Committee staff. For more than three decades Darden dared not change jobs until "I sought Bryce's views."[10] Darden is typical of legions of Washington Beltway associates who brag about being charter members of the Bryce Harlow Fan Club, remarking, "Despite his great intellect and judgment within a rather small physical stature, he never manifested anything like what I shall term, for lack of a better description, a Napoleonic complex."[11]

One of the congressmen Harlow worked closely with in the late 1940s was Republican Dewey Short of Missouri. Short was a storied character who was both a Shakespearean scholar of note and clergyman who could quote scriptures for hours at a time. Short, also an accomplished actor and great orator, had one great shortcoming. He drank entirely too much. Harlow recognized Short's talent for public speaking and was instrumental in Short being hired by the War Department as a civilian public relations speaker after being defeated for re-election to the House. Harlow recommended Short for the job only upon his promise to never drink on the job.[12] Short kept his promise and was an elegant addition to the War Department. Washington insider Edward McCabe later commented that Harlow's salvage of a broken-spirited ex-congressman was "a great credit to his ingenuity and also his innate goodness as a person."[13]

Harlow, an Oklahoman always, made lasting friendships with new Oklahoma congressmen Carl Albert and Tom Steed. Harlow was able to assist Oklahoma in upgrading facilities and assignments for Tinker Field, the state's largest employer.

Harlow's long hours as head of the Armed Services Committee staff limited his time with his wife. However, Betty fully supported her husband's responsibilities and planned quality time for them on weekends and when Congress was in recess. The Harlow family grew when Betty gave birth to a son, Bryce Larimore Harlow, January 21, 1949, in Oklahoma City.

Even though the Harlows lived in Washington, it became necessary for Betty to return to Oklahoma a few weeks before Larry was born in early 1949. Betty was RH negative and there was concern over her third baby's survival. Bryce wanted Betty to have the baby at University Hospital in Oklahoma City, one of the few hospitals in the nation to offer a total body transfusion procedure for RH negative babies.[14]

Harlow's popularity in Washington spilled over into Oklahoma. Several leaders in the Sooner State suggested he run for either the United States Senate or House from his native state. However, Harlow spurned attempts to enter the political arena as a candidate. He was flattered by the opinions of those who thought he could win any race he entered, but he was not willing to drag his family into the war of politics.

The late 1940s, according to Harlow, gave rise to unwanted change at the seat of government. Post-war America was prosperous and government by the people and for the people turned into "government for sale." Harlow saw a black cloud settling on the District of Columbia, a stomach-turning era of coming corruption that affected all branches of government.

Harlow was nauseated by the congressional process in 1951 when a member of President Harry Truman's cabinet lied while testifying before the House Armed Services Committee. Harlow sat in the committee hearing room and got physically ill as the witness lied. The incident took the heart out of Harlow and his love for public service. Shortly thereafter, Harlow resigned, loaded up the family, and headed back to Oklahoma City.

HARLOW EMBODIED FREEDOM'S FIRST PRINCIPLES: HONOR,
INTEGRITY, AND RESPONSIBILITY.

DAVID E. JONES, FOUNDER
THE FUND FOR AMERICAN STUDIES

Harlow settled down into the comfortable role of leading the Harlow Publishing Company in Oklahoma City. He joined the Oklahoma City Chamber of Commerce, was a frequent speaker at civic clubs and church socials, and worked in charity drives such as the Community Chest.

Harlow had become disenchanted with the direction of the Democratic party during his last few months in Washington. That disenchantment led to him changing his party registration from Democrat to Republican in 1950. Harlow saw one man on the political horizon whom he thought could put America back on the right track. That man was Dwight David "Ike" Eisenhower.

"Ike" was a household name in the United States after World War II. A military hero of the highest order, Eisenhower served as Army Chief of Staff and President of Columbia University. Harlow, who had met Eisenhower many times during his stint at the Pentagon and worked for him briefly after he replaced George Marshall as Chief of Staff, followed Eisenhower's career with great interest.

When Eisenhower accepted President Truman's offer to command the newly-formed North Atlantic Treaty Organization

(NATO) in 1950, he offered Harlow a job as an assistant. Harlow considered the job for a moment, but Congressman Vinson considered Harlow too important to his committee and refused to allow any such transfer.

In 1951 Harlow wrote Eisenhower with comments on his opposition to centralization of the federal government and the need for a strong defense in Europe. Some congressional leaders saw no urgent need for the United States to involve itself in strengthening the military defense of European allies. Harlow suggested, and Eisenhower agreed, that it was not merely enough to talk about preserving freedom. Something had to be done.

Harlow was concerned that the United States had only two divisions stationed in Europe in 1951, hardly sufficient military

might to spurn any attempted invasions from the east. Eisenhower thanked Harlow for his thoughts on the defense of Europe and asked him to draft formal recommendations for improving America's relations with its allies in northern Europe.

Harlow, and most other astute political observers of the time, saw Eisenhower as the only Republican who could win the White House in 1952. Eisenhower had been urged to run for president for years, even before Truman won re-election in 1948. Eisenhower received a longhand note from Truman just before Christmas, 1951, in which the President expressed a desire to return home to Missouri. Truman desperately wanted to keep any isolationists out of the White House and wanted to know Eisenhower's intentions. Truman implied that Eisenhower's answer would have a definite influence on his decision.

On New Year's Day, 1952, Eisenhower replied to Truman's letter. Excerpts from the reply explained Eisenhower's mood:

> There has never been any change in my personal desires and aspirations, publicly and privately expressed, over the past six years or so. I'd like to live a semi-retired life with my family, given over mainly to the study of, and a bit of writing on, present day trends and problems. But just as you have decided that circumstances may not permit you to do exactly as you please, so I've found that fervent desire may sometimes have to give way to a conviction of duty.[1]

Reluctantly, Eisenhower accepted the call and conviction of duty and was elected President in the general election of 1952, defeating Democrat nominee Adlai Stevenson by more than 6.6 million votes.

GOP presidential candidate General Dwight D. Eisenhower appeared in 1952 in Oklahoma City with Donald Kennedy, left, later president of Oklahoma Natural Gas Company, and Eisenhower's old friend, Streeter Flynn, right. Courtesy *The Daily Oklahoman.*

Within days Eisenhower began selecting cabinet and staff members to surround him in his presidency. It was a dangerous time for the world. Fighting raged on a bloody front in Korea as the United States committed its forces to thwart the scourge of Communism. Iran's oil resources had been nationalized and the country was teetering toward Communism. Mainland China had fallen to the Communists and American ally, Chiang Kai-shek, had fled to the island of Formosa. Eastern European countries were leaning heavily toward complete Communist control. Against that backdrop, Eisenhower carefully searched for the right people to lead the free world.

After he selected John Foster Dulles as Secretary of State, Charles E. Wilson as Secretary of Defense, and Douglas McKay as Secretary of the Interior, Eisenhower set about choosing the White House staff. For years he had been in contact with the Executive Office of the White House and had a general idea about the system, or lack of system, under which it operated.[2] Eisenhower chose his presidential campaign manager, former New Hampshire Governor Sherman Adams, as White House Chief of Staff, or Assistant to the President, and gave him cabinet rank.

Adams, a former clerk in a Vermont logging camp, entered politics in 1940 when he was elected to the New Hampshire House of Representatives. He later represented his home state in the 79th Congress and was Governor of New Hampshire when Eisenhower tabbed him as his personal campaign manager in the 1952 race for the White House.[3]

On December 2, 1951, Eisenhower, with the full consent of President Truman, arrived in Korea for consultation with the South Korean President and military leaders who believed they were making no headway in the police action. Accompanying the President was retired Major General Wilton B. "Jerry" Persons, one of Eisenhower's most astute and trusted associate.

It was during the Korean trip that Persons suggested that a congressional liaison office be established in the White House. Government had expanded rapidly in the previous decade and the expansion made the President's relations with congress more important than anytime before in history. Because of the complexities of the modern-day world, an efficient White House staff that could work closely with a Democratic congress was a necessity if Eisenhower was to fulfill his wish of courageously leading the American people into a new era.

General Persons accepted Eisenhower's invitation to head the White House congressional liaison office. Persons was uniquely qualified for the job. He had gained the respect and trust of Eisenhower in a similar role at the Pentagon and while serving as an assistant to Eisenhower at NATO.

Persons began the selection of a staff. The first name he thought of was Bryce Harlow, his former associate in the congressional relations office at the Pentagon during the war. Through appropriate channels, Persons cleared his selection of Harlow all the way to the President-Elect who was elated at the prospect of Harlow joining his White House team. Eisenhower called Harlow "an expert on military affairs and a competent writer."[4]

Persons began calling Harlow in Oklahoma City. Time after time Harlow rejected the offer to return to Washington. He was now 35-years-old, established in the publishing business, and the father of three young children. Harlow was flattered by the opportunity to become part of the inner circle of a President in whom he greatly believed but he and his family were happy with their world in Oklahoma City.

After six weeks of calls, one even from Eisenhower himself, Harlow bowed to the pressure of conviction and accepted the White House appointment. He later explained his reasoning, "Every citizen must establish that there is a genuine need for service. Then, if you are truly pressed by the White House, and particularly by the President personally, and you discover your presence is genuinely and ardently desired, you have to say yes, as a responsible citizen."[5]

Victor Harlow played a major role in his son's decision to go back to Washington. The elder Harlow simply said, "It's your civic duty. You can't say no to the White House."[6]

In late December, 1952, Harlow and his family once again

packed their personal belongings and headed for a new life in the hub of the free world, Washington, D.C. As soon as Harlow arrived at the presidential transition office, it was decided that he would handle White House relations with the House of Representatives and Gerald D. Morgan, a successful lawyer who had been one of the drafters of the Taft-Hartley Act, would act as the President's liaison with the Senate.

This latest move of Harlow and his family to Washington was the third trip halfway across the continent from his native Oklahoma. In his heart, Harlow knew it would be his last journey, for he would never live in Oklahoma again.

A Different World

HARLOW HAD AN EXTRAORDINARY TALENT FOR WRITING CLEAN
CLEAR PROSE, AND IT WAS A JOY TO WATCH HIM TAKE
SUBMISSIONS FROM THE DEPARTMENTS, OFTEN HEAVY WITH
"OFFICIALESE," AND IN HIS WORDS, "CUT THE CRUD OUT."

GENERAL ANDREW J. GOODPASTER

The White House is only a few blocks from the United States Capitol. However, the two icons of American government are in two very different worlds.

Before 1952, Harlow had spent all of his time in Washington, D.C. on Capitol Hill, in day-to-day dealings with Congress. His new assignment took him to an office in the East Wing of the White House.

The White House congressional liaison office was a new experiment in the American presidency. It was the first time that a President formally set up a mechanism to allow the free flow of information to and from the Congress. All Presidents had recognized the need for good relations with Congress, but none before Eisenhower created a special staff to handle the relationship.

Harlow came well-prepared to his new job at the White House. The leadership of the House of Representatives was virtually the same as when he left the Armed Services Committee two years earlier. Harlow spent long hours renewing his friendships with dozens of House members in strategic positions. He also spent days in briefing sessions with cabinet officials and top leaders of the new administration to formulate what would become Eisenhower's domestic and foreign policy. Harlow was also called upon by Eisenhower to assist in drafting personal statements, speeches, and answering the enormous amount of communication that arrives in the Oval Office.

The month before Eisenhower took office, Harlow visited the White House to survey his new office quarters. He met with old friend John Steelman, President Truman's White House Chief of Staff, who took Harlow aside and said, "Now, Bryce, I want to strongly urge that you let me know now if you want this place painted and where you want the telephones. Once you move in, you will have no time whatsoever even to think about painting, or moving anything, much less where you want the phones located."[1] Harlow did not fully grasp Steelman's warning until he actually entered his office the first day after Eisenhower was inaugurated. Steelman was right. The phone never stopped ringing from that day until Harlow's last day in the White House.

Harlow was now a Washington insider, a member of an elite group of only a few men who successfully held high positions in both the legislative and executive branches of government. Many who preceded and followed Harlow in the White House were swept up in the importance of their jobs and became "yes men" for their Presidents. Not Bryce Harlow. His new position changed neither his principles nor his candor.

Harlow's candor led to the most memorable moment of his first official meeting with President Eisenhower. In the first months of the 1953 congressional session Harlow was able to obtain House approval of a bill important to the President. Eisenhower invited Harlow to the Oval Office to express his appreciation. After pleasantries were exchanged, the conversation turned to Congressman Carl Vinson whom Eisenhower called a "crotchety old goat." Harlow rose to defend Vinson, his close friend and mentor. Harlow, said, "Mr. President, you're dead wrong." Eisenhower was anything but happy with his young upstart congressional liaison contradicting his views about Vinson. Harlow never regretted standing up for his friend. In an interview many years later, Harlow said, "It takes courage to do it if you know you should. It may hurt you, but if you don't do it, you can't live with yourself."[2]

Shortly after Harlow entered his White House position, Congressman Vinson gave him a state-of-the-art wire tape recorder and told Harlow to record everything going on around him, saying, "You must do this for history. You are going to be around some incredibly important things. For history's sake, you must record what you see and do."[3] Harlow recorded his thoughts on the tape recorder for two weeks then returned it to Vinson. He told Vinson, "I can't do it. I am privileged to be involved in things and they are dependent upon confidentiality. I have no right to reveal those things that I am privy to as a result of my public position."[4]

Eisenhower's four decades of military service affected all phases of his administration. The new President discovered that one man, a non-political federal employee called the Executive Clerk of the White House, was in charge of supervising the mechanics of the White House operation. Eisenhower commissioned a study that resulted in the creation of a military-style command function in the White House, to keep staffers from walking over each other and prevent duplication of effort. Eisenhower chose Paul T. "Pete" Carroll to oversee the new White House secretariat. It was Carroll's job to clear all communications to the President and coordinate cabinet operations. When Carroll died of a sudden heart attack 18 months into the administration, the President selected Colonel Andrew J. Goodpaster as his replacement. Both men were Harlow's confidants.

Goodpaster fit perfectly into Eisenhower's White House line-of-command system. In addition to his military experience as a member of Eisenhower's NATO staff, Goodpaster had empathy and intelligence to virtually anticipate Eisenhower's attitudes toward and responses to issues. One *New York Times* writer called Goodpaster Eisenhower's "alter ego."[5]

The White House staff was very structured and disciplined, a reflection of its leader. Harlow liked the working conditions of a tightly-run staff. He later said one of the great threats to any President is the lack of regularized procedures. Because the pressures of the job are so relentless and intense in the White House, Harlow believed that if mechanisms were not in place to control the flow of movement and information, a President could not make informed decisions during times of crisis, and the country would suffer.[6]

Harlow came to the White House as a loyal servant to the President. He had no hidden agendas, no desire for stardom, and no secret ambitions of being on the cover of national magazines. He had only one goal, to serve the President as efficiently and professionally as he could.

Eisenhower was Harlow's hero. In his lifetime, Harlow knew and worked for several presidents. But Eisenhower was always his favorite. In 1967, Harlow reflected upon his former boss:

> I think it was his personal appearance, in part. He looked somewhat like an American eagle as he stood taking the "Hail to the Chief," standing at attention, as a great commander of armed forces for many years, with his military bearing—very impressive. The crowd liked that. Very dignified, very impressive man standing there, and you could tell he was commander in chief of the armed forces, just looking at him. Standing, facing sternly the flag of the United States while the band played. I'm talking about the symbolism of the Presidency. He looked the part. and he had this astoundingly mobile face, which can look craggy one minute and the next minute that warm, friendly grin of Ike of Kansas. The smile would melt audiences. They loved that, loved his appearance, liked him. He radiated friendliness and genuineness, and the third quality was, he was innately very modest. They liked that. The people always believed that he might make a mistake, but he wouldn't make a mistake in his heart. Here is a fellow who is telling us exactly what he thinks is right for the country. You put that with a pleasant personality capable of being a fierce

commander, and you've got quite a combination. I think it's the most wonderfully rounded personality I've ever known.[7]

Harlow took his responsibility as Eisenhower's link to the House seriously. He was fully aware that a hostile party, the Democrats, controlled Congress for six of Eisenhower's eight years in office. Harlow was respected by leaders of both parties but respected the innate differences and built-in hostilities that result from one party winning the White House and the other party ruling Congress.

The normal bickering between branches of government is magnified when leaders come from different parties, from different philosophies. Harlow took great pain to smooth the communication with the House, to avoid what he called "hardening of the political arteries," that would result in such hostility that great issues affecting the country could be terribly mishandled.[8]

Harlow attacked the problem of potential hostility between a Democratic House and a Republican President head-on. He advised the President to avoid extreme partisanship to prevent alienation of his relationships with the leaders of the other party in Congress. At the same time, Harlow counseled congressional leaders to mute their criticism of the President in the interest of the nation. Students of Harlow's methods can recite many instances when both sides of the President-Congress equation heeded his advice and the nation was better for it.

Eisenhower was in a unique position in his relations with Congress. He was for most of his life non-political. Some of his best and longest friends were Democratic members of Congress who had tried to convince him to run for President as a Democrat. Also, he enjoyed tremendous prestige and popularity among American citizens. He was a national hero and leaders in Congress were hesitant about attacking him personally. More often than not, congressional leaders unhappy with the administration, attacked the President's subordinates, such as Sherman Adams, instead of criticizing the popular President.

In Volume One of Eisenhower's memoirs, *Mandate for Change,* the former President shared a memo Harlow wrote to him outlining the dangers of what he called divided government:

> [D]ivided government—with the Congress in one party's hands and Executive Branch in the other's—is ordinarily the most costly and least efficient arrangement our citizens can have. It produces bills passed only for political advantage, no matter what their fiscal impact; it blocks bills needed by America, only because their passsage might credit the administration; it harasses through investigations, through excessive demands on administrators, through misrepresentations, and ends up leaving the people utterly confused as to who did what to whom. In short, it exalts the petty, demeans the noble, rewards irresponsibility, makes a virtue of stagnation, and bamboozles the public.[9]

One of the methods Harlow used to prevent a divided government was his arrangement of secret meetings between Eisenhower, House Speaker Sam Rayburn, and Senate Majority Leader Lyndon Johnson. Every few weeks, Harlow arranged for a "bourbon and branch water" meeting among the three most powerful leaders in the world. The late afternoon meetings allowed the President to open the door to working together with the Congressional leaders by personally explaining his views on the major issues of the day.[10]

Eisenhower was born in the district Rayburn represented in the House and Johnson called Eisenhower "Captain Ike" for years before he ascended to the presidency. Johnson and Rayburn insisted that the White House meetings be kept secret for the fear of being seen with Eisenhower, considered by many Democrats as "an apostate to the Democratic party," a reference to his choosing the Republican banner for his presidential aspirations.

The everlasting skirmish between an American president and the Congress was later described by Harlow, "Into this uproar, and between the uncontrollable crises abroad, the White House tries to intrude enough common purpose to get a recognizable program enacted, realizing that every victory will be balanced by some defeats. And, I assure you, as ruminatively I rub my scars, that when the opposing party controls the Congress, you will have chicanery of every conceivable kind."

Harlow continued his description of battles between the president and Congress:

> It is a form of insensitivity and sadism, not unlike little boys pulling wings off of flies. Popular recommendations from the President are increased by his Congressional opponents to the point of unacceptability, then returned with a broad partisan smirk for a veto. Unpopular recommendations required in the national interest are tabled and demagogically reviled. Opposition leaders invariably take credit for praiseworthy administration initiatives. Politically motivated investigations multiply like rabbits. Friendly across-the-aisle relations persist through it all, however, for as the pros say, politics is politics, and these tortures are clinically dispassionate. They are political, not personal."[11]

Harlow concluded, however, that despite the chaos in the chess game between Congress and the President, enough cooperation existed to transact the essential business of government.

Veteran Washington reporter for *The Daily Oklahoman*, Allan Cromley, arrived in Washington shortly after Eisenhower took office. Cromley and Harlow struck up a lasting friendship. Once Harlow explained to Cromley his job dealing with a second session of Congress, "What I do now is energetically apply poultices to sores accumulated during the first session."[12]

Cromley recalled a near crisis at the White House early in Eisenhower's first term when Harlow invited many of the administrative assistants to members of Congress to the White House. The assistants lined up, waiting to enter the east wing where Harlow's office was located. Harlow received an urgent telephone call from Mary Jane McCaffrey, first lady Mamie Eisenhower's secretary, wanting to know why the large group was hovering at the White House entrance.

Mrs. McCaffrey relayed Harlow's answer to Mrs. Eisenhower who suggested the assistants leave since she had two small groups arriving at the same entrance. There was a stalemate as Harlow stood his ground against an increasingly impatient first lady. Harlow sat with his feet on his desk as the door to his office slowly opened. It was Mrs. Eisenhower, who demanded to know what was going on.

Harlow explained to the first lady how important the administrative assistants were to getting her husband's programs favorable attention on Capitol Hill. When Harlow added that sending the assistants away could do serious damage to relations with Congress, Mrs. Eisenhower gave in.[13]

After a few months as Eisenhower's liaison with the House of Representatives, Harlow was asked by Chief of Staff Sherman Adams to become chief speechwriter. Harlow at first resisted, not because he was uncomfortable writing speeches, but because he would be required to reflect the views of his hero, the President. Technically, Harlow was a master speechwriter. He had written thousands of speeches in his service at the Pentagon and the House of Representatives. But writing for a great man who happened to President was a unique challenge.

After Adams promised Harlow that he could spend as much time as he wanted with Eisenhower when working on major speeches, Harlow accepted the new assignment. He continued his liaison with the House but shifted his primary responsibility to drafting major speeches for the President.

Harlow's first speech assignment for the President came within hours of Adams' request of Harlow to turn his attention to speech writing. Eisenhower accepted an invitation to speak at a meeting of the nation's newspaper editors, the first major address of his presidency. Harlow was shocked that the job of drafting such an important address fell on his shoulders.

Adams informed Harlow that the subject Eisenhower wanted to talk to the editors about was "the chance for peace." Harlow went to work. Against a historical backdrop of a world war still fresh in the memory of all and the fright of another global conflict eminating from the Koreas, Harlow read everything Eisenhower had said or written about world peace. After three drafts, "The

Chance for Peace" speech was approved by the President. Harlow's words reflected Eisenhower's deep desire for peaceful co-existence with America's world neighbors:

> . . . The free world weighs one question above all others: the chance for a just peace for all peoples. To weigh this chance is to summon instantly to mind another recent moment of great decision. It came with that yet more hopeful spring of 1945, bright with the promise of victory and of freedom. The hope of all just men in that moment, too, was a just and lasting peace. The eight years that have passed have seen that hope waver, grow dim, and almost die. And the shadow of fear again has darkly lengthened across the world. Today the hope of free men remains stubborn and brave, but it is sternly disciplined by experience. It shuns not only all crude counsel of despair, but also the self-deceit of easy illusion. It weighs the chance for peace with sure, clear knowledge of what happened to the vain hope of 1945.[14]

Eisenhower was extremely pleased with his new speech writer. He scrawled Harlow a hand-written memo that simply said, "Good job! You think like I do!"[15]

Working at the White House was anything but comfortable. Harlow's two staff responsibilities required his presence from 18 to 24 hours many days. There was never an ebb in the flow of pressure because "all of the concentrated energies of the world and of America combine into the White House."[16] Harlow often remarked that the only object of a day's labor at the White House was to arrange the several crises into some priority list, or simply put, "prioritize your crises." The incredibly high-level pace of domestic and international activity dictated the necessity for a well-oiled staff mechanism to handle the information flow to the President.

Harlow survived eight years on the President's staff. He was young and withstood the vigorous daily routine. Reflecting on the vitality of a presidential staff, Harlow later said, "A wise President would sit down with his staff from the beginning and tell them,

'I'm replacing you in three years because you're going to be a cinder. Most of your ideas will have been used or rejected. Your energies will have been dispelled. You'll be exhausted. You will need to get out, get new perspectives, and get your batteries recharged. You will come in, and we will agree on your departure time, so you can plan against it.' "[17]

Harlow's workday at the Eisenhower White House began before 7:00 A.M. He had a working breakfast at 7:30 A.M. at least four days a week, often with congressional leaders or federal government agency heads pursuing White House approval of projects or policies.

Leaking of sensitive information was not a major problem in the Eisenhower Inner Circle. Harlow and his contemporaries followed Eisenhower's example of complete honesty and trust. Harlow was not afraid to discuss the most sensitive topics with fellow senior staffers. He believed that the coin of the political world is a person's word. "It's the only major profession left," Harlow remarked, "where you never sign a contract. It's just your given word that is your bond. If you dare break it, it will destroy you."[18]

Harlow never wrote a speech for Eisenhower without fully researching the subject and intended audience. He wanted to do his job well and spent as much time with the President as he could, in Washington, and on trips outside the capital city, so he could become Eisenhower's alter ego and know what words the President had trouble with, what sentence structure best fitted his speaking style. To gain more knowledge about the President's views, Harlow was invited to attend all major meetings in the White House, Cabinet meetings, National Security Council meetings, and conferences with administration and congressional leaders.

Eisenhower called Harlow his "meat and potatoes man," happy with Harlow's down-to-earth, realistic style of writing. Eisenhower was that kind of man. He did not want fancy speeches, just plain-language expressions of his feelings about America's future.

Harlow wrote Eisenhower's speeches for a multitude of situations, from a Chamber of Commerce convention talk to the State of the Union address, the most difficult speech to prepare.

Anatomy of a State of the Union Address

IF YOU ARE WRITING FOR THE PRESIDENT OF THE UNITED
STATES, THE DOCUMENT HAS GOT TO BE ABSOLUTELY ACCURATE.
THERE IS NO ROOM FOR FLAWS.

BRYCE HARLOW

Most Americans' knowledge of a State of the Union address is limited to listening to or watching the speech delivered by the President after being ceremoniously ushered into the House chamber in the United States Capitol. But the hour or two of explanation of how our nation is faring is only the finished product of a complicated, months-long process involving hundreds of people.

Harlow's most arduous task as a presidential speechwriter was the drafting of the annual State of the Union address. Eisenhower's first State of the Union, delivered in January, 1954, began its life among Harlow's late-night doodles three months before.

When speechwriter Emmet J. Hughes resigned his White House position on September 24, 1953, Harlow was elevated to chief speechwriter and given the title of Administrative Assistant to the President. He was sworn in by the President on October 24 and went to work immediately on the State of the Union address.

The address began to take shape with a "continuing procession of paragraphs and notes and ideas and suggestions and requests from the President."[1] Harlow met with Eisenhower to "pick his

Harlow spent hundreds of hours writing and researching the issues of the day to prepare President Dwight D. Eisenhower's State of the Union addresses. Harlow's almost unquenchable thirst for knowledge was a prerequisite for such a high-level White House job. Courtesy *The Daily Oklahoman*.

brain" to develop a definitive list of major-subject topics for development and to answer a series of questions: What would be the unifying theme of the speech? Would Eisenhower be talking principally of foreign affairs? If so, what aspect of it? If the focus was to be on domestic affairs, was it civil rights, the state of the economy, or the plight of the farmers, or all of the above? Harlow's oft-quoted description of a State of the Union address was, "trying to accomplish, in a concerted single purpose, a message comprehensible by the American people that makes good sense and will rally the country."[2]

While Harlow worked on the State of the Union address, the Bureau of the Budget gathered information about the policies and aspirations of the hundreds of federal agencies clamoring for mention in the State of the Union. Harlow received hundreds of memos and calls from agency directors desiring "their place in the sun."

Harlow's already long days were filled with conferences with cabinet officials or White House staff members and trips to the Library of Congress to seek specific information for him to be able to shed light on some new presidential or staff idea. One early December morning found Harlow in conference with one cabinet member and four others waiting in his outer office for their chance to present ideas for inclusion into the President's speech to the nation.

Harlow became the "sifter" of information for the State of the Union. He treasured his time alone with Eisenhower and believed he knew what the President was trying to accomplish in building the State of the Union address from the ground up. In sifting topics, or determining the extent a topic would be treated in the speech, Harlow risked a cabinet member going over his head, directly to Eisenhower. Even though that occasionally happened, Eisenhower usually accepted Harlow's recommendations.[3] Left to explain cuts of material to cabinet officers, Harlow, the suave, master communicator, explained that it was not possible to include all of their wants and wishes in the speech as the President demanded an address that he could deliver in less than two hours without boring the nation to tears.

In December, 1953, President Dwight D.
Eisenhower called Harlow and his team
to Augusta to work on the State of the
Union message. Left to right, Jack
Martin, Arthur S. Fleming, Henry Cabot
Lodge, Eisenhower, Harlow, Sherman
Adams, Gerald D. Morgan, and Joseph
M. Dodge. Courtesy Dwight D.
Eisenhower Library.

Harlow worked at his manual typewriter
in his White House office late into the
night several times each week, preparing
speeches and information for use by the
President. Courtesy *The Daily
Oklahoman.*

Harlow was often overwhelmed by the State of the Union project. His job was simple, "Avoid the temptation of attempting to
capture in that message every program of significance of the administration, because it would be more likely to confuse than to
enlighten the country."[4]

Harlow's first draft was a conglomeration of almost 100,000
words, messages from several dozen agencies proud of their programs. Harlow began paring the message to his ultimate goal,
6,500 words, enough for an hour-long speech, with deductions for
splattering of anticipated applause.

Eisenhower strongly desired input from Republican congressional leaders on his first State of the Union address. On December 17, 1953, he convened a three-day conference attended by Republican leaders, key presidential staff members, and Harlow, who was feverishly taking notes. The President led aggressive discussions on proposed legislative programs and the direction he intended to take the country. Republicans held only a thin margin in both houses of Congress and Eisenhower asked his fellow Republicans to seek bi-partisan support for many of his ideas.

Eisenhower asked Harlow to seek early comment on the speech from Eisenhower's trusted friend, Henry Cabot Lodge, Jr., the United States Representative to the United Nations. On December 18, Lodge wrote Harlow, "I think you are off to a fine start and with the two insertions which I suggest, and the few changes, I believe you have got a splendid document."[5]

Harlow worked through the Christmas vacation on the speech. On December 28, unhappy with his third draft, he wrote to General Persons, "In its present form I am dissatisfied with these sections: housing, veterans, taxation, defense—and, as always, agriculture. I am not sure that all of these need substantial change but I am going to try in the time left to strengthen these various sections without increasing the length of the speech (which will be the neatest trick of the year)."[6]

In the week following Christmas, Harlow disseminated his fourth draft to a pre-determined, high-level list of officials chosen by the President to review the document. They included Secretary of State John Foster Dulles; Secretary of the Treasury George M. Humphrey; Secretary of Defense Charles E. Wilson; Attorney General Herbert Brownell, Jr.; Postmaster General Arthur E. Summerfield; Secretary of the Interior Douglas McKay; Secretary of Agriculture Ezra Taft Benson; Secretary of Commerce Sinclair Weeks; and Secretary of Labor James P. Mitchell.[7]

Within days Harlow received responses from cabinet members. Keeping with the general theme of world peace, secretaries Dulles and Wilson objected to a paragraph that appeared braggadocios, in their opinion, of American military power. Harlow had written,

"The first atomic artillery shell has been fired, releasing explosive energy equivalent of many tens of thousands of the largest cannon on earth simultaneously firing conventional shells. Capital ships are being converted to launch guided missiles. In two weeks the first atomic submarine will be launched and work on the second was begun three months ago." Harlow bowed to the recommendations and deleted the paragraph, inserting instead, "Since our hope is peace, we owe ourselves and the world a candid explanation of the military measures we are taking to make that peace secure. As we enter this new year, our military power continues to grow."[8]

Secretary Brownell, Vice President Richard Nixon, and Republican congressional leaders asked Harlow to emphasize the need for a closer watch of internal security in the United States. Nixon had won acclaim as a Communist-fighter in 1948 and 1949 as a member of the House Committee on Un-American Activities. As Eisenhower's running mate in 1952, Nixon built upon his anti-Communist reputation.

When Nixon reviewed Harlow's draft, the Vice President suggested that the President promise the American people that additional funds would be sought from the Congress to establish tougher standards for a new employee security program. Nixon pointed out that more than 2,000 employees had been terminated by the federal government in 1953 because of their suspected ties to the Communist Party. Harlow added tough language to the draft, "We should recognize by law what is plain to all thoughtful citizens—that we are dealing here with actions akin to treason—that when a citizen knowingly participates in the Communist conspiracy he no longer holds allegiance to the United States."[9]

When Eisenhower edited the fourth draft of the message, he suggested to Harlow even more far-reaching language to express his commitment to rid the government of subversives. The final draft asked Congress to enact legislation providing that "an American citizen convicted of conspiring to advocate the overthrow of our government by force or by violence be treated as one who has renounced his allegiance to the United States and had forfeited his citizenship."[10]

President's notings

Draft No. 1
December 16, 1953

When
~~It was~~ eleven months ago, ~~when~~ last ~~I had the high honor to~~

~~appear before the assembled Houses of~~ the Congress ~~to present my~~ *my* views

on the state of the Union, ~~then~~ the conduct of government had just

been transferred, for the first time in two decades, from one of our

great political parties to the other. Thus my first message was, of

necessity, largely an expression of basic viewpoints and broad objectives

rather than the exposition of a detailed, comprehensive program.

Today, ~~therefore, I am especially happy that as I again come~~

~~before the Congress,~~ I am able ~~not only~~ to present a message relating

substantial progress ~~in the preceding twelve months but,~~ *of* much greater

bring
importance, a message of ~~good cheer --~~ of justifiable hope -- of confidence

for the year that lies ahead.

There has been heartening improvement in almost every area of

domestic and international concern during the past year. Bloodshed has

stopped in Korea. There, one aggression has been thwarted and others

made less likely. The forces of freedom in Korea, in Southeast Asia,

in Europe -- everywhere -- today are more vital, stronger, more assured.

Among scores of free nations, among hundreds of millions of troubled

peoples, the conviction is growing that mankind will not consume

Pencil changes made by President Dwight D. Eisenhower on Harlow's first draft of the
1954 State of the Union address. Courtesy Dwight D. Eisenhower Library.

UNITED STATES REPRESENTATIVE
TO THE UNITED NATIONS

December 18, 1953

Dear Bryce:

Herewith my comments on the State of the
Union Message. I enclose an original for the
President's use in case he wants to see it
himself and a carbon for you.

As you can see, I think you are off to a
fine start and with the two insertions which I
suggest, and the few changes, I believe you
have got a splendid document.

Cordially yours,

Henry Cabot Lodge, Jr.

Enclosures.

Bryce N. Harlow, Esq.,
    Administrative Assistant to
        The President,
            The White House.

Comment: This simply takes out a few "I's".

DETERMINED TO BE AN
ADMINISTRATIVE MARKING
E.O. 12065, Section 1
By _____ NLE, Date 7/30/79

Harlow received early response to his drafts from Henry Cabot Lodge, Jr., the United
States Representative to the United Nations. Courtesy Dwight D. Eisenhower Library.

On New Year's Eve, Harlow flew to Augusta, Georgia, where Eisenhower and his family were spending the holidays. Harlow and Eisenhower sat on the porch of the Eisenhower cottage that overlooked the famed Augusta Golf Club, home of the Masters Golf Tournament, and made last-minute changes to the voluminous message that was nearly a finished product, save expected recommendations from cabinet members.

On January 4, Eisenhower summoned Harlow and other key staff members to the Oval Office to consider a novel request. Should he deliver the State of the Union at night and on television? Eisenhower and Harlow argued against it. Press Secretary James Hagerty thought the increased national audience would be helpful to the President and provide popular support for his proposed legislative agenda. In the end, Eisenhower disapproved the idea because he thought it would reflect badly upon Congress.

On the day before the State of the Union, Eisenhower called Harlow and his cabinet into session to "practice" the speech on them. Cabinet members made notes and talked frankly with the President about the content of the address. Eisenhower accepted or rejected ideas and turned to Harlow with instructions to make still more changes. Working into the night, Harlow polished the final-final draft, incorporating changes telephoned to him by Eisenhower who had retired to the family quarters of the White House.

The following day, January 7, Eisenhower went to Capitol Hill and delivered the Harlow-written speech, although handwritten changes were made to the final draft even as the President motored from the White House to the Capitol. Harlow sat in the House chamber and listened intently to the President, noting every time Eisenhower deviated from the script.

The 1954 State of the Union was well-received. Proposals were made to fortify the national economy and upgrade Social Security and health and welfare programs. Eisenhower proposed construction of the St. Lawrence Seaway, a massive joint project between Canada and the United States to open up 2,000 miles of the Great Lakes and the St. Lawrence River to seagoing ships.

Young + Martin opposed to use of exact figure

Brownell and Humphrey favor its use

Internal Security

Under the standards established for the new employee security program,
~~The new security program has already separated more than 2000~~
2288 employees have been separated from the Federal Government. Our national
~~employees from the government.~~ /\The investigation of new employees and *security demands that*

Brownell
Young
Sen. Ferguson

¹ᵉ evaluation of derogatory information respecting present employees

be expedited and concluded at the earliest possible date.
~~impose a heavy administrative burden.~~ I shall ~~later~~ recommend that the

Congress provide additional funds where necessary to speed these

important investigations. *

Turn now from the special security problems of the Federal Government
to a matter relating to American citizenship—
~~Quite apart from the special security problems of the Federal~~

Government, the subversive character of the Communist Party in the

United States has been clearly demonstrated in many ways, including

court proceedings. We should recognize by law what is plain to all

thoughtful citizens -- that we are dealing here with actions akin to

treason -- that when a citizen knowingly participates in the Communist

conspiracy he no longer holds allegiance to the United States. *

I recommend that Congress enact legislation to provide that a

citizen of the United States who is convicted in the courts of hereafter

conspiring to advocate the overthrow of this government by force or

violence be treated as having, by such act, renounced his allegiance to

the United States and forfeited his United States citizenship. *

In addition, the Attorney General will soon appear before

ʳᵘʳ Committees to present his recommendations for needed additional *legal*   *Nixon*

Harlow made pencil changes on working drafts of the State of the Union address based upon review and input from various sources. On this Internal Security section of the 1954 address, he has noted the source of suggested changes, including "Nixon" on the last line. Courtesy Dwight D. Eisenhower Library.

Assembly. A truly constructive reply by the Soviets will make

possible a new start by which the world can turn toward an era of

peace, and away from the fatal road toward atomic war.

Defense

Since our hope is peace, we owe ourselves and the world a

candid explanation of the military measures we are taking to make that peace

secure.

Our military power, as we enter this new year, continues to

grow. The first atomic artillery shell has been fired, releasing

explosive energy equivalent to many tens of thousands of the largest

cannon on earth simultaneously firing conventional shells. Anti-aircraft

units are being strengthened by revolutionary new weapons. Capital

ships are being converted to launch guided missiles. In two weeks

the first atomic submarine will be launched and work on the second was

begun three months ago. The Air Force will have 115 operating wings

by June 30 instead of 110 wings orginially anticipated. Additional

B-47 wings are ready for action. The new B-52 long-range jet bombers

go into production this year. As will be seen from my budget message,

the air power of our Navy and Air Force is receiving heavy emphasis.

Dulles
Wilson

Harlow's seventh draft of the State of the Union address included specific details of the buildup of the American defense structure. The paragraph was deleted at the suggestion of Secretary of State John Foster Dulles and Secretary of Defense Charles Wilson. Courtesy Dwight D. Eisenhower Library.

January 2, 1954

Dear Mr. Harlow:

Here are suggestions for the foreign affairs portion of the State of the Union message. These are based upon the fourth draft. I trust that they can be taken into account in the final draft.

Sincerely yours,

John Foster Dulles

Mr. Bryce Harlow
The White House

Secretary of State John Foster Dulles was a key person designated by Eisenhower to review Harlow's drafts of the State of the Union address. Courtesy Dwight D. Eisenhower Library.

The President spent an inordinate amount of time in his State of the Union message on American agriculture, a subject close to Harlow's heart. Harlow had received substantial input from the Oklahoma congressional delegation whose members represented thousands of farmers in the Sooner State who were worse off in 1954 than in 1947. Eisenhower cited statistics that a farmer could buy a pickup truck from selling nine bales of cotton in 1947, but by 1952, the same truck cost 14 bales. The agriculture portion of the State of the Union, fondly referred to as the "Harlow Plan" by presidential assistants during drafting of the speech, recommended modernized parity and flexible price supports for the nation's farmers. The speech set the tone for Eisenhower's firm belief in private enterprise, not rigid governmental price supports, as the answer to farmers' problems.

With his first State of the Union message under his belt, Harlow took a few days off to catch up on family time with Betty and the children. Later, he reflected on the enormous power thrust upon a presidential speechwriter, "The speechwriter in the White House can have a very, very substantial influence on the policy, either by the methodology of presentation of the material, or by the inclusion or exclusion of ideas; and by the fact that he has to work so intimately with the President. In the preparation of these documents, he can influence very substantially what ends up in a Presidential statement."[11]

Harlow was now a key member of Eisenhower's team, and he loved every minute of it.

CHIEF SPEECHWRITER

HARLOW WAS INVARIABLY THE ONE MAN WITH A SHARP PENCIL
AT THE END OF THE ROAD WHO POLISHED UP THE PRODUCT
WITH THE PRESIDENT, TO HIS SATISFACTION.

EDWARD A. MCCABE

"Presidential speechwriters," according to former presidential aide and author Martin Anderson, "are a rare breed. There is no formal course of study, no training available, no books to read."[1] A speechwriter must make believe he or she is the president, know his policies and nuances completely, and be able to imitate his writing and speaking style, "then write the words that will become an important part of history."[2] When Anderson later became a speechwriter for Richard Nixon, Harlow told him, "Remember, whenever you write for a president you can be forgiven for not being eloquent or brilliant, but you will never be forgiven for being wrong."[3]

Presidential speechwriters are such an exclusive group that a special club, the Judson Welliver Society, was formed. Welliver was the first full-time White House speechwriter, in the administration of President Calvin Coolidge.

An unseen, but necessary, quality of a successful presidential speechwriter is trust. Harlow had an uncanny ability to earn and sustain the trust of Republicans and Democrats alike. He considered trust his primary asset to Eisenhower. Harlow, who came to Washington a Democrat, changed party affiliation before the

Eisenhower election, and did so without alienating any leading Democrats. Harlow's longtime friend, Melvin Laird, a Wisconsin Republican congressman and later Secretary of Defense in the Nixon administration, surmised that Harlow's success may have stemmed from his conservative upbringing in Oklahoma "A Democrat from Oklahoma was always more conservative than a Wisconsin Republican," Laird said.[4]

Historian Kevin Lynch wrote of the diminutive presidential counselor from Oklahoma, "For Harlow, trust, not money, made Washington go round. Though it has probably always been fashionable to dismiss politicians as corrupt, he believed that politics, when practiced properly, could be the most honorable of professions. He delighted in the fact that politicians seal an agreement by giving their word to one another, not by signing a contract or bringing in lawyers."[5]

Harlow's ability to work both sides of the aisle did not prevent him from being extremely partisan in selling Eisenhower's programs and ideas to Congress. William Bragg Ewald, Jr., a member of Harlow's White House speechwriting staff, described his boss as "Eisenhower's taproot into the Republican Party—the articulate, facile, bare-knuckled partisan. . . coloring the Democrats all black, the Republicans all white; the loyalist standing four-square always with the team."[6] Ewald coined the word "Harlowizing" to describe Harlow's knack of knowing what Eisenhower wanted in a speech and conveying that information to research assistants and other speechwriters.

Ewald joined Harlow's team on April 5, 1954. He walked through the iron gate outside the East Wing of the White House and climbed a flight of stairs into Harlow's tiny office overlooking the roof of a passageway from the East Wing to the White House residence. Ewald will never forget the conversation, " 'Gabe [president assistant Gabriel] Hauge tells me you'd like to work in this vale of tears,' Harlow said, walking around the desk to shake hands. His shortness struck me (I'd never have dreamed he had captained the varsity tennis team at the University of Oklahoma), and his warm and engaging southern-western manner. He spoke of the hazards of working on speeches: 'After everybody has mouthed and penciled up anything you write,' he said, 'if there's a single word in there that you wrote to start out with, it's only an accident.' "[7]

Ewald, in his 1981 book, *Eisenhower the President: Crucial Days, 1951-1960,* wrote of Harlow, "He was all meat and potatoes—solid legislative proposals, tough argumentation, facts and figures and political statistics (what one partisan called 'Republican statistics' to nail the Democratic hogwash). Singlehandledly as Ike's main speechwriter after Emmet Hughes's departure in October, 1953, Harlow had written up in final form the Eisenhower 1954 legislative program, first in the State of the Union, then in a mitrailleuse clatter of special messages on agriculture, labor relations, social security, health, housing."

Ewald also wrote, "This bone-crushing months-long process—draft after draft, quibble after quibble over each word—produced the most massive set of specific proposals Ike would ever send to the Hill."[8]

Ewald's perspective of Harlow is unique and historically important because Ewaid occupied a small room in the White House next to Harlow's office for several years. The day he came on board he was ushered into his office by Harlow's secretary, Mary Nichols, who told Ewald he could see the south lawn of the White House from his tiny window and could engage in "President-watching, when he's out there hitting golf balls in the afternoon."[9]

Harlow was a great teacher and mentor for his assistants. Ewald's first assignment from Harlow was to do a rough draft of a speech for the International Conference of the World Council of Churches. Ewald sat at his typewriter and pounded out page after page of information about the merits of the council. When he presented his first draft, Harlow asked him to stand in the far corner of his 14 foot-by-14 foot office and read the speech aloud.

The speech was a thoughtful essay on freedom of mind and the infinite worth of the individual but "rang no bells, went nowhere, bent no ears back."[10] Harlow paced the office and asked, "Have you ever been to Jerusalem?" Ewald replied he had not. Harlow recited the details of a trip to the Church of the Holy Sepulcher with a group of congressmen years earlier. Harlow suggested a new approach for the speech, with a new beginning, "Eight hundred years ago a throng of Europeans, moved by their religious faith, left Europe, endured enormous hardships, and went into the Middle East."[11] With his new Crusades theme, Ewald took Harlow's suggestions and turned out another draft.

Harlow, always conscientious to seek input from knowledgeable sources on the White House staff, sent the speech to every "semiprofessional religious member of the administration—Ezra Benson, of the Mormons' Council of Twelve; Gabriel Hauge, eminent Lutheran; Arthur Flemming, leading Methodist; and assorted Presbyterians, Episcopalians, and Catholics."[12]

The final speech ended up containing "a little big of everything. . . the crusades, a section on foreign aid. . . and a long section on the need for peace."[13]

Washington lawyer Edward McCabe observed Harlow in his role as presidential speechwriter, "Bryce was Eisenhower's favorite and was the person to whom the President would always turn. He might try somebody else to start a preparation on a major talk on

Harlow was greatly trusted by President Dwight D. Eisenhower. As Ike's administrative assistant, Harlow daily sat in on high-level meetings at the White House. One newspaper said Harlow was one of only a handful of men who had close daily contact with the Chief of State. Courtesy *The Daily Oklahoman.*

something but it seemed the President invariably ended up with Bryce tidying up what somebody else had begun and had not quite caught the flavor of what Eisenhower thought he needed."[14]

Harlow, the gifted and fertile writer, taught his underlings with a passion, imploring them to write as "though you're arguing with somebody, driving, polishing, toughening, livening all the way." Fred Seaton, a former United States Senator from Nebraska and Eisenhower presidential assistant, is among the legion of Harlow admirers. Seaton, who sat through long White House meetings building a major speech from ground up, once remarked, "Harlowizing, at its extreme, could result in blood flowing in the gutters, virgins raped on every street corner, rockets fired off, purple in every sentence."[15]

Self-mockery was a tool used by Harlow to make his audiences at ease. It did not matter whether the audience was one cabinet member or a convention of the League of Women Voters. He was courtly and soft-spoken. When speaking of his five-foot-four frame, he told people he was born in Oklahoma during a drought. Another story about his short stature was that he had been six-feet-four-inches when he first came to the nation's capital but was worn down by his years of travel on Pennsylvania Avenue, the road between Capitol Hill and the White House, because "it is paved with sandpaper and there are rats, excuse me, I mean rasps, at both ends."[16]

Harlow valued his young speechwriters because he knew he could not spend sufficient time to research, write, and revise the dozens of speeches and hundreds of position papers on issues and congressional bills required by a president each year. Methodically, when given a speech assignment by the President or senior White House officials, Harlow assigned one of his staff members to begin the process.

In 1954, the nation's farmers were suffering because of low prices, loss of fertile land due to poor conservation, and excessive crop production. Eisenhower had promised in his State of the Union message to do something about the problem. He asked Harlow to draft a working paper to support legislative proposals meant to promote private enterprise over government subsidies as the solution.

Harlow asked Milt Hill to gather information about conservation programs of the United States Department of Agriculture. Hill wrote Harlow, "As an old Oklahoma farm boy, or reasonable facsimile thereof, you can appreciate what's happening in the flatlands, which are now sifting dust. To many of us who remember the 'Dust Bowl' days, this represents a failure of 20 years of attempts to make a conservation program work."[17]

With the drought in the Midwest worsening, television anchors fed viewers a constant diet of film of blowing topsoil on the evening news. Hill warned, "The Democrats are ready to blame the current situation on the present administration... It is obvious to any Kansas farmer plodding through the sandrows of dust that something went wrong someplace."[18]

Harlow took the information from Hill and contacted the President's brother, Milton Eisenhower, a conservation expert at Penn State College and former president of Kansas State College.[19] With Dr. Eisenhower's help, Harlow and other staff members wrote and produced a television special featuring the President and Agriculture Secretary Ezra Taft Benson explaining why changes were needed in America's farm program.

Eisenhower, walking the political tightrope between a free market and government subsidies for farmers said, "Agriculture is one of the most vital parts of our economy. Farmers in America have done a remarkable job in building wealth from the soil. . . . They have responded to the call of their government for increased production whenever it has been needed."

The president continued, "Now that our need for certain commodities has leveled off, the Government should assist in making necessary adjustments. I do not believe we are providing this assistance when we encourage production for which there is no market. Farmers deserve something better than this. It is my determination to see that they get it."[20]

The words were vintage Harlow, a simple meat and potatoes explanation of the Eisenhower farm program.

MCCARTHYISM AND BEYOND

IN DEALING WITH CONGRESS, NO MATTER HOW TEMPTING IT IS
TO MAKE A DEAL, DON'T EVER PROMISE SOMETHING YOU CAN'T
DELIVER.

BRYCE HARLOW

In the early 1950s, the junior Republican United States Senator from Wisconsin, Joseph McCarthy, made headlines with extravagant and often baseless charges that Communists had undermined the effectiveness and security of the federal government. Protected by congressional immunity, and speaking under a cloak of authority from his position as chairman of the Permanent Investigations Subcommittee of the Senate Committee on Governmental Operations, McCarthy accused individuals and groups of subversive activities, searched for Communists and spies in the Army, and attempted to unearth Communist books in American-sponsored libraries overseas.

President Eisenhower became an enemy of McCarthy during the 1952 presidential campaign when Eisenhower refused to endorse McCarthy, even though they were both Republicans. McCarthy, angered by Eisenhower's actions, began to include the President and his associates in all-out attacks after Eisenhower took office in January, 1953.

For most of his first year in office, Eisenhower refused to directly attack McCarthy, believing that his response to McCarthy's wild allegations would result in even more publicity for the Wisconsin lawmaker. White House staff meetings often boiled with controversy as to the proper way to respond to McCarthy. Eisenhower preached restraint, writing later in his memoirs, "Lashing back at one man, which is easy enough for a President, was not as important to me as the long-term value of restraint, the due process of law, and the basic rights of free men. That is why I condemned book-burning, rather than bandying about the names of the men of the moment who would burn the books."[1]

Harlow was one of the few White House insiders who originally agreed with Eisenhower's policy of restraint toward McCarthy and "McCarthyism." In a May 31, 1953, speech Harlow drafted for Eisenhower to deliver on the occasion of the 250th anniversary of Columbia University, McCarthy was mentioned, but not specifically by name. "Amid... alarms and uncertainties, doubters begin to lose faith in themselves, in their country, in their convictions. They begin to fear other people's ideas—every new idea," the President said. He concluded, "They begin to talk about censoring the sources and the communication of ideas... Without exhaustive debate—even heated debate—of ideas and programs, free government would weaken and wither. But if we allow ourselves to be persuaded that every individual, or party, that takes issue with our own convictions is necessarily wicked or treasonous—then we are approaching the end of freedom's road."[2]

Dissatisfied advisers and friends continued to plead with Eisenhower to directly attack McCarthy. When McCarthy threatened to subpoena White House staffers to testify before his subcommittee investigating subversive activity in the Army, Harlow and other White House officials believed war had been declared by McCarthy and convinced Eisenhower to reverse his plan of attack.

Feeling that McCarthyism was taking its toll on the country and that no one was safe from McCarthy's reckless charges, Harlow drafted a statement for Eisenhower to use to rebut a claim made by McCarthy that Great Britain's trade with Communist China was sufficient grounds for the United States to withdraw all aid from its English allies.

William Ewald, Jr., kept a diary of staff meetings during the McCarthy attack on the Eisenhower administration. Ewald and Harlow joined forces against other aides in a heated argument about whether or not Eisenhower should call McCarthy by name. Ewald wrote in his diary November 30, 1953, "Big rhubarb. Finally agreed to have press conference. The men have really separated out from the boys."[3]

The next day Harlow reviewed Ewald's rough draft of a presidential response to McCarthy. Ewald labeled Harlow's "inexorable logic" as helpful to the process. On December 2 Harlow and Ewald presented the President with a final draft. Aide Jack Martin told the President that a vacuum existed in the country because of the scourge of McCarthyism and that unless the President filled it, somebody else would. Eisenhower was uncomfortable with the speech and once slammed the speech back at Ewald, saying, "I will not get in the gutter with that guy."[4]

At his news conference, Eisenhower justified his name-calling of McCarthy, "To ignore this incident would simply add to the confusion which apparently exists in the minds of many people in this country and abroad."[5]

Eisenhower's direct attack on McCarthy was contained in a four-paragraph statement written by Ewald and polished by Harlow and other aides. The statement released to the press read in part, "By implication, the Senator would have us believe that it is the foreign policy of the United States to attempt to treat allies as satellite dependents... At times we may dislike, we may even deplore, certain actions by our allies, and at such times we have always exerted the diplomatic pressure which the occasion warranted, but always within the framework of that ally's independent sovereignty. In other words, we have treated them as we would expect them to treat us."[6]

McCarthy's reign of terror subsided in 1954 when his conduct was condemned by his fellow Senators and he was stripped of his committee chairmanships. Without influence garnered from almost daily attacks on Communists, McCarthy turned to criticizing Eisenhower's farm program. The President asked Harlow to respond to a letter from McCarthy in which the Wisconsin Senator charged that Wisconsin dairy farmers were being asked to take less for their labor while continuing to face the same taxes and the same cost of production.

Harlow penned an exhaustive response to McCarthy's letter. Filled with detailed statistics and policy-points, the letter met head-on McCarthy's recommendation that the government step up subsidies. Harlow wrote, "There can be no argument that deeply rooted conditions handed down from previous years have created a farm picture today which does not reflect the over-all stability, health and promise that all of us are determined it shall achieve." He continued, "But there should also be no argument that not war, not drought, not blind adherence to programs foredoomed to failure except in time of war or drought, can be our devices to inspire hope and confidence among our farming people. The Administration program was and is sound. We shall continue doing everything we can, without political fanfare and without looking to national or international catastrophes for solutions, to build a dependable, prosperous and satisfying future for all of the nation's farmers."[7]

In July, 1954, Harlow was given the task of drafting a major speech for the President who had been invited to address the annual convention of the American Legion. Eisenhower, long a favorite of veterans' groups, asked Harlow to drop all other projects and work full time on the speech.

Harlow began assembling information from the Pentagon on the Eisenhower Administration's record of support for the American military establishment. Harlow was assisted in the project by speechwriters C.D. Jackson and William Ewald, Jr.

Harlow and his staff completed a first draft of the American Legion speech on July 31. Harlow asked White House Special Assistant Robert S. Kieve to solicit comments on the speech from Secretary of State Dulles, Secretary of Defense Wilson, Attorney General Brownell, and other cabinet members and White House aides, including Earle D. Chesney. Chesney responded, "I believe your thought about the President opening his remarks by praising the American Legion for what they have done is splendid as it gets them into the proper mood. . . These men have a high sense of responsibility. They do not expect special rewards such as bonuses or pensions for such service. . . A message informing this group of the seriousness in our world affairs and keeping them on the team with a caution to always be alert should have not only a sobering effect but might stop the clamor for more pensions in every session of Congress."[8]

Chesney's memo is a typical example of the wide range of responses Harlow received during the critical last days of preparing the speech for the President.

Another Eisenhower worked closely with Harlow on the 1954 American Legion speech. Major John S. D. Eisenhower, the President's son, was assigned to the White House. The younger Eisenhower, in a memo to Harlow, recognized his amateur status in speech writing, "The corrections and comments made on this speech. . . are submitted for what they are worth. . . the third draft appears to me to be still beset with many high-minded generalities which, although it is well to restate them succinctly to round out our case, should not be dwelled on."[9]

John Eisenhower enjoyed working with Harlow. He was comfortable with his belief that Harlow was totally loyal to his father and his programs. Because young Eisenhower was on active duty as an infantry major, he questioned how much he should get involved in helping Harlow produce speeches, writing, "I am not over-eager to do the fire-building myself, being in uniform."[10]

Secretary of State Dulles suggested that the draft of the American Legion speech was "a bit McCarthyish in its tone and indicative of intolerance."[11] Dulles was concerned about language promising stepped-up internal security to prevent Communists from infiltrating the federal government. Harlow, and ultimately Eisenhower, adopted Dulles' suggested language, "Our nation is too strong to give way to a panic of fear which would undermine the very principles on which our institutions rest under the guise of preserving them. That indeed would be penny-wise and pound foolish. I hope I can count on the fighting support of the American Legion in a balanced approach of this matter."[12]

After all comments and suggestions were filtered by Harlow, a final draft was presented to the President. On August 27, in Denver, Colorado, Eisenhower was cheered loudly as he opened his speech, "With you, I give thanks that, at last, we can come together at a time when the sounds of battlefields everywhere in the world have been stilled."[13]

In December, 1954, Harlow was given additional duties at the White House. Eisenhower asked Harlow to assume the responsibility as liaison between the President and the hundreds of departments and agencies of the executive branch. Harlow accepted the official designation outlined in a memo from the President on December 4.

Electric power generation became a political football in 1954 when Eisenhower objected to a proposal by the Tennessee Valley Authority (TVA) to build a new generating plant in Memphis, Tennessee, at a cost of hundreds of millions of dollars for the taxpayers. The TVA was established in 1933 principally to control floods, preserve farmland, and improve navigation. However, by 1954, the bulk of the TVA's budget was spent to produce power.[14] The President suggested that private power companies be given an opportunity to build the power plant and sell electricity for distribution by the TVA, thus saving taxpayers a large capital outlay.

The plan sounded good on paper and reflected Eisenhower's philosophy of creating a partnership between the private sector and government to deliver electric power to every home in America. The plan worked out to accomplish the partnership was known as "Dixon-Yates," named after Edgar H. Dixon and Eugene Yates, the leaders of two large southern utilities that provided the capital to build new generating plants.

Soon after the deal was struck, allegations of conflict of interest were made by Democratic leaders and private businessmen who were cut out of the program. Harlow, in a 1985 letter to Tennessee Governor Lamar Alexander, described the festering scandal, "The fangs of the media vampires were full out and adrip with venom as the search escalated for victims."[15]

MY FELLOW VETERANS

For the <u>third</u> time since World
War II, I am honored to join a national
convention of the American Legion.

With you, <u>I give thanks that</u> --
at last -- we can come together at a time
when the sounds of battlefields,
everywhere in the world, have been stilled.

In ~~so great~~ a gathering ~~of veterans,~~
it ~~is~~ fitting ~~to talk of~~ our international
~~goals~~ and ~~of our~~ nation's security.

Stories surfaced in August, 1954, that reported Dixon and Yates had won the contract because one of their cohorts was a personal friend to Eisenhower. When the integrity of the White House and the President's support of the partnership was questioned, it became necessary for Eisenhower to issue a public statement. Harlow, Press Secretary James Hagerty, General Persons, and Gerald Morgan turned out a brief statement, called by Harlow, "a mealy-mouthed, evasive, convoluted, turgid, bureaucratic squid squirt, intended to block out all possibility of further suspicion."[16]

The staffers took the statement to the Oval Office and sat quietly while the President read their handiwork. Within a few moments, that frankly seemed like hours, the President threw the statement over Hagerty's head into the middle of the Oval Office. Eisenhower was livid. "With his blue eyes flashing, his 5-Star look on, his face brick red, he tongue-lashed us," Harlow recalled.[17]

Eisenhower shouted, "You listen here boys. I'll never put out any drivel like that as long as I'm around this place. You've got to understand that the right thing to do in cases like this is always to tell the truth. Put out the facts very fast, don't get cute about it, just say exactly what the facts are, and make it as simple as you can and short as you can. That way the whole damn mess will blow over and be gone in a week or 10 days and the public will back you for being honest about it. . . . Do it this way—like you boys have it here—and we'll be up to our necks in trouble and we will deserve it."[18]

Harlow, Hagerty, and other staff members filed out of the President's office "chastened and embarrassed but with a lesson in responsible leadership."[19]

Eisenhower was right. He told the American people exactly what happened and the entire controversy died within a few weeks. The Dixon-Yates contract was canceled by the Atomic Energy Commission. The United States Court of Claims awarded the two businessmen nearly $2 million in damages because of the government's actions resulting in the cancellation of the power contract. Eisenhower's original partnership idea was revived and the City of Memphis decided to build its own power plant, relieving the TVA of the responsibility to win congressional approval for the project.

THE POWER GAME

HE KNEW POLITICS, THE BEST SENSE OF THAT WORD, THE
ARISTOTLEAN SENSE. HOW DO WE ORDER OUR LIVES TOGETHER,
HOW DO WE ORGANIZE OUR STRUCTURES TOGETHER?

CHARLES W. COLSON

Integrity is the one word that best describes the life and times of
Bryce Harlow. Early in his political career, in a town one historian called "a crock pot of liars," Harlow established, and lived by, his motto, "Trust is the coin of the realm."

Being close to the President of the United States means being close to power, more power than most men can ever dream of. The politics of Washington, D.C., an ever changing landscape of action amidst the babble, is mastered only by a few who handle the power gingerly and with respect.

Bryce Harlow has been described as one of the most significant power-brokers in the nation's capital in the 20th century. How did the son of an Oklahoma publisher reach such heights to be able to influence decisions that affect the future of the world's greatest nation? The answer may be found in one word. . . integrity.

Harlow once said, "Integrity is power. They are one and the same."[1] Harlow's integrity was never in question, by Democrats or Republicans. He played the national game of federal government politics at its highest level. He never lost sight of how important his word was, even though politics often becomes intertwined with power plays, especially in Washington. Harlow recognized his limitations in advice to all who came to work in the White House, "Never confuse yourself with your job. It may be important. You are not."[2]

Somehow Harlow escaped from the battles of the Eisenhower administration unscathed. While Harlow's physical stature was slight, his integrity was far above the maddening political combat.

Washington Post columnist Mark Shields was a Harlow fan. He called Harlow "a consensus All-American of leading authorities . . . no one better at the delicate art of White House-congressional relations. . . word which you could always take to the bank." Shields wrote in 1981, "There were no demons in Bryce Harlow's political world. He kept no enemies' list because he did not believe in enemies."[3]

Former *New York Times* reporter and Pulitzer Prize winner Hedrick Smith wrote about the power game in Washington:

> Politics in Washington is a continuous contest, a constant scramble for points, for power, and influence. Congress is the principal policy arena of battle, round by round, vote by vote. People there compete, take sides, form teams, and when one action is finished, the teams dissolve, and, members form new sides for the new issues. Of course, team competition is our national way of life, but rarely does the contest take place at such close quarters, among people who rub elbows with each other, professionally and socially, day in and day out.[4]

Harlow wielded tremendous power in the Eisenhower White House because of his close working relationship with the President, a relationship based on absolute mutual trust. It is an old axiom in Washington that on substantive issues, the quality of staff that surrounds a President makes or breaks the man and his legacy. Harlow protected Eisenhower at every fork in the bureaucratic road. And he did it without ever compromising his principles or his mission of giving his all to his assigned responsibilities.

The American President represents power, not only in Washington, but wherever he travels or speaks. Harlow got a taste of the traveling power center when he accompanied Eisenhower on several campaign trips during the 1954 election. The President attracted overwhelming attention everywhere he went. Every word was reported by newspapers, radio, and television. Harlow reasoned that a President was so much more powerful than the Congress as a whole because of simple numbers. The President was one man, easy for people to focus on. The Congress was a conglomeration of 535 men and women, difficult for citizens to recognize as a power center. The third branch of the federal government, was often looked at as "an aloof and anonymous body."[5]

In the summer of 1954 Eisenhower was perceived by many as not excited enough about stumping for Republican congressional candidates. Harlow, who was asked to oversee the writing of dozens of campaign speeches that year, met with aides William Ewald, Jr. and Bob Kieve to draft the script for a campaign film to be made in the White House Rose Garden. The placement of a comma caused consternation for the speech-writing team. The suspect sentence read, "All of us who believe in the aims of this [Eisenhower] program should join together to elect Republican Senators and Congressmen, who will work effectively with leaders of the Executive Branch toward fulfillment of that program."[6]

The comma after "Congressmen," Ewald observed, meant Eisenhower supported only candidates who would work with him and support his programs. Kieve disagreed and the comma stayed in the statement that was released to the press. Sure enough, grammarians wrestled with the implication of the comma and asked White House Press Secretary James Hagerty for clarification. Hagerty told a reporter, "It means exactly what it says."[7] The matter was cleared up for the press with Vice President Nixon's declaration that the White House endorsed all Republican candidates.

Harlow accompanied Eisenhower and his family on a vacation to Colorado in late summer. Harlow took up residence at Lowery Air Force Base in Denver to make consultation on campaign statements and speeches easier.

Some of Eisenhower's advisers, including Henry Cabot Lodge, suggested that the President would be better off with a Democratic Congress. Harlow vehemently disagreed and set out to defeat that kind of "wrongheaded thinking."[8] He drafted concepts for speeches that would capitalize on the high public trust enjoyed by Eisenhower, "an immense political reservoir," and the President's "uncanny way of sensing the feeling of the general public."[9]

Eisenhower scheduled a major campaign address in California in mid-September. Harlow recognized the speech as an opportunity for the President to break out of the doldrums in a lackluster campaign and push hard for a Republican Congress. Harlow went to work and "turned out a ringing pro-Republican slasheroo—a speech that went crashing forward, extolling all the miracles the Republican 83rd Congress had performed for the people, predicting how much more of the same the party stalwarts could accomplish in the next two years, and stomping all over the Democrats."[10]

Eisenhower totally agreed with the direction of Harlow's draft. By the time *Air Force One* headed for Hollywood, the President's metamorphosis on the issue of campaigning for Republicans was complete. The speech in California brought down the house and Republican pollsters grinned.

Harlow began rolling out a series of blockbuster speeches to a variety of audiences. The theme of the speeches was simple: a Republican Congress to work closely with Eisenhower spelled victory for the American people. Harlow was the key architect of Eisenhower's words on the campaign trail. It was not uncommon for Harlow to work until 1:00 A.M., take a nap on a beat-up leather couch in his office, and awake at 4:00 A.M. to review the latest draft of a speech typed by the all-night typing pool in the basement of the Executive Office Building. Harlow, always revered by his assistants, more than once reviewed a final draft of a speech as the sun rose in the eastern sky. By 8:00 A.M., the President met with Harlow in the Oval Office to review a pending speech or statement.

In October, Harlow's mission was "barreling down the turnpike."[11] Eisenhower was a bit uncomfortable with the totally partisan message of Harlow's speeches that warned that a Democratic victory would precipitate "a cold war of partisan politics between the Congress and the Executive Branch. . . We won't get anywhere with red lights at all the governmental crossroads."[12]

Some of Eisenhower's speeches were a result of the combined effort of Harlow and Kevin McCann. When Eisenhower requested a eulogy to former Democratic presidential aspirant Al Smith of New York, the speech was "a sandwich: McCann music on the outside, Harlow meat in the middle." After ringing generalities written by McCann, Harlow hit home with specific facts and figures.

Between August 1 and November 1, Eisenhower made nearly 40 speeches, all written by Harlow, for Republican candidates. No other President had ever done so much for his party in a non-presidential election year. Eisenhower was fatigued by the thousands of miles of travel. As he finished an election eve broadcast, he took out his frustration over partisanship on Harlow. The President exploded, "I don't see how you write a goddamned thing with so many people telling you what to do." Eisenhower reflected on his own brief career as a speechwriter for General Douglas MacArthur in the Philippines, "One thing I know, if you put ten people to work on a speech, they'll kill anything in it that has any character. Now the next time you write something that has any character, you bring it right in here. Don't you show it to anybody."[13]

Eisenhower's words in his weary state "stung Harlow to the quick." William Ewald, Jr., later eloquently described the presidential barrage of words directed at Harlow, "Ike was weary—weary with talk, weary with partisanship, weary for the moment with the devoted, brilliant, and selfless man who more than anyone, in his five-foot, four-inch frame, embodied the vital political process. In that particular season, between Dwight Eisenhower and Bryce Harlow, as between Socrates and Alcibiades, there never could be total peace."[14]

After a good night's sleep, it was business as usual the next day between the President and his trusted adviser. Their work went on, for the Republicans lost control of the Senate and House by a narrow margin.

After the election, new faces appeared in Congress and Harlow

began acquainting himself with freshmen members of the House and Senate. He needed the help of Cabinet officers to carry the Eisenhower program forward on Capitol Hill. He set up Saturday morning meetings at the White House with congressional liaison staff members from a dozen major federal agencies. The purpose of the weekly gathering was to make certain that the Cabinet

A 1960 cabinet meeting at the White House. Harlow (standing, far left), was required to attend all cabinet meetings, often briefing the President and cabinet members on pressing issues. Courtesy Dwight D. Eisenhower Library.

agencies of government fully understood the position of the White House on pending legislation.

Clyde A. Wheeler, Jr., a northwest Oklahoma native, was a special assistant for congressional liaison for Secretary of Agriculture Ezra Taft Benson. Wheeler had served on the staff of Oklahoma Congressman Page Belcher after graduating from Oklahoma A & M University with a master's degree in political science. Wheeler attended the Saturday morning skull sessions with Harlow and recalled, "Bryce went around the room and asked each of us who we had been talking to on the Hill, who was backing our programs, and who was against us. He always let us have our say before smoothly setting out the Eisenhower agenda and how it affected each agency."[15]

Eisenhower and Harlow strongly believed that the White House should stay out of day-to-day congressional dealings of cabinet departments. Harlow recognized that the over-all Eisenhower Administration programs could best be sold to Congress if each cabinet member and his legislative liaison had significant contact with individual House and Senate members.[16]

Every administration legislative proposal, of course, was related to the work of one or more cabinet departments. Thus there was the need for legislative aides on the staff of each member of the Eisenhower cabinet. However, some legislative matters were so central to the President's program that the White House staff, rather than the cabinet department staff, took the lead in handling those matters with Congress. Edward McCabe explains, "Whence came the informal White House staff distinction between 'Presidential' legislative items and 'departmental' legislative items. An arrangement such as this might normally suggest friction or conflict between the White House and the departments. However, thanks in great part to Eisenhower's openness and to the collegial approach of Bryce Harlow and his White House staff colleagues, no such friction or conflict ever developed."[17]

There was no shortage of "Presidential" legislative items during the Eisenhower years. Harlow and his able staff oversaw the job of taking the President's message to Capitol Hill on issues such as major tax legislation, the interstate highway program, mutual security, reorganization of the military, and labor-management reform legislation.[18]

FAMILY MATTERS

HARLOW WAS THE CONSUMMATE PRESIDENTIAL STAFFER, A
SKILLFUL SPEECHWRITER, SEEKING TO HAVE A SPEECH SAY
EXACTLY WHAT THE PRESIDENT WANTED.

WILLIAM SAFIRE

No one questioned Harlow's total devotion to both his incredibly important job in the White House and his family. Harlow was never around his children very much during the week because of his long hours so he sought special projects to afford quality time with the children on weekends.

Betty cooked dinner in shifts, the first for the children at 6:45 P.M. "if Bryce is not in sight" and the second when he arrived home at 7:30 or 8:00 P.M., or later, "according to the dictates of national affairs."[1] Betty's favorite meal to prepare for the family was beef stew, because it improved with age in a pressure cooker should her husband's schedule delay his eating until the wee hours of the morning.

Betty was not the extrovert her husband was. She sometimes was frustrated that she was not using her journalism education but accepted her role as the captain of the household. She was happy to curl up in bed with a good book while her husband was off solving the problems of the world.[2] Betty's children described her in retrospect as a wonderful and devoted mother, "always willing to drop whatever project she was involved in to counsel one of her children."[3]

Betty did have a political side. She once told an interviewer after her husband signed on with the Eisenhower administration, "He did the volunteering, and then left town on business and speech-making, leaving me to do the door-to-door political canvassing."[4] Betty was active in Republican politics at the precinct level and worked as a volunteer in several state and congressional campaigns.

The family's oldest daughter Margery, or "Peggy," was taught to read by her father at age two. She remembers Harlow reading the newspaper and magazines to her, rather than the "See Jane run" books. Harlow had a great sense for fun and rough-housing with his children. He never yelled at them, but when his voice dropped a notch and his words were quieter, the children knew they were in trouble.[5]

Betty took care of the day-to-day disciplining of the Harlow children, bringing in their father for major decisions or punishment. Harlow's "piercing glare" was usually enough to melt Peggy if she was in trouble. Once she was cleaning out an aquarium and her pet snapping turtle bit her. Peggy exclaimed, "Damn turtle!" Harlow quietly, but sternly, said, "We don't talk like that in this house." Peggy got the message.[6]

Harlow dealt with his children as he did with leaders of government. . . rationally. When his daughters complained that "other girls were getting to go" somewhere, Harlow sat them down and said, "I don't care what other parents are doing. It is not in your best interest to go to that dance. That's the final word."[7]

One advantage of having the President's speechwriter as her father was evident when Peggy was writing term papers. Harlow spent considerable time with Peggy, making certain she understood the meaning of every word she used.

Peggy looked like her mother but was closest to her father. Daughter Trudy was just the opposite, looking more like her father but developing a closer relationship with her mother.[8] Peggy followed in her father's footsteps in public service and graduated with a master's degree in public administration from George Washington University. During college she worked for the Republican National Committee and on the staff of United States Senator Everett Dirksen, Republican from Illinois. She later worked with her father on the Nixon transition team, was press secretary for Republican United States Senator Peter Dominick of Colorado, and was legislative liaison for Vice President Spiro Agnew.[9] Peggy raised six Harlow grandchildren, Robert, Charles, Mary, Susie, Libby, and Bill Knight.

Trudy nurtured a close, "affectionate" relationship with her father, who consistently demonstrated his love for his wife and children both with words and actions.[10] Harlow was protective of his daughters, sometimes "puritanical," especially when he questioned their need for makeup and things teenage girls cherish. Harlow had high expectations for his children and warned of early romances that might interfere with their education.

Trudy graduated with a degree in history, and a minor in political science, from an exclusive girls school, Converse College, in Spartanburg, South Carolina. During college she had complete access to her important father at the White House. Even in the middle of a moderate national crisis, Harlow never refused a phone call from his children. Harlow was a faithful letter writer to his children, even though his epistles were dictated to his secretary Sally Studebaker, who was considered by Betty and the children as part of the Harlow family.[11]

Trudy also followed the road of public service laid down by her father, working for the National Republican Congressional Campaign Committee, the Republican Boosters Club, United States Senator Edward Gurney of Florida, the National Park Service, and was, in 1999, Chief of Public Affairs of the United States Geological Survey. In the middle of her professional service, Trudy gave the Harlows two grandchildren, Elizabeth Kirby Lunger and Richard Theodore Lunger, III.[12]

The Harlow evening meal often turned into a debate. Harlow intellectually challenged his children. He made them think about any statement or opinion they made. He gently forced them to talk about the issues of the day.[13]

On Sunday afternoons, Harlow often gave the command for

the family to pile into their automobile for "family time." With Harlow at the wheel, and children fighting over turf in the back seat, the Harlows traveled within a reasonable driving distance to Civil War battlefields, the Smithsonian, or just some interesting back road around the nation's capital. When the fighting in the back seat arose above a clamor, Harlow stopped the car and ordered one of the children to the front seat.[14]

Son Larry developed an early interest in the Civil War after watching a television show called "The Gray Ghost," a saga about Confederate guerrilla fighter John Singleton Mosby. Harlow recognized Larry's interest in the Civil War and brought books about battlefields home for Larry to read. Often, the living room table of the Harlow home was piled high with a couple of dozen Civil War books.

Harlow bought a World War II mine detector and used it to search the many Civil War battlefields in Virginia, West Virginia, and Maryland, within driving distance of the Harlow home in Arlington, Virginia.

Larry had to earn his weekly trip to a battlefield. He spent all week studying the battle to learn of specific locations where he and his father might uncover artifacts. He pored over maps larger than he was, looking for places of intense combat or ridges where cannon balls may have fallen into a gully and covered over with the next rain.

On Friday night or Saturday morning, Harlow quizzed Larry to determine if he knew enough about a particular battlefield to visit. When Harlow was convinced that Larry sufficiently knew a potential site, they loaded the 60-pound metal detector into the back of their station wagon and headed off to learn history firsthand. A hot spot for the adventurers was near Harpers Ferry, West Virginia, only a short distance by two-lane road from Washington. The area was home to the Shepherdstown (Botler's Ford) and Sharpsburg battlefields. Often, at the end of the day, the Harlow station wagon was full of pieces of shrapnel and grape shot. Later, when Harlow purchased a more sophisticated metal detector, the scavengers were able to find and recover lead bullets. The Harlows' greatest find was on a day when they uncovered a cannon ball and three mini balls in one outing. Their priceless treasure trove remains in buckets in Larry's garage 40 years later.

It was not uncommon for the Harlow men to spend all day Saturday and Sunday afternoon, after the family attended morning services at Rock Springs Congregational Church, treading slowly over the fields and hills where Union and Confederate soldiers had battled for the life of America almost a century before.[15]

Larry, before age ten, became an expert on the Civil War. When he accompanied his father on an occasional trip to the White House on Saturday to just "goof around" or swim in the White House swimming pool, his expertise was sought by the leaders of the free world. Eisenhower's military aides, and the President himself, loved to try to stump Larry with questions about Civil War battles. Larry did not recognize the import of spending valuable minutes and hours with Eisenhower, one of history's great military minds, talking about the Civil War.

Larry usually went to the White House alone with his father because his sisters were off doing things that teenage girls do.[16] The youthful Civil War legend even served a useful purpose occasionally for the President and his father meeting on some high-level subject in the Oval Office. Once Larry was assigned the responsibility of watching the Army-Navy game on television in the Roosevelt Room near the Oval Office. His duty was to report to the President as soon as either team scored. The White House was a pleasant place for Larry to visit, "a family atmosphere where secretaries wore white gloves, linoleum floors graced working areas, and none of the present rigidity, tenseness, and moment-to-moment crisis atmosphere."[17]

Betty Harlow and the children accepted their husband's and father's higher public purpose. Betty was a peaceful woman who, without gripe or complaint, took on the great burden of raising the family without Harlow around. Harlow's staff once gave him a cartoon of himself on the telephone saying, "Betty, keep dinner warm. I'll be home later."[18] Larry accepted his father's busy job without question. He was taught, just as his father was taught by his father, that "the greatest pleasure in life comes from being of service to others."[19] All the Harlow children genuinely believed, and practiced, that concept.

Harlow encouraged his children to become involved in the world around them. He and Betty taught the children to read at an early age. He insisted they read the daily newspaper and take advantage of their constant exposure to the leaders who made policy that affected the future of the human race. Larry developed a good taste for public service early in life. He used his father as a model to promote integrity in his own dealings with government and the private sector. He was an aide to United States Senator Howard Baker and lobbied for the Environmental Protection Agency (EPA) and the Grocery Manufacturers of America. Larry headed up the first congressional relations office at the Federal Trade Commission, served as a special assistant for legislative affairs to President Ronald Reagan, and was associate director of the Office of Management and Budget (OMB), in charge of OMB's relations with Congress. In the administration of President George Bush, Larry was Deputy Undersecretary of Treasury. He presently is Executive Vice President of Timmons and Company, one of Washington's leading government relations consulting firms.

President Eisenhower was a grandfather figure for young Larry. Both his real grandfathers were back in Oklahoma, so Eisenhower, "a larger-than-life figure," was important in Larry's life. Larry observed and copied his father's reverence for the President.

After the 1960 presidential election, Larry, age 11, accompanied his father who had been summoned by Eisenhower to Augusta, Georgia, for a special meeting on overseas events of importance to the nation. The meeting was set for a Saturday afternoon so Larry and his father took their metal detector and searched a nearby battlefield. A signal from the detector became stronger and stronger. Larry kept digging until his father bolted from his position over the detector and said, "Oh my God. Look at the time. I have a meeting with the President in 90 minutes." Larry wanted to continue the hunt but his father and he frantically piled dirt in the hole they had just dug.

Larry holds the metal detector as his father digs for a hidden relic in a Civil War battlefield. The hobby was a tremendous learning and bonding experience for both father and son. Courtesy *The Daily Oklahoman*.

Harlow, described by his son as an "Oklahoma driver... My dad could drive, really fly," jumped into a Secret Service Mercury convertible he had borrowed and raced toward Augusta.

Five minutes late, the Harlows rushed into the Eisenhower house on the 19th green at the famed Augusta Golf Course where the President was visiting with General Al Gruenther, George Allen, and General Howard Snyder, the President's personal physician.

After Harlow explained where he and Larry had been, Allen asked if General Sherman came through Augusta in his famous March to the Sea. General Gruenther stopped the President from answering the question and said, "Wait a minute, Mr. President. There's no sense in amateurs answering questions like that. Let's hear from a real expert, Larry."[20]

The room turned toward Larry as Harlow nervously awaited his son's answer. Larry replied, "No, General. He bypassed Augusta and went straight to Savannah." Eisenhower smiled and said, "That's exactly right." Larry recalled, "You could have scraped my father off the ceiling."[21]

Larry was asked to wait for his father, the President, and military aides, on the front porch of the house. When the meeting broke up, Harlow, a bit pale, looked at his son and said, "Larry, get up, you are in the President's chair." Eisenhower followed Harlow out the door and insisted his young friend stay seated in his chair. The President sat down next to Larry and began and began a conversation, "Larry, why did Lee go to Gettysburg?"

Larry gave the President a textbook answer about the need for shoes and General Ambrose P. Hill's advance getting sucked in too far, throwing troops in, and not realizing where the high ground was. Then Eisenhower proceeded to give Larry a 45-minute explanation of the political purposes behind General Robert E. Lee's invasion of the North. Larry was captivated.

As Larry and his father left Augusta that day, Harlow jammed on the brakes and screeched to a stop a few blocks from the Eisenhower house. He looked at his 11-year-old son and said, "I hope you realize that half the people in the world would give their right arm for an uninterrupted hour with that man."[22]

Later, the Harlow Civil War battlefield scavenging team searched Eisenhower's farm at Gettysburg, Pennsylvania, for Civil War relics. The farm was only a few miles from the site of the Battle of Gettysburg.

The 1956 Campaign

Eisenhower was a trained leader, trained in the skill of discarding the trivial and snatching the significant.

BRYCE HARLOW

In late1955, President Eisenhower decided to seek a second term in the general election scheduled for the following November. Harlow and key White House staffers geared up for the campaign.

In February, the first political crisis of the election year reared its head. Democratic congressional leaders slammed Eisenhower for inviting Saudi Arabian King Saud to the White House for peace talks. Eisenhower countered, "You don't promote the cause of peace only by talking to people with whom you agree."[1]

When the Saudi entourage, in its ceremonial robes and hoods, descended upon the White House for the state visit, resentment was stirred up in Congress and the State Department by the pro-Israel lobby. The United States was considering voting sanctions against Israel unless it withdrew from Egyptian territory occupied on the Gaza Strip and along the Gulf of Aquaba. Eisenhower was faced with a tough decision, support the United Nations and Egyptian President Gamel Abdel Nasser and alienate Israel, or back Israel and undo all the progress Eisenhower had made with King Saud and other Asian and African nations who threatened to buy their arms from Russia rather than the United States

Secretary of State Dulles and United Nations Representative Henry Cabot Lodge, Jr., flew to Georgia where Eisenhower was vacationing and convinced the President to take a stand against Israel, and against the Congress, that overwhelmingly supported Israel's claim of sovereignty over the disputed territory.

Harlow was awakened in the middle of the night by Eisenhower who asked Harlow to set up a meeting "to have it out" with the leaders of both parties in Congress. On February 20, Harlow was present in a tense and strained meeting in the Cabinet Room at the White House. Harlow, Arthur Minnich, James Hagerty, General Persons, and General Goodpaster were the only White House staffers present at the summit between Eisenhower and Democrats like Lyndon Johnson, Carl Hayden, Mike Mansfield, Sam Rayburn, and John McCormack and Republicans William Knowland, Everett Dirksen, Charles Halleck, Leverett Saltonstall, and John Vorys.

Vice President Nixon sat silent through the two-and-a-half-hour meeting. Eisenhower, however, opened with a "strong and explicit" explanation of why he was in favor of putting pressure on Israel to comply with the United Nations demand for an unconditional withdrawal from the occupied territory.[2]

With Eisenhower's position made crystal clear to congressional leaders and Israel, Israeli Prime Minister David Ben-Gurion announced the following day that his government wanted to work with the United States to reach an understanding about the situation.

Harlow wrote Eisenhower a blistering speech on the importance of America condemning the hostile takeover of territory from other nations. Nine days after Eisenhower delivered his television speech on the controversy, and before the United Nations voted to invoke sanctions on Israel, Golda Meir, the Israeli Foreign Minister, announced that her government would make a full and complete withdrawal from Egyptian territory.

Harlow played a key role in the political future of Vice President Richard Nixon in 1956. Eisenhower was not totally settled on keeping Nixon as his vice president. Robert Anderson, a Texas conservative serving as Deputy Secretary of Defense, was a close friend of Eisenhower and was rumored to be waiting in the wings for the GOP vice presidential nomination should Nixon be shipped off to a cabinet position. Some of Eisenhower's advisors supported the President's personal contact with Anderson about the issue. Eisenhower told Harlow that Nixon might be better off as a cabinet official because, in his his four years as vice president, "He hadn't run anything" or even been "a corps commander." Harlow is generally credited with convincing Eisenhower to keep Nixon on the Republican ticket, calling any move to dump Nixon "politically impractical."[3]

In the 1956 campaign, Eisenhower laid down a strict set of guidelines for Harlow and other White House writers:

• Every speech must relate to the welfare of the people, rather than the role of government.

• The administration must stand on its record of peace, prosperity and progress. That record must be wrapped in a package intended to show the paramount importance of the people and the subordination of the government.

• The Democrats and their leaders are not to be wantonly attacked. All speeches must take a positive approach and must show what the administration has accomplished, its plans for the future.

• Appeals to any one group were to be avoided. Problems that confront one segment of the population should be presented in relationship to problems facing the nation as a whole.

The newly-announced policy for speechwriting prompted *New York Times* reporter James Reston to call the new policy "Give 'em Heaven," rather than the "Give 'em Hell" policy of President Harry Truman.[4]

Harlow headed a prestigious team of speech writers. Dr. Kevin McCann, on leave as President of Defiance College in Ohio, was an industrial engineer and publisher of weekly newspapers in Illinois. He was noted for his knife-edged wit.

Emmet J. Hughes, a Princeton University graduate and former writer for *Time* and *Life* magazines, was one of the top specific idea writers for Eisenhower in the 1956 campaign.

Arthur Larson combined speechwriting with his normal chores as Undersecretary of Labor. He was Dean of the Law School at the University of Pittsburgh before joining the Eisenhower Administration.

Gabriel Hauge was the economic specialist of the writing team. Hauge taught economics at Harvard and Princeton and was a campaign adviser to Republican presidential nominee Thomas E. Dewey in 1948.

Known as a perfectionist "who strives to see that the President uses exactly the right word in the right place," Robert Cutler, a Boston banker and lawyer, served as the secretary of the National Security Council from 1953-1955.

The laborious process of a campaign speech began when some political strategist in the Eisenhower camp booked a campaign appearance. If the site was approved by Eisenhower, political planners in Eisenhower's campaign headquarters and the Republican National Committee decided upon a theme for the speech. If there was no agreement, Ike's opinion was the tie-breaker.

Once a writer was assigned a particular speech, heavy research began, with input from federal agencies and cabinet members, much like input solicited in the formation of a State of the Union address. The first draft of the speech was read during a meeting in Sherman Adams' office with Press Secretary Hagerty putting in his two cents worth about possible headlines from the speech.

Once the speech won acceptance from staffers, it was taken to the President. Eisenhower, with blue pencil in hand, looked over a speech, writing his changes in the margin and across the top and bottom of the pages.

On top of his double-duty summer in 1956, Harlow had to break in a new secretary. She was Sarah Jane Studebaker who had been labeled "Sally" by a junior high school gym teacher because he believed she was too small to be called Sarah. Sally, a native of Granite City, Illinois, and a graduate of Brown's Business School in St. Louis, Missouri, already worked in the White House as a secretary to Eisenhower's military aide Brigadier General Robert Schultz.

When Harlow's secretary resigned, Sally was encouraged to apply for the position. She had never met Harlow before the job interview because she worked in the East Wing of the White House and Harlow's operation was in the West Wing, nearly a city block away.

Sally walked into Harlow's office and was surprised when he stood up. She was accustomed to tall men around the the White House and now understood why people were overheard saying, "Who is that little man with all the big answers?"[5]

Harlow interviewed several applicants but hired Sally who officially joined his office July 1, 1956. One of Sally's big shocks came when she discovered Harlow could write better shorthand than she could. The secretary Sally replaced told her, "If you take shorthand, do it on your lap. Don't put your notepad on the desk because he will look at it and tell you where you made a mistake."[6]

Harlow put Sally to work right away. He dictated mountains of memos, letters, and drafts of speeches. He was a stickler for detail and kind to his secretaries and assistants. He was on the phone 90 percent of the workday at the White House, talking to congressmen, their staffers, and federal agency representatives.

Harlow was impeccably honest. Sally remembered a time when the President and Mrs. Eisenhower were given wine on a visit to Switzerland. Sally's old boss, Schultz, brought her back a case of wine that she offered to share with Harlow. Harlow would not initially accept even a bottle of wine, announcing, "I don't take gifts."[7] Sally had a difficult time getting rid of the wine so Harlow finally took a bottle, which remained in his bottom drawer until he left the White House. Harlow and Sally worked together well and formed a professional relationship that would span decades.[8]

Harlow was the architect of a major farm speech delivered by Eisenhower in Peoria, Illinois, and on nationwide radio and television networks, on September 25, 1956. Because of his background as an expert on agriculture-related legislation, Harlow always took the lead in speeches concerning the administration's farm program. In the Peoria speech, Eisenhower cited four years of accomplishment in eliminating stifling wartime controls and regaining lost foreign markets.

When Eisenhower campaign officials chose Oklahoma City as the site of an October 29 speech, Harlow was called upon to draft a major campaign speech to be made in his home state. Harlow asked the Defense Department for current statistics on federal expenditures at Tinker Air Force Base, Fort Sill, and other military reservations in the Sooner State. He also requested information from Civil Aeronautics Board official Herbert Hyde, a native of Oklahoma City, about programs to improve Oklahoma's airports.

A week before the speech, Oklahoma Republican State Chairman Walter E. "Gene" Curry sent Harlow a long list of topics that should be included in the presidential address. It was Curry's opinion that the most important campaign issue in Oklahoma was United States Senator Mike Monroney's support of Democratic presidential nominee Adlai Stevenson's stand to limit hydrogen bomb testing. Curry also suggested that Eisenhower stress the need for a two-party system in Oklahoma, because the state had never elected a Republican governor. Oklahoma Democrats had warned voters that if Eisenhower was re-elected, masses of workers at Tinker Air Force Base would lose their jobs. Curry recommended a strong denial of any cuts at Tinker and assurance of continued aid for areas of Oklahoma hit hard by a searing drought.

Harlow sorted through the stack of suggestions for the Oklahoma speech and, with cigarette in hand, began pecking at his trusty typewriter, cranking out a speech that began with a defense of Eisenhower's first four years in office. The speech contained a strong denial that Tinker Air Force Base would be hit with cuts, calling such a rumor "political bunk."[9] Harlow also filled the President's address with promises to Oklahoma farmers that federal help would lessen their burden caused by the drought.

In addition to normal speechwriting duties in 1956, Harlow assisted Melvin Laird, a key member of the Republican Platform Committee. Harlow and Laird became close friends. Eisenhower, a

President Dwight D. Eisenhower throws out the first ball to launch the 1956 baseball season at Griffith Stadium in Washington, D.C. Washington Senators' manager Chuck Dressen, left, and New York Yankees' manager Casey Stengel flank the President. Harlow is just to the right behind Stengel. Courtesy Dwight D. Eisenhower Library.

shoo-in as the GOP nominee, wanted Harlow present at Platform Committee meetings so that his programs and policies were one and the same as the official Republican platform.

As the presidential campaign wound to a close in the first week of November, Eisenhower and his staff were fatigued, yet optimistic of a landslide victory. Their efforts were rewarded as American voters stamped their approval on the programs of the President and elected Eisenhower to a second term.

A SECOND TERM

My dad had a feel for politics as the result of his years
working in the War Department in the thirties.
However, he didn't like politicians much, and I think
Harlow was able to temper that prejudice a little.

JOHN S.D. EISENHOWER

Eisenhower was the first American president affected by a constitutional amendment limiting a president to two terms. Many observers pegged Eisenhower immediately a lame duck and predicted he would have little influence on the Democratic Congress. Harlow believed differently. He was confident that the American people would support Eisenhower's attempts to make the country a better place to live and that Democratic legislators would bow to pressure from their constituents to work with the Republican president.

As Congress reconvened in January, 1957, Harlow was given additional responsibilities to coordinate the flow of information from the White House to congressional leaders. Harlow developed the agenda and often guided the discussion at a weekly meeting between Eisenhower, House Minority Leader Charles Halleck and Senate Republican leader Everett Dirksen. The meeting was held every Tuesday morning at 8:30 A.M. when Congress was in session.

Harlow arose at his Arlington, Virginia, home at 6:00 A.M., waited for the three children to catch buses to three different schools, and then was driven in a chauffeured government car to

Harlow congratulates Eisenhower after the President took the oath of office for his second term in January, 1957. Courtesy *The Daily Oklahoman.*

Harlow's secretary, and later his wife, Sally Studebaker, hands Harlow yet another telephone message, 1957. Courtesy *The Daily Oklahoman.*

the White House. On Tuesdays, before the 8:30 meeting with legislative leaders, Harlow coordinated the President's breakfast with two different members of Congress each week, an effort by Eisenhower to keep in close contact with legislators whose votes would make or break his legislative program.

On Wednesday mornings each week, Eisenhower held a 10:00 A.M. news conference. The great number of news conferences held by Eisenhower came from his conviction that informing the public was essential. Harlow's Wednesdays began with a 7:30 A.M. staff breakfast to make last-minute additions or deletions to material which had been prepared throughout the last week for the President's news conference. Press Secretary James Hagerty was in

With cigarette in hand, Harlow makes a point as he addresses a White House news conference in 1958. Harlow was seldom seen without a cigarette as he went from one phone line to another, throughout his long days as counselor to President Dwight D. Eisenhower. Courtesy *The Daily Oklahoman*.

CONGRESSIONAL LEADERS MEETING

Tuesday, June 5, 1956 -- 9 a. m.

AGENDA

1. Postal Rate Legislation

2. Highway Legislation

3. Foreign Aid

4. Senate Report

5. House Report

One of Harlow's famous "doodles" drawn on the agenda page of a June 5, 1956, meeting with congressional leaders. Harlow was a compulsive doodler, evidencing his powers of concentration and precision. Courtesy Dwight D. Eisenhower Library.

charge of preparing a briefing folder for the President. However, the folder was not completed until Harlow and other aides discussed potential questions from reporters. A half hour before the news conference, Hagerty, Harlow and a handful of key aides trooped into the Oval Office to present the President with a brief outline of expected topics.[1]

Harlow, largely because he grew up in a newspaper publisher's home, defended the right of reporters to ask the President anything, anytime, as long as the answer did not endanger national security. Harlow once told an interviewer, "It is a pillar of our freedom that the reporter can press a public official to respond, even reluctantly."[2]

On Thursday of each week, Harlow was required to attend the meeting of the President and the National Security Council. On Fridays, Harlow's day began early, preparing the agenda for a weekly cabinet meeting.

Despite predictions that Democrats would run all over Eisenhower's legislative programs, the Republican president actually won approval of key legislation and used his veto power to force compromise on many issues. Harlow worked night and day to keep lines of communication open with legislative leaders. He set up elaborate, bipartisan meetings on world problems such as the crisis that occurred when an American U-2 spy plane was shot down over the Soviet Union. Harlow invited 38 leaders from both sides of the aisle to participate in the special meetings which became regular as seemingly insurmountable questions of national defense and foreign aid faced the nation.

Harlow's influence in the White House and on national and international affairs was greater during Eisenhower's second term. One newspaper story said Harlow had more influence on presidential decisions than anyone on the White House staff. Harlow was the President's chief lobbyist and the "bridge" between the White House and Capitol Hill.

Harlow spent many hours each week with Eisenhower during his second term. After the President suffered a stroke, he had some difficulty orally expressing his thoughts and turned more to the written word. Harlow called Eisenhower "a tough editor, sensitive to phrasing and emphasis and documentation."[3]

Eisenhower was a religious man but shared an unusual belief with Harlow while working on a speech in 1957. Harlow had helped write a "Back to God" speech for the President in 1954, a hard-hitting message urging the American people to remember Abraham Lincoln going to his knees to pray during the Civil War, the Mayflower Compact, and the Pilgrims longing for religious freedom. However, three years later, in discussing an upcoming speech with the President, Harlow suggested language to the effect of asking God to help us do the right thing as leaders of the country. The President looked over the speech, sat back, and said to Harlow, "Bryce, I won't say that that way. You'll have to change that, because, you see, what I happen to believe is, the good Lord deals us a hand and it's up to us to play it."[4] It was the only time Eisenhower talked with Harlow about his religious convictions.

There are many people who testify of Harlow never shunning anyone because of status. Former United States Senator Howard Baker first met Harlow at a White House dinner. Baker was present only because his wife Joy, the daughter of longtime Illinois Republican Senator Everett Dirksen, had managed the invitation. Baker, a young lawyer in awe of the powerful gathering at the White House, recalled his first impression of Harlow, "He was easy and conversational and paid some attention to me and Joy, who were clearly the least important and youngest people in the place."[5]

Harlow's congressional liaison staff during the last years of the Eisenhower administration consisted of Clyde A. Wheeler, Jr.; Edward A. McCabe, an Irish Philadelphian; and Jack Z. Anderson, a former congressman from California. The Harlow team chalked up a respectable batting average in selling the Eisenhower program to a Democratic Congress.

Working in a high-profile job in the White House was anything but boring for Harlow. When he arrived at his office after meetings, there were always 10 to 15 phone call slips on his desk.

On September 24, 1957, by Executive Order 10730, Eisenhower federalized the Arkansas National Guard and sent soldiers to Little Rock to enforce a federal court's integration order at Central High School. Arkansas Governor Orval Faubus defied the court order and refused to allow the students admitted. Eisenhower, a strong believer in equal education for all, saw no alternative but to use the power of his office to force Arkansas to integrate its public schools.

Harlow quickly drafted a message for the President to use in a live radio and television broadcast from the White House within hours after the Executive Order was issued. In an intellectual speech about freedom and the fight against lawlessness, Eisenhower told the nation, "Disorderly mobs have deliberately prevented the carrying out of proper orders from a Federal Court. . . Whenever normal agencies prove inadequate to the task, the President's responsibility is inescapable."[6]

Eisenhower blamed the discontent in Little Rock and in other hot spots around the world on the influence of communism, saying, "The divisive force is international communism and the power that it controls. The designs of that power, dark in purpose, are clear in practice. It strives to seal forever the fate of those it has enslaved. It strives to break the ties that unite the free. And it strives to capture, to exploit for its own greater power, all forces of change in the world, especially the needs of the hungry and the hopes of the oppressed."[7]

Harlow was at the White House when a fire storm of controversy erupted over Eisenhower's use of federal troops in Little Rock. Democratic United States Senator Richard Russell of Georgia called Harlow with his denunciation of Eisenhower's action, charging that the move was similar to Hitler's use of storm troopers.[8] Harlow drafted a response from the President to Russell which was sent by telegram from the United States Naval Base in Newport, Rhode Island, where Eisenhower was visiting. In part, the telegram read, "When a State, by seeking to frustrate the orders of a Federal Court, encourages mobs of extremists to flout the orders, and when a State refuses to utilize its police powers to protect against mobs persons who are peaceably exercising their right under the Constitution as defined in such Court orders, the oath of office of the President requires that he take action to give that protection. Failure to act in such a case would be tantamount to acquiescence in anarchy and the dissolution of the union."[9]

When Eisenhower returned to the White House the following day, he had on his desk Harlow's summary of telegrams received from congressmen. Some were favorable to the White House position, some were not. Senator John Sparkman demanded immediate withdrawal of troops and accused the President of breaking his word on using force to promote integration of schools. Harlow characterized Sparkman's telegram as "political diatribe." Senator John McClellan, another Southerner, said he deplored Eisenhower's decision and keeping troops in Little Rock was aggravating the situation and offered no hope for a permanent solution.[10]

Concerned with the legality of the President's action in Little Rock, Harlow asked Attorney General Brownell for his opinion.

Harlow, left, receives a golf putter for President Dwight D. Eisenhower from Oklahoma Congressman John Jarman and his wife, December, 1957. Courtesy *The Daily Oklahoman.*

Brownell replied to Harlow in a September 28 memo that the Executive Order was legal in all respects and could not be challenged in court.[11]

One afternoon in 1957, Eisenhower told Harlow he looked tired and should get some exercise by using the White House putting green. Harlow reminded the President, "Not everybody around here plays golf." Eisenhower said, "What's your game?" Harlow replied, "Tennis."

"Then go play tennis," Eisenhower said. Harlow told the President that the tennis courts at the White House were in complete disrepair and had been designed with gutters running down the baseline. Harlow said, "You could break your ankles playing on those courts."

Ike, with the power of the presidency of the United States behind him, simply said, "Well, then, fix them." Harlow said, "Is that an order General?" Eisenhower, with a glint in his eye, shot back, "Yes, Harlow, that's an order."[12]

That night Harlow had architects from the General Services Administration in his office with blueprints for new tennis courts. Within weeks the White House tennis courts were completed and Harlow took up the game again, although his dedication to work left him most days just looking out the window at the court and wondering what if would feel like to have a racket, rather than a telephone, in his hand.

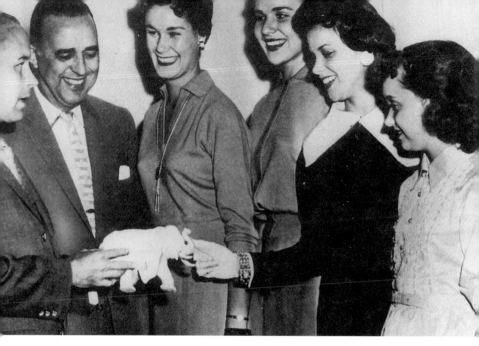

Oklahoma Day in Washington, D.C. took a group of Sooners to the White House in September, 1957. Left to right, Harlow; Lou Allard, chairman of Oklahoma's Semi-Centennial Commission; Charlotte Holloteter, Blackwell; Kay Camp, Waukomis; Cecille Roberts, Norman; and Libby Horne, McAlester. Miss Roberts was named Queen of the Day and Misses Holloteter and Camp were her attendants. Courtesy *The Daily Oklahoman.*

Years later, James D. "Mike" McKevitt, a longtime lobbyist and Harlow's close friend, approached their mutual friend, Vice President George Bush, with a proposal to name the White House tennis courts after Harlow. Bush said, "Great idea. Go do it." However, when McKevitt contacted the White House Historical Society, he was firmly rebuked because of the long-standing policy of not naming anything on the White House grounds after individuals other than presidents and first ladies. Not to be deterred, Bush and McKevitt had a brass plaque made proclaiming the courts as the "Bryce Harlow Tennis Courts." The plaque was hung near the tennis courts.[13]

Except for maintenance and the addition of a cabana/dressing room, the White House tennis courts remain, more than 40 years later, as Harlow designed them.

The year 1957 was demanding upon Eisenhower and his staff. From his farm at Gettysburg on December 30, the President wrote to Harlow, "Together we have spent twelve months in the onerous, demanding, often confining but always rewarding, work of the Federal government. So I want to try once more to tell you of my lasting appreciation of the great service you are rendering. . . Above everything else, I want to thank your for your dedication to our country's welfare and for the unswerving loyalty which have characterized your work in my behalf. . . My confidence in the future stems, in great part, from my knowledge that the Administration is rich in its possession of men of character, ability, and integrity."[14]

HELP FOR OKLAHOMA

HARLOW WAS UNIQUE IN THE SENSE THAT HE WAS INVOLVED IN
SENSITIVE POSITIONS ALMOST ALWAYS ON BEHALF OF SOMEONE
ELSE OR SOME OTHER ISSUE.

HOWARD BAKER

Harlow was given an opportunity to help his native Oklahoma during the state's semi-centennial in 1957. As part of the year-long celebration, 26-year-old female pilot Jerrie Cobb, a native of Norman and graduate of Oklahoma City's Classen High School, planned an all-out assault on the world's nonstop distance record. The record, in the 3,858 to 6,613 pound weight class, was held by a Russian Air Force officer who flew 1,236 miles. Cobb intended to fly from Guatemala City, Guatemala, in Central America, to Oklahoma City, a distance of 1,504 miles.[1]

Cobb's world-record attempt ran into a major problem when she discovered federal regulations would force her to land in Dallas, Texas to clear United States Customs and pass inspection of the United States Public Health Service. Jack Leach, the chief of the semi-centennial press section, called on Harlow to break through the sea of red tape that threatened Cobb's plan. After Harlow made visits to top officials at several federal agencies, Cobb was cleared to fly past Dallas and on to Oklahoma City. Harlow's answer to the dilemma was simple. Federal customs and public health officials were temporarily assigned to Oklahoma City for one day, the day Cobb flew her Aero Commander, named "Boom-town I," across Guatemala, the Gulf of Mexico, Mexico, Texas, and into Oklahoma City, in eight hours and five minutes. The historic flight was closely followed by a cadre of Oklahoma City newsmen flying in another Aero Commander. Included in the press corps were Don Ferrell of *The Daily Oklahoman*, later Oklahoma Adjutant General, Gene Allen of WKY, Bruce Palmer of KWTV, and Leach.[2]

Two days after Cobb's record-breaking flight, Leach thanked Harlow for his help in a flowery letter filled with descriptive adjectives and dangling adverbs. Floods had hit southern Oklahoma on the day of the flight. Leach wrote, "Starting out about 150 miles from Dallas–Fort Worth, the ground was like a giant sponge which had every pore filled with water. It is utterly fantastic that only a few months ago your good Boss was stalking across parched brown fields which are now lush to the point that mosquitoes are everywhere."

"Every farm pond is full," Leach continued, "The lakes are running over their spillways... Why is it, Bryce, that this country we both love so well endures either feast or famine—it breaks the heart."[3]

Harlow responded, "Once in awhile even the government finds its way clear to do the obvious thing. I am happy the Jerrie Cobb expedition worked out."[4]

In November, 1957, Harlow asked Eisenhower to accept Oklahoma Governor Raymond Gary's invitation for the President to appear during the closing days of the state's semi-centennial celebration. To convince the President to rearrange his November schedule and visit Oklahoma, Harlow obtained a football signed by University of Oklahoma football coach Bud Wilkinson and team members. Eisenhower gave the football to his grandson David and thanked Wilkinson in an October 13, 1957, letter, "David has an ardent interest in the sport... So, to all of you go his thanks and my thanks for this prized gift."[5] With his broad smile and military stance, Eisenhower made a major address to the nation from Oklahoma City on November 13, 1957.

During top-level White House meetings with congressional leaders, Harlow made copious note of the attendees, and made time for a simple "doodle." This 1957 note in Harlow's hand lists the top leaders of the country, President Dwight D. Eisenhower, Vice President Richard Nixon, Senate Majority Leader Lyndon Johnson, House Speaker Sam Rayburn, and many others. Courtesy Dwight D. Eisenhower Library.

In a speech written by Harlow, the President spoke of strong military as a deterrent to the enemies of freedom. Eisenhower said the nation had tough choices to make, "Some civilian programs were desirable but not essential. Some savings would be squeezed out through the wringer and pressure groups will wail in the anguish."[6] Eisenhower promised, however, that America would never sacrifice security just to worship a balanced budget. The message was needed as speculation about the eventual plunging of Russian satellites into orbit over the United States sparked anxiety and feelings of vulnerability in the hearts of Americans.

In early 1958, Harlow was the sounding board in Washington for members of opposing forces in Oklahoma fighting over the expansion of Fort Sill at Lawton. Congress was considering a major expansion of the Army facility which had become the primary training ground for American Army artillerymen. However, Fort Sill officials proposed the purchase of 281,000 acres west and southwest of the existing military reservation in Kiowa, Comanche, and Caddo counties, land necessary for the development of new missile-firing ranges.

A postcard received by Harlow from an Oklahoma woman who opposed the 1958 expansion of Fort Sill. Newspapers identified Harlow as close to President Dwight D. Eisenhower, resulting in a flood of mail for the presidential assistant. Courtesy Dwight D. Eisenhower Library.

In a series of letters, Harlow responded to both proponents and opponents of the expansion plan. W.G. Dudgeon, officer manager of the Kiowa County Farm Bureau, directed a scathing attack of the plan to Harlow. Dudgeon wrote, "You can not imagine the turmoil and the tension that the people in this area are facing. We are all terrified at what is about to happen to us. Talk about a Cold War! That is what we are facing. . . We can not understand the taking of our good productive land for a missile range when we know that the government already owns vast acres of waste land that would be better suited for such an impact area."7

The *Hobart Democrat Chief* plunged head-on editorially into the fight, calling the expansion plan a "fantasy" and a "slur" at "those of us who believe the federal government already owns enough land."8 The Hobart newspaper took a swipe at leaders in Lawton who would benefit greatly by the Fort Sill expansion by writing, "It is not unpatriotic to oppose foolish and unneeded waste in federal government. The purchase of high priced land just for the sake of capital gain to a single city. . . at the expense of such a large segment of the state will not be tolerated."9

Lawton Chamber of Commerce leaders called upon Harlow to convince both Eisenhower and the Congress to support the program. The Oklahoma Defense League (ODL) was formed to promote the expansion. Chaired by Dave Vandivier of Chickasha and Ned Shepler of Lawton, the ODL launched a barrage of news releases citing the economic benefits and military necessity of the Fort Sill expansion. The ODL, buttressed by Executive Committee members and political honchos such as J.M. Sturdevant, Altus; Fred Holmes, Enid; Exall English and J.C. Kennedy, Lawton; James C. Leake, Muskogee; Frank Buttram and Major General W.S. Key, Oklahoma City; R.C. Longmire, Pauls Valley; and Brandon Frost of Woodward, met with Oklahoma Governor Raymond Gary to win his support.

Gary, feeling pressure from citizens living in the towns affected by the proposed expansion, balked, and announced his opposition to the Army purchasing any additional land. The state legislature passed a resolution asking Gary to fly to Washington to talk with the President about the problem. The Governor asked Harlow to set up a meeting with Eisenhower. Within a few days Harlow worked Gary into the President's schedule.

When Governor Gary reached the Oval Office, he was asked to wait outside while Eisenhower completed a conference with Secretary of State John Foster Dulles. Gary, anxious about his first face-to-face meeting with the President, waited for what seemed an eternity. When he was shown into the Oval Office, Gary talked politics for a few moments and then told Eisenhower tactfully that he was opposed to any Fort Sill expansion into the surrounding counties in southwest Oklahoma. The President put Gary at ease when he said, "The Army already owns too much land."[10] However, the Oklahoma Governor was confused when Eisenhower remained noncommittal to Gary's request that the President tell his top generals to forget about the plan. When Gary pressed Eisenhower by pointing out that reporters were waiting outside for an answer, the President said, "Just tell them everything's fine."[11] That is exactly what Gary told the reporters, resulting in Oklahoma newspaper headlines the next day, "Gary Says Everything's OK."[12]

True to his word, Eisenhower axed the expansion project.

White House Reorganization

REAL POLITICAL RELATIONSHIPS ARE NOT GOVERNED BY SOCIAL AMENITIES AT THE WHITE HOUSE. THE KEY TO PRESIDENTIAL INFLUENCE IN THE CONGRESS IS FOUND IN THE PRESIDENT'S STANDING WITH THE PUBLIC.

BRYCE HARLOW

When former New Hampshire Governor Sherman Adams resigned as Assistant to the President in the fall of 1958, Eisenhower restructured his staff. Harlow told the President he was willing to serve in any capacity. The two men talked about the tremendous amount of time each week Harlow spent writing and editing speeches. Eisenhower asked his trusted adviser, Dr. Kevin McCann, for advice on how best to use Harlow's talents. McCann told the President that Harlow enjoyed a phenomenal relationship with leaders on Capitol Hill and it was a waste of this national resource to have him spend most of his time on speeches. Adams urged Eisenhower to give Harlow more power in dealing with Congress, calling Harlow "one of the most adept men in political semantics I ever knew."[1]

Eisenhower took McCann and Adams' advice to heart, and placed Harlow in full charge of the Administration's dealings with Congress. On October 18, 1958, Harlow was sworn in as Deputy Presidential Assistant for Congressional Affairs. Harlow's appointment was part of the sweeping reorganization of the White House by new Chief of Staff General Wilton Persons, with whom Harlow had served since their days at the Pentagon. Robert Merriam became the President's principal adviser on domestic issues and General Andy Goodpaster was named staff secretary and chief adviser on national security.

From his office on the second floor of the West Wing of the White House, immediately above the Oval Office, Harlow put together a team of congressional liaison representatives. One member of the group was former California congressman and apple-grower Jack Z. Anderson. Others were Pennsylvania native Edward A. McCabe, a former staff member of the House Labor Committee. McCabe later became a prominent Washington lawyer with a much-respected expertise in labor law. Earle D. Chesney, a World War II veteran and accomplished artist, and Brigadier General Homer H. Gruenther, who had been with Eisenhower since his first term, rounded out the Harlow team.

Later in 1958, Harlow hired Clyde A. Wheeler, Jr., to handle liaison primarily with the House of Representatives while McCabe concentrated on liaison with Senators on behalf of Eisenhower's programs. Harlow kept the division of duties between Wheeler and McCable quite flexible. For example, on significant agriculture programs, Wheeler covered both the House and Senate because he was an expert about that area of legislation. And labor reform legislation, a major Eisenhower priority, was assigned entirely to McCabe as it moved through both houses of Congress in 1958 and 1959, since his experience in that area was extensive.[2]

Wheeler recalled the daily meetings with Harlow, "We met for breakfast at 7:00 A.M. and received our marching orders for the day. Harlow passed along words of wisdom from Eisenhower and other top officials. By 8:30 A.M. we were on the Hill, buttonholing every member of Congress we could."[3]

Harlow went to great lengths to make certain he and his legislative liaison team stayed out of the limelight. He taught his troops to have a goal of never being quoted by the press. He strongly believed they could be more effective if they worked under the cloak of near anonymity and that only Eisenhower and his chief of staff should speak for the White House.[4]

President Eisenhower
congratulates Harlow after
he was sworn in as
congressional liaison chief
in October, 1958.
Courtesy Dwight D.
Eisenhower Library.

Left to right, Betty, Bryce, Larry, Trudy, and Peggy, at the White House October
18, 1958, as Harlow was sworn in as Deputy Presidential Assistant for
Congressional Affairs. Courtesy *The Daily Oklahoman.*

After the reorganization of the White House staff, Eisenhower's son, John, played a larger role on his father's team. Young Eisenhower looked up to Harlow and watched his every move in handling the heavy affairs of state. During the Berlin Crisis in 1958, Major Eisenhower observed Harlow diffuse a complicated political problem that threatened to sour public opinion of Eisenhower.

Soviet Premier Nikita Khrushchev had given an ultimatum to the United States to withdraw its forces from Berlin. Eisenhower was faced with public opinion polls that said he was failing to make adequate military preparations for a showdown over Berlin. The President insisted on fulfilling his earlier promise to reduce the American military presence in Europe.

Harlow suggested, and Eisenhower agreed, that top legislative leaders should be brought to the White House immediately to plan America's response to Khruschchev. Harlow went to his office and launched a telephone campaign to invite key members of Congress to a meeting the next day in the ground-floor library of the White House.

From the Senate came Alexander Wiley, Everett Dirksen, Lyndon Johnson, Richard Russell, J. William Fulbright, and Leverett Saltonstall. Representatives present were House Speaker Sam Rayburn, Leslie Arends, A.S.J. Carnahan, Carl Vinson, and Robert Chiperfield. The Executive Branch was represented at the high-level meeting by Vice President Nixon, Secretary of State Christian Herter, Defense Secretary Neil McElroy, and Central Intelligence Agency (CIA) Director Allen Dulles.

President Eisenhower gave a general intelligence briefing, covering such subjects as Soviet military strength in the region, political attitudes in Germany, and the size of Allied garrisons in Berlin.[5]

John Eisenhower later wrote how he was shocked by how little some of the congressmen knew about the Berlin situation. As the meeting progressed, however, Harlow and Senate Minority Leader Everett Dirksen pieced together their recommendations for a public statement to be made by the President: (1) The United States had explored the situation and would maintain its responsibility to the people of Berlin; (2) The United States would stand firm, but was willing to negotiate; and (3) Allied military forces were in place and were adequate to defend West Berlin.[6]

Young Eisenhower was also shocked at the frank statements, many laced with political considerations, made by members of Congress at the meeting. He expressed his frustration to Harlow as the two walked out of the meeting. Harlow told Eisenhower in a soothing tone, "You've got to realize John that these are tough birds. They've all risen to where they are over the dead bodies of a lot of opponents."[7]

Nuclear disarmament was a topic of conversation among world leaders in 1958. For more than a year American and Soviet representatives had met to work out details of an arms control agreement. Eisenhower, aware of Harlow's already impossible workload, nevertheless asked his young friend to draft a series of public statements on disarmament.

The horror of World War II was still fresh in the minds of Americans who feared disarmament would place America in a vulnerable position. Harlow drafted a statement for the President that defended his desire to agree to suspend nuclear weapons tests if the Soviet Union would promise the same. Harlow added a paragraph to allay the fear of critics of the policy. The last paragraph of the statement promised, "Until such a first-step arms control agreement comes into force, the United States will, of course, conduct such nuclear testing as our security requires."[8]

After leading newspapers expressed their support for Eisenhower's disarmament policy, the President sent a personal note to Harlow, "Quite naturally I am encouraged by the editorial comment I have seen. . . I well realize that your work on it, added as it was to your already heavy schedule, involved a lot of late hours and extra pressure. This note is simply to tell you that I much appreciate the fine job you did."[9]

One of Harlow's toughest sales job in his congressional liaison career was a Pentagon reorganization plan introduced in the Congress in 1958. Harlow teamed up with new Secretary of Defense Neil McElroy, the former president of Procter & Gamble, whom

Eisenhower had convinced to assume responsibilities for the massive Department of Defense in October, 1957.

Harlow also worked closely on the project with General Andrew Goodpaster, who later characterized the reorganization move as one that "brought us head-long against vested interests in the Pentagon, which sought to water down the efforts that the President's objectives required." Goodpaster said Harlow's "skill and knowledge were crucial" to congressional passage of Eisenhower's sweeping proposals. As Harlow began preparing position papers and speeches for the President, he used his talents, described by Goodpaster, of "writing clear prose, it was a joy to watch him take submissions from the departments, often heavy with 'officialese,' and in his words, 'cut the crud out.'"[10]

Eisenhower, the commander of the largest military force ever assembled during World War II, had lived with subject of military reshuffling for years. He knew what he wanted to do and appointed an advisory committee to help draft a reorganization plan. On January 25, 1957, Eisenhower, Harlow, and Goodpaster went to the Pentagon to meet with Secretary McElroy and his top staff.

The military reorganization plan was complicated but essentially concentrated more authority in the Secretary of Defense and subtracted powers from the Army, Navy, and Air Force chiefs of staff, instead vesting more power in the Joint Chiefs of Staff (JCS). Critics claimed the plan would set up the Secretary of Defense as a czar or dictator.

Harlow's job was made tougher when Eisenhower was belligerent in an early April news conference when he declared he did not care how strong or how numerous were the congressional opponents to his plan. *The Daily Oklahoman* assessed Harlow's job: "It won't be soft soap that Harlow will be peddling on Capitol Hill. It will be hard facts, presented with a deep background knowledge of Congress and the defense establishment."[11]

In addition to carrying Eisenhower's water on military reorganization to Congress, Harlow was charged with the duty of providing a technical explanation of the plan to members of the press. In May, 1958, Harlow drafted a summary of Eisenhower's Pentagon-reshuffle plan for the press. The summary pointed out that the President supported a concentrated or unified command structure with a Joint Chiefs of Staff (JCS), "If the unified commands are to act quickly, decisively, and with the fullest possible flexibility, they must have a direct channel of command from the Secretary of Defense through his military advisors. Thus the ability of the JCS to render to the Secretary the most able military advice that can be obtained, both for strategic planning and for operation of the combatant forces."[12]

The heart of Eisenhower's military reorganization proposal lay in the concept of a unified command. The President reasoned, "Separate ground, sea, and air warfare is gone forever. In the future the unified command will provide the cutting edge of our military machine."[13]

Harlow began the overwhelming job of talking with members of Congress, one-on-one about the merits of the President's Reorganization Plan. Harlow suggested Eisenhower set up "a luncheon or stag dinner" with leading publishers and broadcast executives such as DeWitt Wallace of *Reader's Digest;* Elliot Bell of McGraw Hill; Henry Luce and David Sarnoff; union leaders such as AFL-CIO President George Meany; and business and chamber of commerce leaders to drum up support for the plan. Harlow was elated on April 10 when he learned that the American Legion National Security Commission adopted a strong statement in support of the reorganization program.[14]

The difficulty of Harlow's job of getting as much of the reorganization plan through Congress as possible was described by Goodpaster, "Here Bryce's abilities absolutely shone in turning around, almost completely, the top Congressional leaders, individuals committed to leaving things as they were. Other than the President himself, no one but Bryce could have done it. Bryce was the key figure."[15] After months of long days and nights of negotiations, Eisenhower's Pentagon reorganization plan, the Defense Reorganization Bill was passed by Congress and signed into law by the President on August 6, 1957.

Toward the end of the Eisenhower administration, Harlow convinced fellow Oklahoman Clyde A. Wheeler, Jr., to run for Congress in Oklahoma's sprawling Sixth Congressional District. Harlow drafted, and the President signed, a strong letter of endorsement of Wheeler's candidacy. In this photo taken at the White House in early 1960, Eisenhower says goodbye to Wheeler, his wife Barbara, and children, left to right, Clyde A. Wheeler, III, Jane, and Ruth. In the November, 1960 election, Wheeler apparently won the Sixth District seat by 120 votes. However, a controversial recount gave a 76-vote victory to Democrat Victor Wickersham. Courtesy Clyde A. Wheeler, Jr.

Facing: As the Congress began reworking Eisenhower's military reorganization plan, this cartoon appeared in the *San Francisco Examiner.* Courtesy Dwight D. Eisenhower Library.

Harlow worked feverishly to convince members of Congress in 1958 to add Alaska and Hawaii as states of the union. Eisenhower fully supported the idea and asked Harlow to coordinate the legislation adding the two new states through the congressional process. There was opposition from both parties. Southerners opposed the addition of new members of Congress that might defeat their attempts to hang on to segregation. Republicans feared Alaska would go Democratic and Democrats feared Hawaii would become Republican. After much debate, Congress added Alaska as the 49th state in 1958 but put off the admission of Hawaii.

In 1959 Harlow assigned Clyde Wheeler, Jr., to push the Hawaii statehood bill. It was a cause close to Wheeler's heart. He was educated fully on the subject by one of his best friends at Oklahoma A & M who had chosen the issue as a dissertation subject.

"And All I Wanted Was a Little Gas!" By Burris Jenkins Jr.

The hard work of Wheeler, Harlow, and McCabe paid off. Congress passed, and Eisenhower signed, legislation admitting Hawaii as the 50th state in March, 1959.[16]

A spy-plane incident marred improving relations between the United States and Russia in May, 1960. A U-2 aircraft, more of a flying glider than a conventional airplane, went down over Russian territory during a reconnaissance flight. The U-2 program had begun four years previous with the intent of gathering information about the predicted buildup of the Soviet military machine. Somehow, the United States had kept the flights of the U-2 secret until pilot Francis Gary Powers went down and was held by Soviet authorities.

At first, the National Aeronautics and Space Administration claimed the U-2 was conducting high-altitude weather research. However, Soviet Premier Nikita Khrushchev displayed pieces of the downed airplane on television and bitterly accused the United States of spying on his country.

Harlow and Secretary of State Christian Herter suggested to Eisenhower that he tell the public the truth, that America had successfully spied on Russia for four years. Eisenhower asked Harlow to draft a statement. Harlow went back to his office and began writing.

Because Eisenhower had been silent for days, and allowed the world to believe the initial story about the U-2 being involved in weather research, Harlow feared the storm that lay ahead. He struggled with the speech. Henry Bellmon, Oklahoma Republican chairman and later governor and United States Senator, happened to be at the White House that day to visit Harlow. Bellmon remembers Harlow as writing feverishly, then tearing the paper out, crumpling it and throwing it away, again and again, then writing something new. In describing Harlow's frustration at his difficult task, Bellmon later recalled that it was the only time he ever saw Harlow flabbergasted.[17]

Old colleagues doubt Harlow was ever really "flabbergasted," but if he were then, it would have been with good reason. Edward McCabe opined:

Bryce knew 1960 was, as he would put it, a year divisible by four, a Presidential election year. He was well aware that politics that year would not 'stop at the water's edge,' as was often the case in earlier times. The entire Democratic election appratus would be all over Eisenhower and Vice President Richard Nixon, charging them with reckless foreign adventures that damaged American prestige in the world. . . . There was insufficient time to blunt that sustained attack before the voting in November. Bryce knew this. He could have been further dismayed when some also charged the President with being untruthful, in that the administration waited several days before correcting the cover story that the U-2 was a weather reconnaissance plane."[18]

Eisenhower admitted Russia's allegations about the U-2 incident. Pilot Powers was humiliated in a television trial and imprisoned. He was freed years later after Eisenhower left the White House.

Lost in the political clamor of 1960 was the fact that the United States gained intelligence of enormous value to military security planning from the many photographs of Russian military activities and installations taken by the U-2 flights.

But the facts were submerged in the political rhetoric. Even the towering stature of Eisenhower, or the formidable communication skills of Harlow, could not change the picture in the short run.[19]

Harlow's prestige grew enormously during his service in the Eisenhower White House. He influenced the lives of many people, including teenager David Lyle Boren who enjoyed talking politics with Harlow and Melvin Laird. Boren, a high school student with great political ambition, was the son of former Oklahoma Congressman Lyle H. Boren, a close friend to both Harlow and Laird. Young Boren met with Harlow and Laird who tried to convince him to register to vote as a Republican, predicting that Boren's home state of Oklahoma would someday be Republican and that the Democratic party would eventually adopt policies and programs that would be less compatible with Boren's own views.[20]

Boren, influenced by his Democratic parents and the realities of the Democratic voter-base in Boren's home base of Seminole County, Oklahoma, registered as a Democrat and was elected a state representative, Governor, and United States Senator in Oklahoma before resigning to become president of the University of Oklahoma.[21]

Boren never forgot principles taught him by Harlow who recognized that the country must come first, that sometimes partisanship must be cast aside for the good of the nation, when leaders were compelled to reach out to the other side of the political aisle. Boren followed in the footsteps of Harlow in becoming a champion of bipartisan cooperation. Boren said this was the most important aspect of his entire political career, influenced absolutely by Harlow. As a confidant and sounding board for Republican Presidents Gerald Ford and Ronald Reagan, Boren well remembered advice given him by Harlow decades before.[22]

In 1960, Harlow received the Minuteman Award, the highest honor of the Reserve Officers Association of the United States. Presenting the award was Colonel Jesse B. Stuart, a colleague of Harlow who had been wounded in the Battle of Normandy, and whose first visitor, after being transported from a field hospital to Walter Reed Army Hospital in Washington, was Harlow.

Colonel Stuart said of Harlow, "The record of his achievements speaks rather eloquently. But the record does not sparkle as does his personality. . . . It is not as stout as his fine character, which is the bedrock of every good American's nature. It does reflect the polish and deftness of his diplomacy, which turned the tide for us many a time when the issues were shadowy. . . . Bryce Harlow is an incorruptible patriot."

Procter & Gamble

HARLOW WAS RESPONSIBLE, KNOWLEDGEABLE. HE KNEW THE
RULES AND ABIDED BY THEM CONSCIENTIOUSLY. YOU COULD
ALWAYS TRUST HIM IN ANY LOBBYING ACTIVITY THAT HE WAS
DOING IT PROPERLY.

PRESIDENT GERALD R. FORD

Neil Hosler McElroy was Harlow's link to the private sector. McElroy, a native of Cincinnati, Ohio, joined Procter & Gamble in 1925, fresh out of Harvard. He began his illustrious career at P & G as an advertising mail room clerk for $100 per month. In just 23 years he became president of the giant consumer products company.

Procter & Gamble began operations in 1837 on a small scale with partners William Procter and James Gamble boiling animal fats in a giant iron kettle over a wood fire behind their small shop in Cincinnati. Procter and Gamble used the fats to manufacture candles and soap which they peddled to area businesses in a wheelbarrow. The two young entrepreneurs constituted but one of 18 candle-making operations in Cincinnati in 1837. Their company was not only the lone survivor, but Procter & Gamble endured wars, depressions, riots, panics, periods of unbelievable shortages, and became one of the largest and most successful corporations in America.[1] In 1998, P & G employed 110,000 people worldwide, marketed 300 brands to nearly 5,000,000,000 consumers in 140 countries, and amassed $37 billion in sales.[2]

During the Civil War P & G produced millions of candles and bars of soap for Union soldiers. Even when Confederate troops approached Cincinnati, and martial law was declared in the city, P & G remained open. An unexpected advertising boost for the company came from free publicity supplied by the wooden crates in which soap and candles were shipped to the front lines. When emptied of their products, the crates were used by soldiers for chairs and storage containers. The black letters proclaiming "Procter & Gamble" on the sides of the crates were a constant reminder of the company's importance in the new economy that would grow after the war.

In 1879 P & G developed a new white soap that actually floated in water. Harley Procter's quest for a name for the new product ended one Sabbath during a church service. The minister read from the Psalms, "All thy garments smell of myrrh and aloes and cassia, out of the ivory palaces whereby they have made thee glad."

One of Procter & Gamble's most successful products was Tide. This is the store poster introducing the new product in 1946. Courtesy Procter & Gamble.

Three generations of Procter & Gamble leadership. From left, Howard J. Morgens, Richard Redwood Deupree, and Neil McElroy. McElroy led P & G from 1948-1957 with time out to serve as Eisenhower's Secretary of Defense. He was Harlow's link to the private sector. Courtesy Procter & Gamble.

Procter focused on the word "ivory," which meant to him "purity and luxury." Thus was born Ivory soap, a leading seller in the soap industry for more than a century.[3]

Neil McElroy moved up the corporate ladder at P & G throughout the 1930s and 1940s as the company introduced products such as Tide, Spic and Span, and Ajax that became part of the American language.

In 1948 McElroy was named president of P & G. Under McElroy's leadership, Procter & Gamble went Hollywood, sponsoring and producing television dramas and entertainment. The soap opera was born and P & G soon produced more filmed entertainment than any major movie studio.[4] The company's first long-running television drama was "Search for Tomorrow."

Harlow first met McElroy in 1954 when Eisenhower appointed him chairman of a White House Conference on Education. Eisenhower knew that McElroy was dedicated to public education. Both his parents had been teachers and he had chaired educational fund-raising campaigns in the Cincinnati area for years. McElroy's organizational talents in bringing more than 2,000 educators to Washington for the White House conference caught Eisenhower's eye. One publication called the conference "the most massive and searching consultation on United States education in history."[5]

In 1957 Eisenhower summoned McElroy to the White House with another request. The President wanted the P & G chief to become Secretary of Defense, replacing Secretary Charles Wilson. McElroy was stunned but decided he could not turn down the leader of the country. In August, the United States Senate confirmed Eisenhower's nomination of McElroy who was sworn in on October 9, 1957, to lead America's complicated and growing military establishment.

Harlow and McElroy worked long hours together, discovering they had much in common. Both believed in excellence in education, hard work, the use of ingenuity in handling problems, and absolute honest dealings in every situation. The reorganization of the Pentagon threw Harlow and McElroy into the same smoke-filled rooms night after night as the largest restructuring of the military might of the United States proceeded through Congress.

A great mutual respect developed between Harlow and McElroy. Harlow was impressed with McElroy's strong, candid leadership capabilities. McElroy was intrigued with Harlow's wide-ranging and comprehensive knowledge of the Department of Defense, information he had gleaned from his years of service at the Pentagon and as staff director of the House Armed Services Committee. Often McElroy bypassed his own speech-writing staff at the Pentagon and called upon Harlow to draft speeches and position papers.

In 1959, McElroy resigned his position as Defense Secretary and returned to Procter & Gamble as chairman of the board. He was awarded the Medal of Freedom by President Eisenhower for his outstanding service to his country.

As the end of Eisenhower's second term neared, Harlow wondered about his future. He wanted to stay in Washington. However, the 1960 presidential election cast uncertainty upon his options. Everyone predicted a close race between Vice President Richard Nixon, the GOP nominee, and United States Senator John F. Kennedy, the Democratic standard-bearer. Harlow was respected greatly by Nixon and would have been asked to stay in a Nixon administration should the vice president win the presidential race. However, there was a wide chasm between the political ideologies of Harlow and Kennedy and Harlow would never be asked to be part of a Kennedy administration.

Harlow's uneasiness over the possibility of continuing in a political job led Harlow and McElroy together. As McElroy assumed the top leadership at P & G, a new management problem evolved. The federal government was becoming more involved in controlling manufacturing and sales of consumer products. Congress, feeling pressure from consumer-advocate groups, began to create and pass legislation that placed strict controls on everything from drugs to food and shampoos. The Food and Drug Administration was born and P & G no longer had the luxury of depending only upon excellent management of consumer demand to succeed in the household products, paper, and food business. As Harlow saw it, "More and more our products, our personnel, our processes, our profits, our planning, our policies were being swept into the federal orbit. Increasingly there was need for on-the-spot professional counsel on how our company should comport herself with the testy goliath pacing the Federal District."[6]

McElroy understood the new game-plan. P & G would need to develop a mechanism to provide correct and current information on its products to Congress and federal and state government agencies that were beginning to make rules that affected the day-to-day manufacturing and sales of its products, and ultimately its bottomline profit. In the past Procter & Gamble had extensively tested its products and launched sales campaigns when a product was ready for marketing. However, in the new age of government regulation, it took the company 12 months to obtain Food and

Drug Administration (FDA) clearance for Head and Shoulders lotion and 18 months to obtain permission from the FDA to sell Scope mouthwash.

The growing lag time from research, to production, to government approval, concerned McElroy who turned for advice to the one man in Washington whose reputation proclaimed him as the most honest and informed communicator with Congress. That man was Bryce Harlow. The two men talked for weeks about the possibility of Harlow launching an intensive effort to communicate P & G's concerns about too much government control to Congress and government agencies. Harlow expressed to McElroy his fear that P & G might want to hire him because of his influence rather than for his knowledge and abilities. McElroy put Harlow's fear at ease when he told him in no uncertain terms that P & G wanted him on its team because of his intrinsic values, not his ability to peddle influence.[7]

McElroy took Harlow to meet with the P & G Board of Directors at the company's headquarters in Cincinnati. At first Harlow was intimidated by the captains of industry gathered around the conference table on the 11th floor of the P & G building. Uncomfortable, facing the stern faces of his potential new employers, Harlow broke the ice, "Well, I'm from Washington, D.C., first in war, first in peace, and last in the American League."[8]

Shortly after Nixon's defeat in the November, 1960 presidential election, Harlow accepted McElroy's invitation to join P & G as the company's congressional liaison, or lobbyist, or officially "Director of Governmental Relations." Harlow often referred to himself as "Procter's biggest Gamble."

At a meeting with the P & G board shortly after his appointment, Harlow suggested board members ask themselves two questions. The first question was "Did we get the best possible man?" Harlow answered the question for the board, saying, "No, and I will not tell you his name." Harlow posed a second question, "How will you, as board members, judge my performance?" Harlow's answer was classic: "When some midguided segment of our vast bureaucracy takes it upon itself to do unwarranted violence to

Procter and you turn this over to your Government Relations office, you must put yourself in the position of a man caught in the jaws of an alligator. The alligator has its teeth into the man's upper thigh and is savoring a full and delicious meal including the full leg and hopefully more. The man, struggling with all his strength and cunning to save his leg, or at least his life, finally jerks free, leaving a severed foot in the alligator's mouth. You must ask yourselves the question—'Did we win or lose?' "9

After the Eisenhower administration wound down in January, 1961, Harlow rented office space in Washington and began the process of setting up P & G's first full-time corporate representation office. He took along with him to P & G his trusted secretary, Sally Studebaker. Harlow had a staff of three: Sally, legislative researcher Lucille Catlett, and secretary Kay McKeon.

Harlow's exodus from the White House moved him only five city blocks, from 1600 Pennsylvania Avenue to the third floor of the Riddell Building at 1730 K Street. Harlow found his new job similar to his White House responsibilities. Where before he had sold programs and ideologies of the Eisenhower administration to members of Congress, he now sold ideas and information about one of the nation's largest corporations to those same elected repre-

Harlow and Sally Studebaker opened the Procter & Gamble government relations office in Washington in 1961. Sally was now accustomed to Harlow's routine, having served as Harlow's secretary in the Eisenhower White House. Courtesy Sally Harlow.

sentatives he had dealt with for more than a decade. Instead of reporting to the President of the United States, he now reported to the President and Board Chairman of the largest soap company in the land.

Within a month after moving into his new office, the Democratic National Committee moved into the same building. Harlow, having spent the better part of the previous decade fleeing Democrats, saw a saving grace when the Federal Bureau of Investigation suddenly rented space on the floor between Harlow and the Democrats.[10]

Harlow's "tiny outpost" kept close tabs on events unfolding in Congress and the administration and work with P & G's top executives to prioritize the matters that deserved their attention and action. Harlow drew upon his personal contacts, trade journals, wire services, congressional reports, and a half-dozen daily newspapers. He was given unlimited access to P & G's technical staff in the home office in Cincinnati when he needed to verify the authenticity or significance of some piece of information that was the latest catch-word or phrase on Capitol Hill.

Years later Harlow looked back at the creation of the P & G office in Washington, "It was programmed initially as merely a periscope, a radar, a forward observer on the Potomac, keeping a weather eye on possible adversarial hijinks in Congress and the federal bureaucracy. But later on, as company goose pimples slowly retracted and as P & G antibodies adjusted to the new Washington presence, the function enlarged, making the office capable of doing as well as looking."[11]

Harlow kept his eyes trained on the Federal Trade Commission, the Federal Communications Commission, the Securities and Exchange Commission, an assortment of cabinet departments, the "unpredictable organism" called the Congress.[12]

Harlow was brilliant at his job. His long hours of face-to-face meetings with congressman and senators had paid off. Harlow knew the names of members' wives, their sporting and hobby interests, and where they stood on most issues that affected his new employer.

Harlow understood the workings of the federal government, saying, "This huge mass of humanity [the Congress]... doesn't mill about like a mob, as it tends to appear to outsiders, but instead functions as a series of inter-related power centers." He explained, "The salvation of the system, and the magic of our political process, is that the dominant influence of virtually all times throughout the Congress is simply this: what do most of the people back home really want."[13]

Harlow had a sixth sense of deciding when to conduct advocacy alone or jointly with other companies or trade associations. Specific situations and the personalities of the decision makers guided Harlow to know whether he should talk to a congressman or regulator alone, over dinner, or whether company leaders and experts should be called in to address a public hearing or conduct a private briefing for a key congressional staff member.

David L. Boren, after serving in the United States Senate from Oklahoma, analyzed Harlow's successful methods of dealing with Congress. Boren said, "In dealing with others he always advised that if you did not agree with someone, let them know up front, avoid anything that might raise an unrealistic expectation on the part of the other party, and express hope that you can help on something else in the future." Boren said Harlow advised him to "give the other person a graceful exit from his position, don't embarrass him or paint him in a corner."[14]

In an oft-quoted essay on corporate representation, Harlow wrote:

> Corporate representation is sometimes dangerous, often frustrating, and always time-consuming and difficult. It calls for an unceasing effort to educate and motivate current and potential allies—and to discourage and befuddle foes. It requires the coordination of personal visits, telephone calls, and letters from top management; the flexing of political muscle in the home districts of particularly recalcitrant members of Congress; the fine-tuning of press relations and advertising; and, throughout, a dogged determination to prevail.[15]

Corporate representation in the nation's capital in the 1960s is only distantly related to the lobbying business in the 1990s. Jane Fawcett-Hoover, the daughter of a former president of Ohio State University, and currently vice president of National Government Relations at Procter & Gamble, joined Harlow's staff in the 1970s and compared the "good old days" of corporate representation with present-day methods:

> In the 50's and 60's, members of Congress came to Washington and often served 20-30 years. There was great continuity and longevity. This is no longer the case. Since 1994 there has been a 40 percent turnover in Congress. As a result, there is far less institutional knowledge. When Bryce was here, long-term members created fiefdoms and communicating with decision makers was more direct. Now, leadership is spread among many more people. Bryce often dealt solely with members of Congress, not their staff. That has changed. We deal with staff as well as members today and information to all is critical.[16]

Fawcett-Hoover, who began her career with P & G as a consumer representative, is one of the many professional lobbyists in Washington who attribute a great deal of what they know about corporate representation to time spent observing and listening to Harlow.

Harlow threw himself into his new job with the same vigor and sense of achievement that had brought him great acclaim in the Eisenhower White House. He already had the respect of members of Congress and fellow lobbyists. His integrity gained him access to the highest leaders of the land, in both the government and the private sectors.

One of the foremost challenges for Harlow's representation of P & G interests was in the field of government pollution regulation. Rachael Carson's controversial book *Silent Spring,* published in 1962, spurred a nationwide protest movement against manufacturers such as P & G who pioneered the use of the cleaning agent alkyl benzene sulfonate (ABS). ABS was a cheap and effective ingredient of many of P & G's products but was criticized by some health officials for leaving residues along the banks of rivers or streams because it was not completely broken down during sewage treatment.

In response to the public outcry, congressional hearings were scheduled. Harlow and his staff provided stacks of technical data that proved ABS was not harmful to the environment. Harlow's personal integrity stood behind the scientific proof and Congress refused to bow to the pressure applied from small public interest groups to prohibit the use of a long list of cleaning agents. However, when foam appeared on streams and waterways, the detergent industry was blamed and P & G and other manufacturers quickly developed alternative chemicals for use in cleaning products.

Harlow, whose integrity was unquestioned, had chosen his employer carefully. He often told friends that P & G was a unique company, built on character and principle, a company he could honestly believe in and represent without compromising his own principles. When federal regulations forced P & G to remove products from store shelves pending investigation of the safety of their contents, P & G President Howard Morgens cited two principles that guided the company, "The first is that Procter & Gamble obeys the law. The second is that we sell products that are safe for use under normal usage conditions."[17]

During his entire 40 years on the national scene, Harlow was a mentor to dozens, and possibly hundreds, of assistants and co-workers. In the complex world of lobbyists, many competitors mimicked Harlow's methods. Harlow always had time to lend a word of advice and a guiding hand to those fortunate enough to learn at his side. In writing this biography, the authors have been contacted by dozens of men and women who have countless reminiscences of the wisdom passed along to them by Harlow over the years.

An example is a story told by longtime Gerber Products Company lobbyist Eugene Hardy. Early in his career, Hardy was terribly upset by House of Representatives rejection of an amendment he supported. Hardy unloaded on Harlow, spewing forth an indictment of the House as an institution. After patiently waiting for Hardy to complete his demonstration, Harlow said, "If you could dismiss the entire House today and tomorrow pick all new members from the same districts, of the same political parties and from the same background, I would venture to say that the result would be the same on this issue you see so important."[18]

Hardy recognized the endurance of Harlow's wisdom when years later he heard the exact same words in a speech by one of the top leaders of the House. Hardy knew the congressman well enough to tell him that he first heard those same words from Harlow. The congressman said, "Who do you think I heard them from?"

Harlow, a wordsmith with a staggering vocabulary, preached to any up-and-coming lobbyist who would sincerely listen, that proper expression often made the difference between success and failure of driving a point home to a member of Congress or government agency official. He insisted that his underlings use correct grammar and style when preparing documents for public consumption.

Harlow vehemently believed that the professional lobbyist performed a function vital to the public policy process. He spent much of his spare time, what little there was, in developing alliances with other lobbyists who were interested in ethical considerations in the profession.

Harlow worked closely with the Business-Government Relations Council (BGRC), founded in 1966 as a non-profit organization to improve business understanding of governmental policies, methods, and operations, and to increase the government's awareness of the role of business in national affairs.[19] Among the founders of the BGRC were Bill Whyte of U.S. Steel, John Rudy of Goodyear, and Laurence I. "Larry" Wood and Gerry Toye of General Electric.[20] Harlow served on the first official governing board of the BGRC, elected to the post in October, 1966. Many of Washington's leading corporate representatives, including founders Whyte and Wood, and Rodney W. Markley, Jr., Fred B. Zoll, Jr., Frank P. Jones, Jr., Emmett W. Hines, Jr., Allan D. Cors,

Don A. Goodall, Wayne H. Smithey, and Theron J. Rice have served terms as president of the BGRC.

The BGRC matured into a strong, influential entitly in the nation's capital. Harlow later recalled, "I saw its ability to contrive useful programs and activities steadily grow. . . I regard it as an extraordinarily successful effort, entirely voluntary, selfless, constructive, and significant. It has powerfully influenced Washington."[21]

As he performed his daily tasks as director of Procter & Gamble's Washington office, Harlow quickly became the unofficial dean of lobbyists in the nation's capital.

IKE'S MAN IN WASHINGTON

HARLOW SERVED EISENHOWER AS SON SERVES FATHER, WITH
MORE ENERGY, DEVOTION, TIRELESSNESS, STREET-WISE
COUNSEL, AND SELFLESSNESS THAN ALMOST ANYONE ELSE.

WILLIAM BRAGG ELWALD, JR.

From his post on K Street at the Washington office of Procter &
Gamble, Harlow became the eyes and ears of President Eisenhower who had retired to his farm at Gettysburg, Pennsylvania.

Eisenhower left Washington with regrets that his Vice President Richard Nixon had lost a narrow bid for the White House to
Senator Kennedy and that little progress had been made in global
disarmament and in reducing the bitterness of the East-West
struggle during his eight years in office.[1] Even though the former
President was officially retired, his decades of service to his country made him much more than a sideline observer sent out to pas-
ture in the valleys of Pennsylvania.

Almost immediately after leaving the White House, Eisenhower embarked on a seemingly overwhelming project, the writing of
his memoirs. He selected William Bragg Ewald, Jr., to coordinate
the writing project. However, it was his old colleague Harlow who
ultimately read, reviewed, and commented on every chapter of
Eisenhower's two-volume epic published in 1963 and 1965.

In the period 1961-1965, hardly a week passed without some
contact between Harlow and Eisenhower and his small staff at
Gettysburg. Harlow's voluminous correspondence file at the Eisen-

hower Library in Abilene, Kansas, is filled with hundreds of typed and handwritten notes that cover an amazing variety of subjects.

Before Eisenhower had time to settle in his Gettysburg home, Harlow began sending him periodic reports on legislation and issues close to the former President's heart. On February 25, 1961, Harlow wrote Eisenhower, "I am toying with a project that perhaps will interest you, that of reestablishing a tight working arrangement with a multitude of organizations and individuals so successfully used in the 86th Congress to hold the boys in line. If this takes on real character, I will let you know. . . My belief is that with just a bit of creative effort, the Congress can be taken entirely out of the hands of the new Administration—a result, to my way of thinking, devoutly to be wished."[2] In the same letter Harlow promised to keep Eisenhower and former Vice President Nixon "informed of significant developments here."[3] Harlow told Eisenhower he was particularly anxious to get to him the kind of information he would find of the greatest interest and value.

Harlow's efforts to keep Eisenhower informed was fully supported by his superiors at Procter & Gamble. "Mr. McElroy [P & G Chairman Neil McElroy] has approved my staying as close as possible to the situation," Harlow wrote.[4]

One of Harlow's personal efforts for Eisenhower in early 1961 was to develop Congressional support for a bill to grant Ike permanent five-star status in the Army. Eisenhower had been made a five-star general as Supreme Allied Commander during World War II, but the rank had never been made permanent for retirement purposes.

When delays hindered the introduction of the five-star bill, Eisenhower let his impatience be known in a letter to Harlow, writing, "I am getting just a bit bewildered by Uncle Carl's [Congressman Carl Vinson] inaction. While the whole matter is not one of life and death, the possibility of keeping with me certain individuals that have been so faithful and efficient over the years is a bit bothersome."[5]

Congressmen Vinson and Les Arends introduced the legislation in the House within days. Covertly, Harlow was able to produce a letter from President Kennedy endorsing the bill. Harlow reported to Eisenhower on March 1, "I engineered this through my replacement on his staff, thinking that since JFK has to approve the bill once it passes and then, no doubt, would issue appropriate comments, we had might as well get him to talk out in advance, thereby smoothing the legislative road. Uncle Carl doesn't know of my involvement in this particular slither and is quite charged up by the President's request for action."[6]

Behind the scenes Harlow worked to speed up passage of the five-star bill. He drafted a speech in support of the bill for Congressman Charles Halleck. Eisenhower commented, "Charlie made a very fine talk (particularly since you wrote it for him). Not only did I like all of it, but I was especially impressed by the fact that he (you) stressed the need for progress."[7]

Eisenhower regularly related to Harlow his most personal feelings, from the physical, "My back is still quite painful, but I am hopeful of returning to the golf course soon,"to sadness, "It is disturbing to learn of the evident increase of mutual antagonism between Ev and Charlie."[8] Eisenhower was upset that Congressmen Everett Dirksen and Charles Halleck were feuding. Eisenhower wrote, "This is something so foreign to my own nature in dealing with my friends that I am baffled in any attempt to correct it. I think I shall send a very short note to Charlie saying that I am hearing from you that he is really on the job and is getting our boys in the House working together."[9]

The tone of letters from Eisenhower to Harlow, and vice versa, supports the theory of Clyde A.Wheeler, Jr., that the former President and Harlow had a father-son relationship. Wheeler said, "Eisenhower regarded Harlow's opinion above all others. They spent hours talking about World War II. Bryce was a walking encyclopedia of the war and enjoyed reminiscing about the battles and people involved in the conflict."[10]

A sincere conveyance of deep appreciation characterized Eisenhower's letter to Harlow after Congress passed, and President Kennedy signed, the five-star bill. Vacationing in Palm Desert, California, Eisenhower wrote, "Life, and particularly work, out

March 17, 1961

MEMORANDUM FOR:

✓ DWIGHT D. EISENHOWER
RICHARD M. NIXON

I attach several items of interest compiled by Steve Hess, some of which might be exploitable by certain of the boys on the Hill and have been passed along to them with that thought in mind.

There is an interesting development, Mr. President, involving your "Farewell Address." At least two vigorous young Republicans in the House (Bob Michel of Illinois and Brad Morse of Massachusetts) have interested themselves in your warning to America against excessive power being accumulated by the military-industrial complex and are girding their loins to raise a rumpus through the Congressional investigation route. Nation magazine, of all things, has suddenly interested itself in the same thing and has run a column on the subject written by Jerry Greene, one of the most conservative correspondents in Washington. Congressional Quarterly, widely read, will run a whole spread on this in its next issue. The point is, this part of the Address turns out to be curiously yeasty, and one can expect some fall-out from it in the Congressional-political area over coming months. All of the interested parties (except Nation, of course!) have been in touch with me about this: I have quietly, without attribution, sought to add fuel to this still small flame.

The Congressional Leaders have at last hired Bob Humphreys as their full-time staff man, much to my relief and gratification. He should do a splendid job, provided they will give him running room, and I would anticipate that within the next month the public imprint of Ev and Charlie will be noticeably more powerful and positive. There is a growing undercurrent of discontent, especially among the new House Republicans (a very large class approximating 40), but including Tom Curtis who is a veritable bulldog, over the leadership (and party) image now being projected by the Leaders, and this could evolve into a serious problem for Charlie, Johnny Byrnes and Les, but my hope is that Bob Humphreys' imaginative help will ease this strain before it reaches serious proportions.

The first page of a March 17, 1961, confidential memorandum prepared by Harlow for former President Dwight D. Eisenhower and former Vice President Richard Nixon. Harlow reported on congressional interest in Eisenhower's warning to America against excessive power being accumulated by the military-industrial complex. Periodic reports from Harlow to Eisenhower and Nixon detailed Harlow's undercover efforts to keep Republican ideology alive. Courtesy Dwight D. Eisenhower Library.

THE
PROCTER & GAMBLE
MANUFACTURING COMPANY

BRYCE N. HARLOW
DIRECTOR OF GOVERNMENTAL RELATIONS

WASHINGTON 6, D. C.

9/6

Annie —

Wouldn't tell DDE that Bourke
Hickenlooper will put a rebuttal to
Anderson in the Cong. Record,
as per DDE's suggestion to me.
I am asking Strauss to prepare
the item for the Senator's use.

Bryce

✗ Strauss, Admiral

Harlow's handwritten note to Eisenhower's personal secretary, Ann Whitman,
telling her not to tell Ike that Iowa Senator Bourke Hickenlooper was putting a
rebuttal to Senator Clinton Anderson's criticism of Eisenhower in the Congressional
Record. The admonition was not successful because the initials "D.E." at the top of
the memo is in Eisenhower's hand, indicating he read the memo. Hickenlooper's
action came after Eisenhower asked Harlow, "Can you think of a Senator who
would like to do a small hatchet job on Anderson?" Courtesy Dwight D.
Eisenhower Library.

here are much more enjoyable and tolerable when there is someone like yourself who diligently keeps me informed on what is happening on the political front. . . . I have received your several letters, cartoons, speech (which I shall read tonight), clippings and copies of drafts, all of which were eagerly digested and absorbed. I just want you to know how much I appreciate your efforts. And, for your tireless work in connection with the legislation to restore my old rank in the Army, you have my special gratitude."11

Harlow always was honest with Eisenhower, even when the news was not good. After Harlow met with Nixon in Washington in September, 1961, to review the progress and popularity of the Kennedy Administration, Harlow wrote, "I have just received an August 19 poll from the Republican Chairman of Minnesota (the poll taken by the *Minneapolis Tribune*) saying that 79% of the people in that area think President Kennedy is doing a good job."12

Harlow and Eisenhower often exchanged gifts, at Christmas and birthdays, and other special occasions. Harlow proudly wore a unique wrist watch he received one Christmas from Eisenhower. The watch was a hollowed-out $50 gold piece that had one side of the coin hinged so that when a button was pushed, the face of the watch was revealed. The watch was given to Harlow without a band. True to his conservative nature, Harlow transferred the somewhat frayed, "definitely sweat-stained but very, very honest" band on his old watch to the new watch.13

Harlow's letters to Eisenhower's flowed like a pleasant conversation between old friends. Here are some examples:

Ran into Sam Rayburn two days ago. He dragged me into his office for a long visit. Said for me to tell you that now that you are out of the Presidency, he intends to call you "Captain Ike" once again. I advised him that you would be delighted and that you have been persistently urging others of your long-time friends to drop the formalities. Mr. Sam, by the way, is having interesting problems, patronage-wise, with the new Administration. His boys aren't getting appointed, and Sam is privately miffed over it. He says he still cannot find out whom the new President depends upon to be his Harlow, and he has a growing concern lest a palace guard so maroon Kennedy that he will start making serious mistakes, especially with the Congress.[14]

Legislatively, things look far from easy sailing for Kennedy. Les Arends believes the conservatives in the House stand a very good chance of controlling most of the issues, but I believe he is a bit over-optimistic about this.[15]

The importance of Eisenhower's pipeline to Washington via Harlow is demonstrated by a June 26,1962, memo from Eisenhower's Chief of Staff at Gettysburg, Brigadier General Robert L. Schultz. The memo outlined specific procedures for the handling of mail received in Eisenhower's office. After listing what personal mail would be left unopened, and what general letters would be screened to determine Eisenhower's possible interest, the memo directed that copies of all letters written by Eisenhower on political subjects be sent directly to Harlow at Procter & Gamble.

After spending eight years serving Eisenhower in the White House, Harlow had a good working knowledge of who the former President liked and disliked. If Harlow heard about the death of one of Eisenhower's colleagues, he reminded Ike to "send a note of condolence to the widow."[16] Harlow also took the heat for Eisenhower when Ike rejected requests from Washingtonians. Once when Eisenhower refused to sign photographs for a congressman who was a member of the John Birch Society, Ann Whitman wrote Harlow on behalf of Eisenhower, "Do you know any diplomatic way to return them?" Harlow accepted the challenge and privately explained to the congressman the rationale of Eisenhower's decision.

Eisenhower leaned heavily upon Harlow's counsel when asked to make public comment on pending legislation or important issues of the day. In August, 1962, House Speaker John McCormack asked Harlow to convince Eisenhower to make a statement in support of a bill providing emergency financial assistance to the United Nations.

Former President Dwight D. Eisenhower at his Gettysburg, Pennsylvania, office in 1967. Left to right, Edward A. McCabe, Harlow, Congressman Charles A. Halleck, and Gerald D. Morgan. Harlow's hand resting on Eisenhower's chair symbolizes how comfortable Harlow felt around the former chief executive. Courtesy Dwight D. Eisenhower Library.

Harlow sent an urgent telegram to Eisenhower. The telegram outlined Harlow's reasons why the statement should be made and contained the draft of the public statement Eisenhower should release. In a process repeated countless times in the years following Eisenhower's exodus from the White House, the former President accepted Harlow's recommendation, and without any editing, released a statement wholeheartedly endorsing congressional action to bail out the United Nations, "This is a measure helping to hold open the door of hope for all mankind in its yearning for a world of peace and justice among nations."[17] The words were pure Harlow.

After President Kennedy's assassination on November 22, 1963, Vice President Lyndon B. Johnson ascended to the presidency. Harlow and Johnson had been congenial combatants for years. Both had admiration and respect for the other's political skills. Harlow never underestimated the slow-talking Texan who easily was nominated by Democrats to run for re-election in 1964. However, Harlow's political ideologies were opposite from precepts upon which Johnson based his policies.

Harlow spent much of the spring and summer of 1964 working with the Republican National Committee to write a GOP platform. Both Harlow and Eisenhower were saddened when Republican presidential candidate Senator Barry Goldwater of Arizona was defeated badly by Johnson in the November, 1964, election.

Harlow made frequent trips to visit his old boss Eisenhower at Gettysburg. It was not uncommon for the retired military legend and former President to reserve an entire afternoon to spend with Harlow, reminiscing about their years in the White House and comparing notes on the latest political gossip.

Eisenhower hesitated to make any major public statement or agree to an extensive interview with a member of the press unless Harlow approved. An example appears in *With Nixon,* a 1977 book written by former Nixon aide and speechwriter Raymond Price. Price, a Long Island, New York, native who honed his journalism skills at magazines and newspapers until being named chief of the editorial page of the *New York Herald Tribune,* remembered his first meeting with Harlow at Gettysburg. "I first met Harlow in Gettysburg in 1964, when I went there to work with Eisenhower on an article he was writing for the *Herald Tribune* on the Republican presidential choice. Eisenhower had asked Harlow to come up from Washington...to advise him on it and to work with us. At the White House Harlow had...been Eisenhower's favorite speechwriter. Over lunch at a little coffee shop across the street from Eisenhower's office, Harlow gave me my first briefing on the subtleties of how to function as a president's—or, in that case, an ex-president's—ghost."[18]

Harlow directed his political efforts, outside his normal lobbying activities for Procter & Gamble, toward electing a Republican president in 1968. As early as March, 1966, Harlow revealed his feelings about Republican chances of recapturing the White House in a letter to Eisenhower:

> Republican Congressional leaders have begun to mind their tongues on Vietnam and largely have stopped attempting to dictate tactics to the Commander-In-Chief. Some six months ago Gerry Ford [Congressman and later President Gerald Ford], Mel Laird [a Wisconsin congressman and later Secretary of Defense],. . . and Dick Nixon, among others, seemed to be wandering into a bellicose stance, portraying the Republican Party as a party of war, not of peace. Now official leaders are deliberately letting the Democrats fight among themselves...The House leadership group has equipped itself better than at any time I can recall with competent research support. In the Senate, the entire apparatus can be summed up in one word— Dirksen. His influence in the Senate and with his Republican associates has grown to an unbelievable degree and he has become a favorite of the press...Finally, the Party folk continuously say that George Romney [the popular GOP Governor of Michigan] and Dick Nixon are the only two choices for 1968. Increasingly people begin to mention a "dream ticket" of Romney-Lindsay [New York City Mayor John Lindsay]. Most of the people I run into believe that Romney will make a very major effort in 1968 if he wins big in Michigan this year; they believe also that he will try hard to force Nixon into a personality contest in the Presidential preferential primaries.[19]

THE NIXON CONNECTION

HARLOW PROVIDED FOUR UNITED STATES PRESIDENTS WITH
MORE ADVICE ON MORE IMPORTANT PUBLIC ISSUES THAN
PERHAPS ANY MAN IN THE HISTORY OF THE UNITED STATES.

MARTIN ANDERSON

AIDE TO PRESIDENTS NIXON AND REAGAN

The paths of Bryce Harlow and Richard Milhous Nixon crossed frequently in the two decades before Nixon was elected President of the United States in 1968. Harlow was a key staff member of the House Armed Services Committee in 1947 during Nixon's first term as a Republican member of the House of Representatives from California.

Harlow had a lasting first impression of Nixon as "unusually gifted, a smart sonovagun, a workaholic, with tunnel vision." Harlow told his colleagues that he thought highly of Nixon, especially in comparison with another congressional newcomer in 1946, John F. Kennedy of Massachusetts. Harlow heard some congressmen refer to Kennedy as "a dope, a totally amoral playboy, a ubiquitous stud."[1]

Nixon also respected Harlow's abilities to influence members of Congress, a respect fostered early in both their careers on Capitol Hill. In 1990, long after the sting of Watergate had begun to subside, Nixon wrote of Harlow in a best-selling book entitled *In the Arena:*

One of the past masters in handling Congress was Bryce Harlow. His advice was always to treat congressmen and senators with "tender loving care." But Harlow was a hardheaded realist. He knew that when the chips were down, few would risk their political futures because of their tender affection for the President. What is decried as horse trading—giving a member something concrete for his vote besides a thank-you letter and a set of cufflinks—is sometimes indispensable in winning a close vote.[2]

Harlow and Nixon had weekly contact during the eight years of the Eisenhower administration. Harlow, as a top aide to the President, attended hundreds of meetings with Vice President Nixon.

Harlow played a significant role in Nixon's campaign for the presidency in 1960. Harlow wrote speeches and position papers and critiqued Nixon's public appearances. Harlow was one of the first close advisers who reluctantly saw Democratic nominee Kennedy pulling away from Nixon in popularity. Reflecting on the magnetism Kennedy used to charm wildly cheering crowds as he crisscrossed the country, Harlow remarked, "Good God, how can you run against that?" as he saw Kennedy and wife Jackie on television smiling and waving warmly to voters. The usual unflappable Harlow's gut feeling was that Nixon's chance to succeed Eisenhower in the White House was slipping away.[3]

After Kennedy defeated Nixon on November 8, Nixon returned to California where Harlow kept him apprised of the political happenings in Washington. Nixon unsuccessfully tried to revitalize his political career by challenging California Governor Edmund G. "Pat" Brown in 1962. Afterward he announced his withdrawal from politics forever and moved to New York City to practice law. As Nixon yearned to return to the political arena, he periodically called Harlow for advice and up-to-date background information on the issues of the day.

By 1966 Nixon was again a major player in the Republican Party. He spoke out on domestic and foreign policy issues and was active in Republican fund-raising circles. His eye was on the 1968 GOP presidential nomination.

Harlow respected Nixon's understanding of Congress. Nixon had served in both the House and Senate and did not cower when an irate congressman shouted into his ear about some executive branch move that did not please him.

Nixon's philosophy on the myriad of issues surrounding national politics was well known to Harlow, who assisted Melvin Laird in behind-the-scenes drafting of the Republican platforms every four years from 1956 to 1964.

Because of his respect for Nixon's leadership potential, his understanding of how Congress operated, and their many years of association, Harlow jumped on the Nixon bandwagon early when he officially announced his candidacy for the GOP nomination at a press conference in Manchester, New Hampshire, February 2, 1968.

Within days of the campaign announcement Nixon called Harlow and asked for his assistance in drafting speeches, in selection of top campaign staff, and in choosing issues to win for Nixon the spotlight in the Republican primary season and ultimately in the general election against incumbent Democratic President Johnson. Harlow asked for, and received, a leave of absence from Procter & Gamble to work in the Nixon campaign full time.

In late March, President Johnson stunned the country by announcing he was directing his full attention to ending the Vietnam War and would not seek re-election. Nixon turned his attention to fellow GOP contenders, New York Governor Nelson Rockefeller and California Governor Ronald Reagan, as United States Senator Robert F. Kennedy and Vice President Hubert H. Humphrey vied for the lead for the Democratic nomination in a divisive struggle that included Alabama Governor George Wallace.

Two assassinations marred the American dream in 1968. Two days after the Wisconsin primary, civil rights leader Dr. Martin Luther King, Jr., was gunned down in Memphis, Tennessee. Only months later, Senator Robert Kennedy fell to an assassin's bullet in Los Angeles, California.

Harlow was instrumental in luring former President Dwight D. Eisenhower, left, to Oklahoma in 1962 to campaign for Republican gubernatorial hopeful Henry Bellmon. In November, 1962, Bellmon was elected Oklahoma's first GOP governor. Courtesy *The Daily Oklahoman.*

Harlow and Nixon met in New York City on July 5 to discuss the possibility of former President Eisenhower actually endorsing Nixon for the nomination before the Republican National Convention scheduled for August in Miami Beach, Florida. Both believed Eisenhower wanted Nixon to get the nomination but, as an ex-President and titular head of the party, Eisenhower might be hesitant to endorse one candidate over another before the convention. At the conclusion of the meeting, Nixon asked Harlow to at least explore the question with the former President.

Harlow phoned Eisenhower, who was hospitalized at Walter Reed Army Hospital in Washington. A meeting was planned to discuss the potential hazard of an early Eisenhower endorsement negatively affecting party unity. Harlow, with his slow, Oklahoma drawl, carried the conversation with the weakened Eisenhower, concluding that everyone expected Eisenhower to back his former running mate for the nomination. Harlow assured Eisenhower that his sources anticipated no criticism from GOP party regulars.

Eisenhower agreed to publicly endorse Nixon, calling on his old friend Harlow to draft the statement for release to the press. On July 15 Nixon visited Eisenhower in his hospital room at Walter Reed. Nixon recalled, "His smile had not dimmed, but the deep wrinkles in his face showed that age and illness had taken their toll. After some small talk, he brought up the question of the endorsement. Our importunings had apparently been effective; without hesitation or qualifications he said, 'Dick, I don't want there to be any more question about this. You're my choice, period.' "[4]

Harlow fine-tuned Eisenhower's statement that was released to the press three days later on July 18. In part, Harlow's words expressing Eisenhower's support for Nixon, read, "I do so not only because of my appreciation of his distinguished services he performed for this nation during my own administration but even more because of my admiration of his personal qualities: his intellect, acuity, decisiveness, warmth, and above all, his integrity. I feel that the security, prosperity, and solvency of the United States and the cause of world peace will best be served by placing Dick Nixon in the White House."[5]

Eisenhower later sent a copy of the Harlow-drafted statement to Nixon with a handwritten note scribbled across the top, "Dear Dick—This was something I truly enjoyed doing—DE."[6]

With Eisenhower's support in hand, Nixon handily won the Republican nomination at the GOP convention in Miami Beach, Florida, where Harlow helped write the platform and wrote a nomination-seconding speech delivered by United States Senator Howard Baker.[7]

During the convention, Harlow incorrectly predicted that Nixon would choose Oregon United States Senator Mark Hatfield as his running mate. Harlow gave the inside tip to reporter Allan Cromley who spent most of the night developing background facts on Hatfield and splashed Harlow's prediction on the front page of *The Daily Oklahoman* the next morning. The vice presidential nominee turned out to be Maryland Governor Spiro Agnew.[8]

Nixon left the convention and squared off against Democratic standard-bearer Senator Hubert Humphrey. Immediately after the Democratic convention, polls showed Nixon leading 43 to 31 percent. However, the gap began to narrow dramatically when Senator Eugene McCarthy endorsed Humphrey and antiwar liberals finally decided to back Humphrey.

Harlow and Melvin Laird were two of Nixon's key campaign veterans in the 1968 race. To keep from feeling isolated from voters, Harlow and Laird alternated traveling with Nixon on the campaign trail. Harlow spent one week with Nixon and one week in the office while Laird took his place on the road. Both men believed keeping in touch with real people was important in their campaign advisory role.

Melvin Laird served a long and distinguished career in the federal government. After winning the Purple Heart in the Navy during World War II, he was elected to the United States House of Representatives in 1952. He was Secretary of Defense from 1969 to 1973, Counselor to the President 1973-1974, served on the boards of many major American corporations, including Phillips Petroleum Company and Northwest Airlines, and served in 1999 as Senior Counselor for National and International Affairs of the Reader's Digest Association. Courtesy *The Daily Oklahoman.*

One of Harlow's chief responsibilities in the Nixon campaign was to monitor speeches written by junior staff members such as William Safire. Safire, later an award-winning columnist for the *New York Times,* once tried to blast third party candidate George Wallace for taking away conservative voters who otherwise would vote for Nixon. Harlow vetoed efforts by Safire to include direct attacks of Wallace in campaign speeches prepared for Nixon. Often Harlow's advice was to "tone it down."[9]

One of Nixon's tactics during the 1968 campaign was to avoid proposing detailed programs of government policies in advance of the election. Harlow thought such specific plans would give Nixon a "quality of arrogance."[10]

Nixon recognized the power of special interest groups in Washington and across the country. He ordered Harlow and other Nixon campaign officials to routinely meet with representatives of interest groups to find out what they wanted "and essentially to tell them that the Nixon administration would fulfill these aspirations."[11] Later, after the election, Nixon attempted to honor the promises, sometimes at a substantial cost to the government.[12]

At election day approached, Nixon feared that President Johnson would attempt to help Humphrey win the election with last-minute spectacular announcements about a possible end to the war in Vietnam. Rumors were rampant that peace talks in Paris, France, were bearing fruit, that an end to the hostility was eminent.

Nixon and his campaign staff decided to bluff Johnson into publicly announcing what progress was being made in Paris. Nixon, through campaign director Bob Haldeman, asked Harlow to contact Republican Minority Leader Everett Dirksen. Harlow was instructed to tell Dirksen to inform President Johnson that Nixon had inside information from Paris, that nothing significant was happening in the peace talks, and that Humphrey and Johnson were playing politics with the war. Johnson did not budge and was non-committal about a quick cessation to bombing.

On October 22, Harlow received critical information from a credible source within Johnson's inner circle at the White House.

Harlow sat down at his ageless typewriter and drafted a quick memo for Nixon's eyes only:

> The President is driving exceedingly hard for a deal with North Vietnam. Expectation is that he is becoming almost pathologically eager for an excuse to order a bombing halt and will accept almost any arrangement. . .
>
> Clark Clifford, [Joseph] Califano, and Llewellyn Thompson are the main participants in the effort. [George] Ball is in also, though somewhat on the fringe.
>
> Careful plans are being made to help HHH [Humphrey] exploit whatever happens. White House staff liaison with HHH is close. Plan is for LBJ to make a nationwide TV announcement as quickly as possible after agreement; the object is to get this done as long before November 5 as they can. . .
>
> White Housers still think they can pull the election out for HHH with this ploy.[13]

Nixon was angry and frustrated. He threatened to call Johnson's hand and even send Harlow to Vietnam to talk to General Andrew Goodpaster "to get a firsthand military view of the situation there."[14] Others on Nixon's staff questioned the authenticity of Harlow's source. Dr. Henry Kissinger had heard nothing of the plan. President Johnson vehemently denied the rumor face-to-face with Senator Dirksen, chiding Dirksen for being taken in by rumors.

However, Harlow's pipeline to the Johnson White House was correct. On October 24, Harlow's source confirmed that a deal to halt the bombing had been struck the day before in Paris. Nixon, deciding that the only way he could prevent Johnson from undercutting his candidacy at the eleventh hour was to publicly announce that a bombing halt was imminent, called Harlow to his office and sought help in drafting a statement.

On October 26, Nixon told newsmen of the "flurry of meetings in the White House" and the hard drive for an agreement before the election, now just days away. Harlow suggested Nixon not directly attack Johnson but veil his cynicism. The final statement read, "I am...told that this spurt of activity is a cynical, last-minute attempt by President Johnson to salvage the candidacy of Mr. Humphrey. This I do not believe."[15]

The Paris negotiations faltered and it became apparent that no announcement would be forthcoming before election day.

In the early hours of November 6, Nixon, confident that he had won Illinois, and thus the election, called Harlow and told him to get Lawrence O'Brien, Humphrey's campaign manager, on the phone. Nixon said, "Bryce, lay it on the line. Don't fool around. Tell O'Brien to tell Hubert to quit playing games." Nixon referred to Chicago, Illinois, Mayor Richard Daley's stubbornness in not releasing the vote count in Cook County, Illinois. O'Brien would not take Harlow's call.[16]

By 8:00 A.M., the Illinois vote was in and the networks declared Nixon the winner in the electoral vote count, with a slim 500,000 popular vote margin. After 22 years of public spotlight, through stunning victories and shuddering defeats, Richard Nixon finally realized his dream. He had been elected President of the United States.

NIXON'S INNER CIRCLE

RICHARD NIXON WAS THE TYPE OF INDIVIDUAL MAN WHO
WANTED TO BE PRESIDENT WITH THE LEAST POSSIBLE
INTERFERENCE FROM OTHER ACTORS IN THE POLITICAL SYSTEM.

BRYCE HARLOW

President-elect Nixon's selection of Harlow as his first major appointee of his administration reflected Nixon's appreciation of his position as the first man in 120 years to begin his White House tenancy with both houses of Congress controlled by the opposition party.

On November 12, Harlow was named Assistant to the President for Legislative Affairs, the second staff member selected after Nixon chose Rose Mary Woods as his personal secretary. The official announcement of Harlow's new assignment was made after he and Nixon met for an hour at the former presidential campaign headquarters, now the transition office, at the Hotel Pierre in New York City.

Several of the country's leading newspapers speculated that Harlow was chosen because Nixon expected a turbulent relationship with Congress because both the Senate and House were controlled by Democrats who had recently fought bitterly against his election. The *New York Times* reported, "Some saw in the appointment a special design of the President-elect to try to symbolize the continuity between the Eisenhower administrations and his own."[1]

The front-page *Times* article applauded Harlow's selection, calling him "the best in the business... He brings to the his job a quality few men have achieved even after years of effort—he has the confidence of both Democrats and Republicans in Congress."[2]

The headline in the Washington D.C., *Evening Star* read, "Harlow Just Cannot Say No to a Call for Public Service." The story described the "bantamweight Oklahoman" as "one of that breed of men who cannot say no to a call for public service...He knows what he is getting into—14-hour work days with 30 telephone calls still not returned when he pulls himself from his desk at night."[3]

Harlow began spending long days, unloading boxes of files and poring over his invaluable congressional contact list in his new office at the Hotel Pierre. The phone began ringing constantly. It was not unusual for Harlow to take 150 phone calls during a 12-hour day. Activity was brisk as Nixon supporters from all 50 states clamored for the President-elect's ear, wanting jobs and positions of influence.

Daughter Peggy had worked on the Nixon campaign and became Harlow's administrative assistant in the transition office. Often working 18 hours a day, Harlow interviewed the giants of the political world. Peggy's main job was to shuttle prospective Cabinet officials and federal agency directors into Harlow's tiny office and place them in the overstuffed chair beside Harlow's desk.[4]

Facing page, top: Harlow briefs reporters outside the transition White House at the Hotel Pierre in New York City, December, 1968. Note the young ABC reporter, Ted Koppel, to Harlow's right. Courtesy *The Daily Oklahoman.*

Facing page, bottom: Harlow took time out from the Richard Nixon campaign in 1968 to accompany former President Dwight D. Eisenhower to the new Eisenhower Library in Abilene, Kansas. Here Eisenhower, left, and Harlow admire exhibits in the massive library and monument built to honor the former military hero and President. Courtesy Dwight D. Eisenhower Library.

Robert Bennett, now a United States Senator from Utah, was one of hundreds of men and women who wanted jobs in the new administration. Bennett had served as corporate representative for the J. C. Penney Company and worked in the campaigns of his father, United States Senator Wallace Bennett. The younger Bennett had told Harlow during the presidential campaign that if Nixon was elected he, Bennett, might be calling for a job. Harlow had urged Bennett to "stay in touch."[5]

Harlow found a job for Bennett as head of congressional liaison at the Department of the Interior. However, Bennett had his eyes on a similar post at the Department of Transportation. Gently, but firmly, Harlow told Bennett that he would be wise to keep a scheduled appointment with Interior Secretary-designate Walter Hickel. Bennett recalled, "Bryce told me that if I was going to turn the job down, I would have to do it directly to Hickel himself."[6] Bennett later turned to Harlow for help when a post at the Department of Transportation became of available.

Harlow received thousands of pieces of mail each week. Peggy, having picked up some of the key Harlowisms of her father, answered hundreds of letters without Harlow ever knowing it. She drafted responses and signed her father's name to mundane correspondence.[7]

Harlow officially took a leave of absence from Procter & Gamble and accepted a $30,000 per year pay cut, from $60,000 to $30,000, the top salary allowed by law for a presidential assistant.

During the transition period after the election and before Nixon took office, Harlow had an occasion to renew his acquaintance with his old boss, General Andrew Goodpaster. Harlow suggested, and the President-elect agreed, that Goodpaster, serving as Deputy United States Commander in Vietnam, would be valuable in working with the transition team to develop a national security plan to be in place by inauguration day. Goodpaster made his headquarters the St. Regis Hotel in New York City where he worked with Dr. Henry Kissinger for five weeks. When the two men needed to know Nixon's thinking about some aspect of the plan, they first asked Harlow.[8]

Harlow, with hands raised in the middle of a story, is the focus of attention of former President Dwight D. Eisenhower and Eisenhower Library staff members, during a visit to the library in Abilene, Kansas in 1968. Courtesy Dwight D. Eisenhower Library.

One of Nixon's first assignments was to force the resignation of Republican National Chairman Ray Bliss. Bliss told Harlow he would not resign, that "the news almost broke his heart," so Harlow set up a meeting between Bliss and Nixon at the Hotel Pierre.[9] At the meeting Nixon explained to Bliss that he was being replaced because he was a "nuts and bolts chairman" and the times now required "someone who can drive home the issues, attack the Democrats."[10]

It was no surprise to any Washington observer that Harlow's job representing Nixon in the Congress would be difficult. One newspaper described the task as "delicate and unenviable."[11] Harlow went into the assignment with his eyes open knowing that he must fashion some kind of an administration majority in a Congress comfortably controlled by the opposition; either that or create a stalemate which would prevent Nixon from realizing any significant part of his legislative program.

As Harlow surveyed congressional election results, he saw hope. The Democrats lost all the southern states, except Texas. Harlow began to map his strategy. His goal was to find some kind of working arrangement with key committee chairmen from states which racked up the huge Southern anti-Johnson administration majority. House Ways and Means Committee Chairman Wilbur Mills of Arkansas, House Rules Committee Chairman William Colmer of Mississippi, and House Armed Services Committee Chairman L. Mendel Rivers of South Carolina had been re-elected but voters in their states had rejected policies of the Johnson administration.

Harlow's master plan was to mold a coalition of Republicans and conservative Democrats, mostly from the South, to be controlling on important votes.[12]

Back home, Oklahoma newspapers took note of Harlow stepping back into the national limelight. The *Oklahoma Journal* reported, "So, if you happen to get to the White House in the next four years, and a small fellow weighing about 140 pounds soaking set, who dresses casually like clothes mean nothing to him (and they don't) but whose eyes of blue sparkle and crackle with intelligence and friendship, that is probably Bryce."[13]

Nixon and Harlow began to quickly assemble a White House staff. Harlow, who had been the youngest staff member in the first Eisenhower administration, now found himself as one of the elder statesmen of an inner circle of advisers chosen by Nixon to surround him. *Chicago Tribune* Washington correspondent Walter Trohan, an obvious fan of Harlow's vast experience in the federal government, said Harlow "was the oldest member of a staff of bright and eager young men. . . Harlow is now a substantial but hardly decrepit 52. . . He isn't a gray beard. His hair may be a bit thinner, but it isn't flecked with gray."[14]

The young Nixon staff, many of whom became famous and still others who became incredibly infamous, began taking shape in the last week of November and in the first weeks of December, 1968. The staff was fully in place when Nixon was sworn in as President January 20, 1969.

Nixon chose as his Chief of Staff 42-year-old Californian Harry Robbins "Bob" Haldeman. Haldeman was an advertising executive when he joined Nixon's team in 1956, was the chief advance man in Nixon's 1960 campaign against Kennedy, and managed the successful 1968 presidential campaign. Haldeman became the gatekeeper, controlling who had direct access to the President. Almost from the beginning of the Nixon administration there were grumblings that Nixon was isolated from his key people because of Haldeman's exercise of power over the President's appointment book.

One of Haldeman's first personnel moves greatly upset Harlow. Rose Mary Woods, Nixon's personal secretary, was denied her request to occupy the office just outside the Oval Office. Haldeman wanted the office himself, to establish himself as the final arbiter of who saw and talked to Nixon. Woods was relegated to a basement office, even though she had faithfully served Nixon for years. *New York Times* columnist and author Tom Wicker observed, "[I]t removed the possibility that Miss Woods would provide back-entrance access to Nixon."[15] Wicker, who interviewed Harlow 20 years after Haldeman's move, wrote that Harlow was still appalled at Nixon's willingness to permit it.

Shortly after the decision by Haldeman, Nixon himself delivered the bad news to Miss Woods. A few minutes later, Harlow was present in the Hotel Pierre elevator with Nixon and Woods. Nixon spoke to Woods twice, with no response, only a grief-stricken glare. Harlow referred to the incident as "the longest elevator ride ever taken by a man who had recently been elected President of the United States."[16]

Professor Henry Kissinger, a longtime national security adviser for Nelson Rockefeller, was named Special Assistant to the President for National Security Affairs. Kissinger, a rare and versatile scholar in foreign affairs, was a full professor at Harvard University's Center for International Affairs and was a recognized authority on Europe. He was 46.

John Daniel Ehrlichman, a fellow UCLA graduate of Haldeman, became the White House troubleshooter from his official position as Counsel to the President. His primary function was to coordinate the development of domestic policy while Dr. Kissinger oversaw the administration's thrust into international affairs. At age 44, Ehrlichman had served as the "tour director" of Nixon's 50,000-mile presidential campaign.[17]

Nixon placed Harlow in charge of preparing an employment package that would entice Professor Arthur Burns away from a standing job offer at Stanford University in California. Burns, the only senior staff member older than Harlow, had written task force reports on several subjects for Nixon during the campaign. Harlow successfully convinced Burns that, as Counselor to the President, he, Burns would have vast influence over the direction of the Nixon presidency. And, Nixon conferred upon Burns the Cabinet-rank title of "Counselor."

Daniel Patrick Moynihan, who lived briefly as a child in Tulsa, Oklahoma, before growing up in a cold-water flat in the Harlem section of New York City, was selected by Nixon as Assistant to the President for Urban Affairs. He came to the White House from Harvard University. Marked by his bow tie twinkling above a striped shirt, Moynihan was eminently qualified for the new position having served as an adviser to both John F. and Robert F. Kennedy and as Assistant Secretary of Labor in the Johnson administration. Moynihan, a liberal surrounded by arch-conservatives in the White House, was an old friend of Harlow. Both had spent years on Capitol Hill and trusted each other implicitly.[18]

Rounding out the inner circle around Nixon were the public relations men, Communications Director Herb Klein and Press Secretary Ron Ziegler.

Heinz Alfred Kissinger, who changed his first name to Henry after coming to the United States, was born in Bavaria in 1923. His family immigrated to the United States in 1938, settling in New York City. From his base at Harvard University, Kissinger became an expert in foreign affairs, lecturing around the world, and served as a consultant to the National Security Council during the Kennedy administration. In 1968 he advised Nelson Rockefeller during his run for the GOP nomination. After Richard Nixon was elected President, Kissinger took a leave of absence from Harvard and joined Nixon's White House team. For the next two decades, Kissinger was the most visible American expert on foreign affairs. He has written extensively on historical and political subjects. Courtesy *The Daily Oklahoman.*

The first full-blown meeting of the new presidential staff occurred in the Sapphire Room at the Hotel Pierre on December 19, 1968. In attendance were Harlow, Haldeman, Kissinger, Moynihan, Burns, speechwriter Pat Buchanan, and Ehrlichman. Harlow, surveying the room, described the staff, "This is a political staff and many of you know many more congressman than I do. These congressmen will call you at the White House, and when it becomes apparent that you cannot help them, they will call me to complain about you." Most of the young staffers thought Harlow was kidding.[19]

The old pro Harlow went on, "Just because of your location at 1600 Pennsylvania Avenue, you are exceedingly important. As a result, you will be sought after. One technique we will see often is this: a congressman will call us, expecting us to say no, since we are the professional mattresses, or soft barrier."

Harlow continued, "Then they will call all the other assistants and go through the same catechism. Do not be taken in. Now that you are in the White House, you are talking with the voice of Jove. You cannot say something like 'I am confident that this will be done' anymore, because that is a canard."[20]

Pat Buchanan, later a well-known author and television commentor, and Republican presidential candidate, remembered Harlow's words of wisdom at the first Nixon staff meeting, "Harlow told us 'Boys, what you have to realize down there [in Washington] is that trust is the coin of the realm. Politics isn't like business where you have to have a signed contract. In politics, when you give a man your word, it should be as good as gold.' "[21]

Author William Safire observed that the purpose of Harlow's speech in the early days of the Nixon staff was to put the fear of power in the new staff members and to block intrusions into his own area of responsibility.[22]

Also in December, President Johnson invited President-elect Nixon and his new staff to meet with Johnson's staff at the White House. Both staffs stood silently on opposite sides of the room, eyeing each other somewhat awkwardly and uneasily. It was Harlow who broke the ice and observed with a twinkle in his eye, "While I see a lot of Texas in the room, there are also some good Oklahomans here and that makes me confident that we are going to get along together just fine."[23]

W. DeVier Pierson, then serving as President Johnson's Special Counsel, recalled, "Bryce's wit and charm paved the way for an exceptionally harmonious transition between administrations of different political parties. Each of us on Johnson's senior staff became very well acquainted with our Nixon counterparts and had thorough discussions concerning every pending matter that might require Presidential attention. By January 20, the torch had been passed in an efficient and cordial manner—with Bryce being the indispensable interlocutor on any sticky problem."[24]

Haldeman's grand staff plan in the Nixon White House was to have five equal assistants, all of whom would be available to him at any time, for whatever tasks might be needed. However, Harlow, the only staffer with real White House experience, disdained the idea from the beginning, pointing out that "there is no such thing as five equal assistants to the President. There will be one who will be more equal than others."[25]

The euphoria Harlow enjoyed by being back in the center of the world's stage lost its glamour temporarily just weeks into the administration. Shortly after Harlow visited an ailing former President Eisenhower on March 28, he received an urgent phone call from John Eisenhower saying his father was dead.

Harlow, at Eisenhower's request, had been one of the last nonfamily members to visit the former President in his last moments of life. After the phone call bearing the bad news, Harlow sat in his office with the door closed for hours, reflecting on the deep loss to him personally, and to the nation. Harlow had lost a supporter, a friend, and the man he most revered in his life, second only to his father, Victor.

After Nixon's first few months in office, The *New York Times Magazine* published a lengthy article, written by reporter Robert B. Semple Jr., describing the weekday meetings of the senior White House staffers in the Roosevelt Room of the West Wing of the White House. The article, noting that Harlow was the only senior staff member allowed to attend any meeting in the White House, said, "Nixon wants Harlow around in part because Harlow, as chief salesman of the President's proposals to Congress, must know something of the origin of the proposals. But Nixon also wants him around because he has no other man on the staff—

with the exception of Moynihan—who is wise in the ways of both the bureaucracy and Congress. Few men have seen Congress from as many angles."[26]

Of Harlow, The *New York Times Magazine* reporter wrote, "Thirty-one years ago a fellow so small you could hardly see him in the daytime emerged out of the hybrid culture of Oklahoma, took a Democratic patronage job in Washington, and never left town again... Such is his familiarity with the subterranean passages of the Capitol that nobody was surprised when Nixon named him to the White House staff before anyone else."[27]

Harlow's soft-spoken, courtly and conservative tactics in dealing with the Congress did not always garner rave reviews from political observers. He was sometimes criticized for failing to do enough arm-twisting on Capitol Hill. Harlow, preferring the softer sell, instructed his staff to avoid threats and direct pressure. In the final hectic days of an early administration surtax battle in the House, Harlow surmised that he needed only four or five undecided Republican votes to pass needed legislation. Some White House aides urged direct pressure from the President. Instead Harlow set up a breakfast the next morning at the White House where a determined Nixon spoke quietly of his needs and the necessary votes were produced.[28]

No member of Nixon's White House staff could match Harlow's experience. Not only could he count noses in Congress when matters were coming to a vote, but his speech-writing background won Nixon's confidence as a principal adviser when deciding what subjects to include in press conferences and major speeches. The *Oklahoma Journal* said, "Not only can Harlow soft soap a recalcitrant senator in a back room but he can stand before an audience of hundreds to lay down the administration line convincingly."[29] In every aspect of his job, Harlow was the complete professional, the ultimate generalist.

In 1999, Pat Buchanan reflected on Harlow's role in the Nixon White House three decades before, "Bryce was a transitional figure. He belonged... to a better era of politics than we have today. Politics today is too crude, too harsh. Bryce was a gentleman in this business and I don't know anyone who did his job better. He belonged to the old school, an honorable school, and in many ways, a far better school than we have now."[30]

Harlow single-handedly maneuvered Vice President Spiro Agnew into a greater position of responsibility in the Nixon White House. Harlow, who had observed Lyndon Johnson "nearly dying of humiliation being Vice President to Kennedy,"[31] went out on the limb for Agnew during a Key Biscayne, Florida, meeting a few weeks before Nixon took office. Nixon had summoned his newest staff members to Florida to organize the White House staff. To a small audience of Nixon, Haldeman, Ehrlichman, and Robert Finch, Harlow proposed giving Agnew an office actually in the White House for the first time in American history. Harlow later said, "I told them I thought it was high time we put the Vice President in the White House, where he can actually help the President: It'll all work much better. He can walk right in and see the President. The President can call on him, and the two staffs will tend to meld and drop the irritation and competition that have been the bane of the office."[32]

Harlow suggested giving Agnew an office in the southwest corner of the West Wing, the office once occupied by Eisenhower's Chief of Staff Sherman Adams. Unfortunately, Haldeman wanted that office and was upset at Harlow. However, Harlow sold the idea to Nixon and Agnew and the Vice President moved into the White House.

Four months later, tired of being badgered and disrespected by Ehrlichman and Haldeman, Agnew "took umbrage and decided to get out of here,"[33] and moved his office and his staff to the Old Executive Office Building.

As the senior member of the original Nixon White House staff, Harlow had his choice of office space. He chose a spacious office, its greatest asset a private bathroom. Harlow knew he had arrived, later recalling, "Kissinger had to come and ask permission to use my john. Haldeman had to ask if it was all right. Now, that's power."[34]

Later, while Harlow was on vacation, Haldeman and Kissinger

moved into Harlow's office, sealed off the entrance into the bathroom from Harlow's office, and opened it out into the small hallway that ran to Kissinger's office. Harlow, not feeling like fighting over the loss of his private bathroom, used the incident for years in speeches, getting a lot of mileage out of stories of "losing his head to Henry Kissinger."[35]

From the very beginning of the Nixon administration Harlow surrounded himself with a small staff of brilliant people. Harlow's first staff member was, of course, Sally Studebaker, who knew his habits, both good and bad, like the proverbial "back of her hand." Harlow then hired as his executive assistant young Lamar Alexander, 28, single, and a veteran of Citizens for Nixon, a campaign organization headed up by former University of Oklahoma football coach Bud Wilkinson. After the campaign Wilkinson contacted Harlow and recommended Alexander, later Governor of Tennessee and a leading Republican presidential contender, for the position as Harlow's assistant.

Alexander described his job with Harlow in the opening days of the Nixon administration as, "I answered his telephone and piled up his unanswered phone calls, and worked with Sally Studebaker to deal with the horde of people who wanted to talk with him and see him, partly because they wanted his advice and partly because he was so much fun to talk to. Bryce's greatest characteristic of all was whenever you got his attention, you had his full attention."[36]

Harlow's first two deputies in the congressional relations office were William E. "Bill" Timmons and Kenneth E. Belieu. Timmons, 38, had 12 years experience on Capitol Hill, including a stint as legislative assistant to Tennessee Congressman Bill Brock, was described later as "one of the class acts of the Nixon White House."[37] Belieu, 55, was a career Army man who retired after wounds from Korea forced the amputation of his left leg below the knee, worked for Senator Lyndon Johnson as a staff member of the Senate Armed Services Committee.

In the summer of 1969, Harlow, during a trip with Nixon to the Kentucky Derby in Louisville, Kentucky, persuaded his old friend Lyn Nofziger to consider joining the congressional relations staff. Nofziger was working in political public relations but agreed to travel to Washington for a grueling interview with Harlow and Haldeman. After the interview Nofziger was hired. Because of his background in newspapers and public relations, Nofziger became part of Sunday afternoon secret meetings at the White House to plan Nixon's public relations strategy.

Nofziger left the White House in February, 1971, to become deputy chairman for communications for the Republican National Committee where he "flogged Democrats in an aggressive, irreverent and sometimes amusing way."[38] Nofziger later served as press secretary, campaign manager, and presidential assistant to President Reagan. After government service, Nofziger opened a highly-successful political consulting firm in Washington.

In August, 1969, Charles W. "Chuck" Colson, a young Washington attorney and former Nixon campaign aide, was asked by Elliot Richardson to consider accepting a position as Assistant Secretary of State for Legislation. Colson, happy with his lucrative law practice, was intrigued by the offer and began the clearance process of both an FBI background check and political screening.[39]

Harlow was assigned the responsibility to interview Colson, as part of the political clearance. Colson appeared at the White House and was ushered into Harlow's smoke-filled office by Lamar Alexander. Harlow asked Colson, "I understand you're thinking of going to the State Department?" Colson answered, "Elliot Richardson asked me." Harlow shocked Colson when he said matter-of-fact, "Well, I'm not going to clear you. If you're going anywhere, you're coming here to the White House." Harlow walked Colson down the hall to Haldeman's office and within a week Colson was the newest member of the White House staff.[40]

Harlow and Colson had known each other casually since the Eisenhower administration. Colson, an administrative assistant to United States Senator Leverett Saltonstall of Massachusetts, the ranking Republican on the Armed Services Committee, had fairly frequent contact with Harlow on Capitol Hill. Colson formed an early impression of Harlow, "He was kind of an unusual fellow in politics. The normal politician wants to impress you with his own influence and importance quickly. Bryce would do just the reverse. He had a particular humility about him. He recognized that he was an assistant, he would sit behind the scenes, always trying to help someone else. Often, you would not know he was in the room. He might be the last person to speak, but usually had the most important thing to say. People listened when Bryce began talking."[41]

Colson, a Bostonian who hated the Kennedys and a Marine officer in his youth, was colorfully described by Dan Rather in *The Palace Guard*, "Colson prided himself on being tough and ruthless in the best knee-to-the-groin fashion. His general view of the world during his White House years can be summed up by the Green Beret slogan he proudly displayed over the bar in his den: 'If you've got 'em by the balls, their hearts and minds will follow.'"[42] Colson was later caught up in Watergate, became a devout Christian, and led a sincere, successful worldwide ministry to prisoners. He would eventually sell more books than his boss, the President.

Colson began working with Haldeman and Ehrlichman, whom he described as "kind of forbidding." Not impressed with Nixon's two senior aides, Colson turned to Harlow who recognized his friend was not entirely happy with his White House assignment. Harlow asked Colson to join his congressional relations staff, "Chuck, you need to come help the President mobilize public policies and politically organize this town."[43]

Nixon wanted reform of the United States Post Office and Colson was assigned the task of developing a game plan. Harlow, "sucking on a cigarette and full of energy," told Colson one morning, "There's going to be a large mushroom cloud go up over the Oval Office because the President wants this legislation and no one is doing anything about it." Harlow and Colson went to the Oval Office where Harlow told Nixon, "Chuck will get this done." From that day forward Colson and Nixon had a special rapport. Colson remembered, "That day when Harlow kind of brought me in and sprinkled holy water on me, Nixon and I began a great, one-on-one relationship."[44] Throughout Colson's three years in the Nixon White House, he often turned to Harlow when he needed help or advice, particularly, Colson said in 1998, "when I got myself into some scrapes in internal political wars."[45]

Harlow met with his staff every Saturday morning in his office in the West Wing of the White House. He and his underlings gathered around a large oval table and spread out piles of paper tracking the President's legislative program. It was not unusual for President Nixon to show up at the weekly Harlow staff meeting unannounced.

Harlow brought other bright, young men to the White House staff. Jay Wilkinson, the son of University of Oklahoma football coach Bud Wilkinson, Dwight Chapin, and Steve Bull joined the congressional relations office staff.

Young staff members such as Nofziger were sometimes given bizarre assignments by Harlow. On one occasion, Harlow was buttonholed at a party by Martha Mitchell, the wife of Attorney General John Mitchell. Mrs. Mitchell complained about being constantly pestered by the press and wanted Harlow to take care of the situation. Harlow passed Mrs. Mitchell off to his assistant, Nofziger. When Mrs. Mitchell called for an appointment, Harlow set her up with Nofziger who spent an hour explaining to the Attorney General's flamboyant wife that she was not required to appear on television, or talk to reporters, or submit to interviews. Mrs. Mitchell thanked Nofziger profusely and "went out and did everything I told her not to do," Nofziger later wrote.[46]

Once when Alexander grew impatient because Nixon was not taking a more aggressive stance on some issue, Harlow told Alexander, "Lamar, you need to remember that just a little tilt here creates an earthquake out there," referring to the awesome influence upon the world economy that any public announcement from the White House had.[47]

By the fall of 1969, the Nixon inner circle lost its first member. Arthur Burns, largely because of disagreements with Haldeman and Ehrlichman, lost his influence with Nixon. Harlow, who many times estimated he spent half his time saving people in the White House, overheard a conversation between Burns and Ehrlichman. Burns argued that a certain program was not in agreement with Nixon's philosophy. Ehrlichman laughed and said, "Don't you realize the President doesn't have a philosophy?" Burns turned to Harlow and sadly observed, "Bryce, if this is true, our country is in serious trouble." Knowing that Burns had lost his effectiveness as a member of the senior White House staff, Harlow engineered his appointment as Chairman of the Federal Reserve Board, a position in which he admirably served his country.[48]

Colson observed how Harlow dealt with Haldeman and Ehrlichman, saying, "Harlow was the consummate politician, he knew how to handle people and situations. Haldeman and Ehrlichman did not. They were tough and ruthless. Harlow handled them well, however. I would watch him sometime finesse them and sort of roll his eyes around at me. When Haldeman and Ehrlichman wanted to ram something down Congress's mouth, Harlow was the voice of moderation."[49]

Left to right, Betty, Harlow, and Sally Studebaker at San Clemente, California, 1969. Courtesy Sally Harlow.

In December, 1969, Nixon named George P. Shultz as Secretary of Labor. Shultz, the only man in American history to hold four cabinet-level positions, considered himself inexperienced in the ways of Washington and listened closely to Harlow's counsel. Shultz remembered, "Harlow told me, in dealing with Congress, no matter how tempting it is to make a deal, don't ever promise something you can't deliver. Never. And always deliver no matter how much pain and agony it costs you. It's the only way to engender trust."[50]

Shultz, who called Harlow "beloved and trusted by everybody on both sides of the aisle," remembered Harlow's admonition to use trust as the coin of the realm and treat everyone with respect. Harlow said, "It's not just telling the truth, it's not misleading either. Little white lies don't help you any. You never know when the guy who is on the other side today is on your side tomorrow. So you fight hard, but you don't burn bridges personally."[51]

Shultz served honorably as Secretary of Labor, Director of the Office of Management and Budget, and Secretary of the Treasury under President Nixon and as Secretary of State in the administration of President Ronald Reagan.

Harlow's influence over decisions of Nixon is demonstrated in a story told by Shultz. Early in the administration, senior White House adviser Arthur Burns was in the Oval Office arguing for the President to intervene and provide a federal government bail-out for the collapsing Penn Central Railroad. All the high-browed economic reasoning for a bail-out was forgotten by Nixon when Harlow walked into the meeting and said, "Mr. President, in their wisdom the Penn Central has hired your old law firm to represent them and under the circumstances you can't touch this with a ten-foot pole."[52] Nixon took Harlow's advice and allowed Penn Central to slip into bankruptcy.

Congressional Battles

THE NIXON WHITE HOUSE WAS THE MOST TALENTED WHITE
HOUSE, ARGUABLY, THIS COUNTRY HAS EVER SEEN IN RAW
TALENT. IT WAS THE CHICAGO BULLS OF POLITICS IN TERMS OF
LOTS OF GOOD PLAYERS AND BRYCE WAS THE FIRST ONE.

LAMAR ALEXANDER

Harlow often used humor to break up the seriousness that sometimes engulfed the legislative process in Washington. Once, when informed that leading senators were irate because a junior White House staffer showed them less than the respect they demanded during a controversy over a presidential nomination, Harlow jumped into the small black White House staff car assigned to him and headed toward the Capitol.

He found the angry senators huddled over cigars and whiskey. Harlow entered the room, dropped to one knee, bowed, and said, "I believe I am in the presence of 155 years of seniority, if I have counted correctly." The sight of the diminutive Oklahoma genius broke up the room. His tactic saved the day and ingratiated him further in the eyes of the battle-scarred senators.[1]

The Nixon administration had the support of most Republicans in Congress. So, to create working pluralities on diverse pieces of legislation, Nixon gave Harlow a special mission to cultivate congressional Democrats. The President asked for a list of the chairmen and ranking minority members of all committees in both Houses, and promised to telephone each one. Harlow remembered the massive project, "He was quite sincerely counting on them to cooperate. Now, we're talking about some thirty-one committees, two members apiece to be called—sixty-two calls by a man who hardly had time to go to the john, plus a score of other leaders. He had to make some eighty calls to do this project. Each call would take at least five minutes, that is four hundred minutes, which is about seven hours. He did exactly that. He called them all. They all were flattered. . . and promised to cooperate as best they could."[2]

W. DeVier Pierson, an Oklahoma City native, and former Special Counsel to President Lyndon B. Johnson, first met Harlow when he arrived in Washington in 1965 to be Chief Counsel of the Joint Committee on the Organization of Congress, a touted project of Oklahoma United States Senator Mike Monroney. Pierson was in awe of Harlow, "He was already a Washington legend. He had built of reputation of legislative skill and absolute integrity during his own service on Capitol Hill. He was a walking encyclopedia of Congressional lore. I turned to him frequently as a wise advisor when the Joint Committee was considering institutional changes in the way that the Congress did its work."[3]

As spring days thawed the cold, harsh Washington winter in 1969, Harlow was brought back to reality as the cooperation promised by congressional leaders faltered. Nixon angered Republicans over Postmaster General Winton Blount's call to depoliticize the postal service. Harlow had warned Nixon not to accept Blount's recommendations because Republicans would be giving up a large slice of political patronage they had won by regaining the White House. Harlow predicted Nixon would be committing "hara-kiri" if he allowed Blount to go ahead with his plans.

Nixon did not listen to Harlow, causing House Post Office Committee ranking Republican H.R. Gross of Iowa, to complain, "That son of a bitch [Nixon] takes away all the job opportunities Republicans have been crying for for a generation."[4]

Stephen Hess, a senior fellow at the prestigious Brookings Institution and author of many excellent works on the presidency and national politics, outlined the traits that made Harlow "the quintessential broker of power:"

First, he was an incredibly skillful negotiator. As go-between, he had an uncanny knack for discerning what was most crucial to each "player." He knew on what point a legislator could afford to give in, and where the legislator would have to stand firm. He understood that the trick was to insure, if possible, that everyone would be able to claim some victory.

Second, he was always a giver of credit. It was Robert Taft, I think, who once said that it's remarkable how much can be accomplished if you let the other fellow take the credit. In a city of great egos, Mr. Harlow's effectiveness was partly based on an unassuming nature. To those who aspire to see themselves on the network news, Mr. Harlow never posed a threat.

Third, he was eminently practical. There was a sign in his office in the Eisenhower White House: "Have you come with the solution, or are you part of the problem?" Harlow had firm views on public issues. But basically, he was a solver of problems.[5]

Harlow sometimes employed unique methods to accomplish an objective. Once he and President Nixon were flying back from Georgia where they had attended an affair honoring long-time Congressman Carl Vinson. Nixon was impressed with Vinson's long service to his country and remarked to Harlow that someday a great warship might be named for Vinson. Nixon said, "What a shame it has to wait until he's dead." Harlow looked at the President and said, "It really doesn't have to wait." Nixon answered, "Bryce, how can you say that? A major warship has never been named after a living person." Harlow, always the man with a workable plan, got in the last word, "Because you, Mr. President, are the President and Commander-in-Chief." After several minutes of silent consideration, Nixon said, "You're right, Bryce, and we'll do just that." Thus, the true story of how the nuclear carrier, *The Carl Vinson,* came about.[6]

Harlow used powers of persuasion to convince Robert Bennett to take a position as congressional liaison at the Department of Transportation. Bennett was stalling, asking for more information about the post, concerned about receiving a lesser title than his predecessor. At a chamber of commerce breakfast, Harlow spotted Bennett and said, with an edge to his voice, "I want to talk to you."[7]

Harlow gave Bennett some fatherly advice, saying, "There are a lot of good people who are standing in line for that job, waiting for you to make up your mind. I am convinced you and [Secretary of Transportation John] Volpe will get along just fine, regardless of what the title is." Harlow emphasized, "The important thing is for you to get oer there and get started." Bennett obeyed his astute friend and resigned immediately from his job at J.C. Penney Company.[8]

Harlow was handed many opportunities in the first year of the Nixon administration to form a bridge between the executive and legislative branches of the national government. Nixon sent 40 domestic proposals to Congress in 1969, including one of the first major tax reform packages since the days of Eisenhower, and 20 proposals dealing with crime and drug and pornography control. Only a handful of bills passed, but Harlow engineered some tactical legislative victories over the Democratic opposition.

Nixon proposed an anti-ballistic missile (ABM) system to strengthen America's negotiating position with the Soviet Union on matters of limiting arms. Critics said congressional support of the plan would undermine United States efforts to ever convince the Soviets to diminish production of nuclear weapons. However, Nixon suggested passage of the ABM "involved the much deeper question of whether Americans still believed that we stood for something in the world and that we must be willing to bear the burden of resisting aggression against our allies and friends."[9]

Harlow and his team blanketed Capitol Hill, armed with facts and figures and whispered rationalizations. Powerful liberal forces, headed by Massachusetts Democratic Senator Edward Kennedy, openly fought the Nixon ABM plan. However, Harlow found a

Democratic ally, Washington state's Henry Jackson, a strong proponent of national defense, to carry the ball for ABM in the Senate.

As the time neared for a critical vote in the Senate, Nixon told Harlow, "Make sure that all our guys are there all the time. Don't let anyone get sick. Don't even let anyone go to the bathroom until it's all over."[10]

Nixon played hardball with Senator William Saxbe of Ohio, who was opposed to ABM. Somehow Nixon discovered Saxbe had a $250,000 campaign debt which was to be paid by the Ohio Republican Party. Harlow suggested that the GOP pay the debt but let Saxbe know he was wrong for opposing the President on ABM. Nixon disagreed, writing on the bottom of Harlow's memo, "Make the deal tougher with Saxbe—he doesn't understand anything else."[11]

When other liberal Republicans such as Margaret Chase Smith of Maine remained opposed to ABM, Nixon wrote Harlow, "Apply the pressure, get the idea across that a no vote would weaken our arms limitation negotiating position."[12]

The long hours of gentle, yet firm persuasion of Harlow and his deputies, and the nightly calls to senators from the President, paid off. On August 6, the Senate split evenly, 50-50. Vice President Agnew cast his tie-breaking vote, creating the final 51-50 tally. Ironically, it was the vote of Margaret Chase Smith that made the difference. Chuck Colson, who worked closely with Harlow in the ABM fight, won Smith over, even though she may have been the only person on Capitol Hill who despised Harlow. Legend had it that Harlow once opposed the elevation of Smith's assistant to brigadier general, creating an unhealable rift between the two.[13]

Colson gave Harlow the entire credit for masterminding the ABM victory, a win described by Colson as "possibly one of the most critical victories in later efforts to end the Cold War."[14]

President Nixon wrote in his memoirs that he was convinced that had the ABM battle been lost in the Senate, America would not have been able to negotiate the first nuclear arms control agreement in Moscow in 1972.[15]

From the beginning of the Nixon administration, the unfairness of the draft became one of the many vehement emotional issues related to the war in Vietnam. Although Nixon was on record favoring an all volunteer army, reform of the draft was one of his highest priorities. The President proposed, and the Congress followed with swift approval, a draft lottery. Special presidential assistant Jonathan C. Rose was given White House oversight of the new lottery's implementation.

General Lewis Hershey, for three decades director of America's Selective Service System, hated the lottery and undermined Nixon's efforts to implement the plan. When Rose approached Harlow with the problem, Harlow's answer was straight and to the point, telling Rose, "It's very simple, you just remove Hershey."[16] Rose believed the firing of Hershey was as remote as removing J. Edgar Hoover as head of the FBI. However, Rose passed Harlow's solution on to Haldeman, who said, "Great, I'll clear Hershey's firing with the President and we'll get Bryce to do it."[17]

Harlow began a series of lengthy meetings with Hershey, finally negotiating a compromise that allowed Hershey to resign as head of the Selective Service System in exchange for a promotion to four-star general and appointment to the new post of Presidential Adviser on Military Manpower Mobilization. Harlow's most difficult task in the negotiations was to smooth over the elevation of Hershey to four stars with Defense Secretary Melvin Laird who did not perceive Hershey in the same category with other four-star generals such as Lucius Clay and George Patton.[18]

Nixon's major domestic thrust in 1969 was welfare reform. The nation's welfare system was a mess, inefficient and inconsistent. Fraud was rampant. Moynihan had convinced the President to support the Family Security System (FSS), or negative income tax. Ehrlichman also supported the controversial welfare reform proposal and pushed for its introduction in Congress.

When Nixon told Harlow in July that he intended to send the FSS to Capitol Hill without any previous consultation with Congress, Harlow resisted, telling the President, through a memorandum to Ehrlichman, "If it is the President's object to loft this program without regard to (1) Republican resentment or (2) likelihood of Congressional approval, I of course understand and readily acquiesce. If however the President hopes for the maximum favorable response from the Republican Party, and if he desires to enact the FSS rather than merely propose it, then I consider the present plans inadequate."[19]

Harlow predicted outloud that a large number of Nixon supporters in the Congress and around the country would react violently to FSS. However, Nixon ignored Harlow's warning, waited until the last minute to inform the Cabinet of his plans. When the plan was introduced to the Cabinet, nearly all were "opposed, skeptical, shocked, or sat in stunned silence."[20]

After a prolonged meeting with the Cabinet, and after Vice President Agnew said FSS would be a political tragedy, Nixon boldly announced he was determined to go forward with his plan, although the name was changed to the Family Assistance Plan (FAP).

Two days later, Nixon publicly announced his FAP proposal, founded on three principles: equality of treatment, a work requirement, and work incentives. Initially, public and press reaction was positive. But then the critics began their assault. The House passed a version of the FAP, but the Senate bottled the measure up until its ultimate death three years later. Nixon justified his vehement support of FAP, "It was ahead of its time. The people just weren't ready for it."[21]

By the summer of 1969, only five months into the administration, Harlow privately expressed concerns to friends that President Nixon was spending too much time with too few staff members, that he was isolated from the real world of dealing with Congress or the pressing issues of the day. *Newsweek* magazine was one of the first national publications to agree with Harlow, publishing an in-depth article entitled "The New Crisis."

Newsweek pointed to narrow Nixon victories in Congress, a bungled attempt by Attorney General John Mitchell to defend the administration's voting rights bill, and ferocious criticism of Health, Education, and Welfare Secretary Robert Finch's announcement of proposed new school desegregation guidelines, as proof of a "leadership crisis of disturbing proportions."[22]

Newsweek quoted one unnamed GOP Senator, who bitterly complained about lack of access to Nixon. *Newsweek* Washington correspondent Henry Hubbard wrote that the whole world, including Congress, was waiting for Nixon to do something, "The President has exerted no leadership over Congress."[23] *Newsweek* posed the question, "Why? Bryce Harlow, the President's top assistant for Congressional liaison, came to town with an excellent reputation for competence, and with excellent personal relationships with Congressmen. . . . Says one who was particularly upset by the troubles, 'Harlow is only one man. The rest of this group is awfully inexperienced.'"[24] *Newsweek* concluded with a sweeping observation, "Harlow is not only one man, he is the only man, save Mr. Nixon, with any truly high-level political experience."[25]

Vietnam was on the weekly White House meeting agenda in 1969. Harlow, having spent his early years in Washington at the Pentagon, was called upon often by senior staffers to comment on Defense Department reports. Harlow was extremely pleased with Nixon's selection of the former Wisconsin cigar-smoking Congressman Melvin Robert Laird as Secretary of Defense. Harlow and Laird were friends of the highest order from Capitol Hill. Each had absolute trust in the other.

Harlow was inundated with phone calls from his first day in the Nixon White House. The sheer volume of calls assured a crisis in communications, making it easier for petty grievances to turn into hurt feelings when a member of Congress wanted to talk to Harlow personally, and could not get through.

Rowland Evans, Jr., and Robert D. Novak, in their comprehensive book, *Nixon in the White House: The Frustration of Power,* wrote of an example of Harlow being caught up in the breakdown in communication, "A new portrait of Richard Nixon was being installed with some ceremony at the new municipal airport in Houston, and the President was invited to attend or at least send a letter of acknowledgment. But when Representative George Bush of Houston tried to arrange it, he found to his dismay that his let-

Harlow appeared on ABC Television's *Issues and Answers* in 1969, answering questions about the Nixon White House and its dealings with the Democrat-controlled Congress. Courtesy *The Daily Oklahoman.*

The 14-hour days and hundreds of daily phone calls to his White House office wore on Harlow. He more than once tried to quit, but President Nixon talked Harlow into staying, convincing him that the country needed him. Courtesy *The Daily Oklahoman.*

ters, and later, his telephone calls to Harlow went unanswered. Bush was a loyal Republican and a Nixon man who would cause no trouble and hold no grudges, but others would and did."[26]

Part of Harlow's problem was trying to initially perform the White House congressional relations job with a small staff, as he had done in the Eisenhower presidency. However, it was a different decade, a new world in American politics and Harlow soon had to hire additional staff to handle the myriad of Congressional inquiries. His idea of "weaning Congress off the teat" did not work.[27]

One of Harlow's difficulties in bridging tensions between the Nixon White House and the Congress emanated from the attitudes of Haldeman, Ehrlichman, and Peter Flannigan, that Congress was an awkward and obnoxious obstacle, a hostile foreign power.[28] Haldeman expressed a take-it-or-leave-it attitude when dealing with Congress. There was no give-and-take. Instead of compromising, Haldeman, Ehrlichman, and Flannigan were convinced that the way to get Congress to approve Nixon's programs was to use public relations and advertising gimmicks to force Congress to accept new ideas. An example was during the ABM fight in the Senate, when Haldeman turned to a Harlow aide during a staff meeting and shouted, "You shouldn't be sitting here, you ought to be up in the Senate telling Hugh Scott how to vote."[29] Harlow knew that "telling" a veteran senator how to vote was a sure way to guarantee his opposition.

Harlow and his congressional liaison team received earfuls of complaints about the attitude of the Haldeman and Ehrlichman. Capitol Hill staff members urged their bosses to talk to Nixon about the serious breach in relations between top White House staff and the Congress. Harlow spent much of his time trying to persuade the less experienced senior staffers that negotiation, not bullying tactics, was the only way to successfully pass any of Nixon's legislative program.

Evans and Novak wrote

> Harlow knew there was no magical way of getting Congress to give Nixon or any President exactly what he wanted. To manage Congress required mostly hard work that would reveal a Congressman's Achilles heel, discover a Congressman's most influential supporters back home, disclose a Congressman's hidden aspirations and thereby offer the raw material of a bargain. But as Harlow once advised Lawrence F. O'Brien, when O'Brien succeeded him as chief White House lobbyist under Kennedy in 1961, "There are no tricks that haven't been tried over and over—stilettos, swords, pistols, poison, rifles, shotguns, cajolery, wheeler-dealing, private meetings, public meetings, secret meetings—all of it has been tried repeatedly by every President. If you think you have a new fix on this deal, Larry, you're nuts!"[30]

Some 1969 observers saw a curious jealousy of Harlow, on the part of Haldeman, Ehrlichman, and Flannigan. Harlow received much attention from Congress and the rest of the outside world and was considered indispensable to the President. The spotlight on Harlow made Haldeman, et al suspicious, and no doubt led to further divisions in the White House staff.[31]

One of the bitterest legislative defeats Nixon suffered while President revolved around his attempt to fill a vacancy on the United States Supreme Court in 1969. In May of that year Nixon nominated D.C. Circuit Court of Appeals Judge Warren Burger to replace retiring Chief Justice Earl Warren. Burger's nomination sailed through the Senate confirmation process.

An unexpected second vacancy on the Court occurred later that year when Justice Abe Fortas was forced to resign. In August, Nixon nominated Judge Clement F. Haynsworth, Jr., of Greenville, South Carolina, and the Fourth Circuit Court of Appeals.

Haynsworth, considered in retrospect by most observers as worthy of Senate confirmation, was caught up in a bitter war between certain Senate leaders and Nixon over the President's desegregation policies and allegations that Haynsworth was anti-labor. Indiana Senator Birch Bayh led an all-out attack on the Haynsworth nomination, accused the judge of deciding cases in which he had a financial interest.

Harlow headed up a White House working group to guide the Haynsworth nomination through the confirmation process in the Senate. Other active members of the group were Assistant Attorney General, and later Chief Justice William Rehnquist; Deputy Attorney General Richard Kleindienst; Senators Robert Dole and Howard Baker; attorney John Dean, who represented Attorney General John Mitchell in the closed-door strategy sessions; and White House staffers Lyn Nofziger, Herb Klein, Chuck Colson, and Jeb Magruder.[32] Chief Justice Rehnquist later wrote, "I remember being impressed by his [Harlow's] knowledge of the Senate, but I was very much a newcomer to the scene and operated on a less exalted level than he did."[33]

Harlow, always good at counting noses, advised Nixon in October to withdraw Haynsworth's nomination. John Ehrlichman, in his book, Witness to Power, reported that Harlow's October count was 52 to 48, against confirmation, and that the situation was "festering."[34] Harlow reported that Delaware Senator John Williams was about to openly oppose the nomination and that several of his close friends would surely follow suit.

Nixon again ignored the advice of Harlow and stood firmly by his selection of Haynsworth. The President sent Harlow, Attorney General Mitchell, and Ehrlichman to meet personally with a group of Republican senators who confirmed Harlow's prediction that support for the nomination was eroding at a maddening pace.

In the following weeks more Republican senators dropped their support of Haynsworth and Nixon had no alternative but to withdraw the nomination. His staunch support of Haynsworth scarred his reputation with Congress. However, the real casualty of the failed operation was Attorney General Mitchell who was widely criticized both from within and outside the administration for his handling of the nomination process.

Nixon was determined to name a southerner to the Supreme

Court. His choice was Judge G. Harrold Carswell who the previous year had passed the confirmation hurdle with flying colors after Nixon had appointed him to the Fifth Circuit Court of Appeals. Harlow was against the nomination because he believed that the same strategy that defeated the Haynsworth nomination would be employed by enemies of the President a second time.

Again Harlow was correct in his assessment. Even though the Senate Judiciary Committee approved Carswell's nomination and sent it to the floor of the Senate, Harlow knew the nomination was doomed. His conversations with Democrats and Republicans alike told him that Carswell could never make it through the full Senate. Harlow reported to Nixon in late March, 1970, that Carswell was "increasingly in bad shape."[35] Harlow was shocked when Nixon loyalist Senator Hiram Fong of Hawaii told him he would vote against Carswell. Harlow told the President, "They think Carswell's a boob, a dummy. And what counter is there to that? He is!"[36]

On April 8, the Senate rejected Carswell's nomination. Nixon announced that he was giving up his fight to name a southerner to the Court. He blasted his opponents, charging them with hypocrisy and false and vicious attacks on his nominees to the high court. He turned to Harry Blackmun of Minnesota as his new nominee. Within weeks, the Senate confirmed Blackmun's nomination. Harlow took the defeat of the two Supreme Court nominations personally.[37]

Jeb Magruder, in his book, *An American Life,* said the real loser in the Carswell defeat may have been Harlow, "a soft-spoken, gracious, politically astute man. . . probably the one man in our Admninistration who was most liked and respected on Capitol Hill."[38] Magruder, who often sought Harlow's advice over lunch, remembered Harlow's words of wisdom, "We're here to bear the brunt of the President's problems. We take the heat, and if it costs us our jobs later, that doesn't matter, we've served our President well."[39]

As the first year of the Nixon administration wound down, Harlow spent some time alone with the President in Florida. He was concerned that Nixon, known as a loner, was spending inordinate amounts of time isolated from key staff and the public. Years later, Harlow ventured an explanation for Nixon's frequent deliberate retreat from family, staff, and friends, when he wrote, "As a young person, he [Nixon] was hurt very deeply by somebody he trusted. . . a sweetheart, a parent, a dear friend, someone he deeply trusted. He never got over it and never trusted anybody again. Since he did not really trust people, people did not really trust him." Harlow continued, "Nixon went up the walls of life with his claws. He climbed to the top on his own, not trusting people but using them to the degree he could, for his purposes. Out of that he got lots of enemies, lots of success, and the enemies finally got him."[40]

Nixon's tendency toward isolationism and retreat would haunt him during the next few years.

Cabinet Rank

HARLOW WAS A MASTER IN HANDLING CONGRESS.

PRESIDENT RICHARD NIXON

President Nixon was aware of the tremendous personal load Harlow carried as his voice in Congress. He also was cognizant that Harlow was leaning toward returning to Procter & Gamble. To trim Harlow's overwhelming telephone responsibilities, and to give Harlow more time to actually advise the President, Nixon decided to shuffle staff members and duties.

On November 4, 1969, Nixon named Harlow and Daniel Patrick Moynihan as Counselors to the President, with cabinet rank. Their pay was raised to $60,000 annually. When a reporter asked Moynihan about two men with Oklahoma connections being elevated to the highest level of government, he cracked, "A southwestern axis has been formed."[1] The White House press release explained Harlow's promotion and new job description, "Harlow will continue policy guidance of the Congressional relations but will be freed from day-to-day operational detail to be more available to the President for counsel on the entire spectrum of national affairs."[2]

Harlow never concealed his desire to return to the private sector, to Procter & Gamble. He enjoyed his independence at P & G. He used his desire to leave the White House as a tongue-in-cheek threat, "Wanting to leave is a source of great power in the govern-

Daniel Patrick Moynihan, left, and Harlow were promoted to Counselors to the President, November 4, 1969, and given Cabinet rank. Moynihan, a liberal Democrat, called Tulsa his hometown, even though he grew up in a succession of tough neighborhoods in New York City. Harlow, the Democrat turned Republican, was the better known of the two new Nixon stars, with deep roots in Oklahoma. Moynihan once said of Harlow, "Principles were his concern, and the principles of self-government and the responsibility of those in power." Courtesy *The Daily Oklahoman*.

ment. If you don't want anything, people can't believe it in the first place. And, secondly, it deprives them of any handles on you. If they move in on you, you just say, 'Be my guest, I want out. Take all of it, not just a little.' And then they look at you and think, 'Uh-oh, there's something dangerous about this one.' "[3]

Harlow was replaced in his job of day-to-day supervision of Congressional liaison three months later by his trusted aide, William Timmons, who had been in charge of White House lobbying in the House of Representatives. Harlow never got away from the problems associated with trying to communicate with 535 members of Congress. He spent much of his workday giving guidance to the congressional relations staff whose members had matured under his tutelage. Timmons subscribed wholeheartedly to Harlow's conviction that the center of Nixon's power must be a Republican center—not Democratic—moving right or left to pick up needed Democratic votes.[4]

Timmons was a native of Chattanooga, Tennessee, who graduated from Georgetown University with a degree in Foreign Service. Before he joined Harlow's White House staff, Timmons was an aide to United States Senator Alexander Wiley and Congressman William Brock and was congressional relations director for the Nixon–Agnew campaign in 1968. He later served as an assistant to President Gerald Ford before founding a very successful public relations firm, Timmons and Company.

Not all of Harlow's moments in the Nixon White House were somber. When he and GOP National Chairman Rogers Morton appeared at a dinner given by the Women's National Press Club, Harlow slipped behind the podium, hesitated until the applause died down, and quipped, "Don't wait for the rest of me. I'm standing up." Harlow then introduced the six-foot-six Morton and said, "Rogers and I have stood eyeball to kneecap ever since 1938 when I first turned to the public treasury for a living."[5] On another occasion, Harlow remarked that he had once been as tall as Morton, but had lost inches to the daily grind of dealing with Congress.

Harlow's ability as a "people person" contributed to his success. Washington insider Edward McCabe, observed, "He was kind and thoughtful, had a good sense of humor, and a light touch to his humor. The subjects were always heavy and important but he did not belittle and never lost sight of the human on the other side of the conversation. He was considerate of others, it did not matter whether they were the President of the United States or the guard at the outer gate."6

"Harlow was liked and respected by everyone," Pat Buchanan said in a 1999 interview, "He was like an honorable small neutral nation in the midst of all the vulcans. He was like Switzerland at the beginning of World War II. He was respected and was considered detached from those of us who clearly had agendas. I had a conservative agenda. Kissinger had his foreign policy agenda. Moynihan had his welfare agenda. Harlow was just someone who was considered an honest broker."7

Aides who worked under Harlow worshipped him. Lamar Alexander talked of Harlow's mentoring, "The year and a half I worked with Harlow, including the six months where I sat at a desk about 15 feet from him, watching and listening to him, was the most valuable Ph.D. in how to do things right rather than wrong in politics, government, than any 29- or 30-year-old person might ever earn."8 When Alexander left the White House to manage the 1970 campaign for the Republican gubernatorial nominee in Tennessee, Harlow insisted that he get to spend five minutes in the Oval Office with Nixon. When Alexander told Nixon he was leaving for politics in Tennessee, the President mused, "The two states with the nutcuttingest politics are Tennessee and Indiana. Be careful."9

Harlow's former colleagues in the corporate representation community continued to seek his counsel even during times Harlow was on the White House staff. Emmett W. Hines, Jr., recalled a phone call to Harlow requesting advice on how to deal with a touchy matter regarding consumer protection legislation that he and Harlow had worked on before Harlow accepted the position in the Nixon White House. Harlow, his integrity always shining through at the strangest moments, said, "Emmett, stop. I can't talk to you about that. When I returned to the White House, I made a commitment that I would not have any discussion with anybody with respect to those issues that my ex-employer was interested in. I can't do that."[10] Hines, not wanting to impair his close relationship with Harlow, stammered a bit, "Bryce, now I understand. I don't want to lose you. What can we talk about?" After a long silence, Harlow responded, "We can talk about girls." Hines got the message, recognized how busy Harlow was, and hung up.[11]

Race relations was an area that Nixon spent a great deal of time in his presidency trying to improve. Blacks had not supported his election in 1968 yet Nixon appointed blacks to high policy places within the government at a greater frequency that previous administrations. In a *U. S. News and World Report* published interview

Harlow aide Lamar Alexander learned well from his mentor. After leaving as executive assistant to Harlow, Alexander was Governor of Tennessee from 1979 to 1987, President of the University of Tennessee, Secretary of Education in the Reagan and Bush administrations, a well-known author, and Republican presidential candidate. Courtesy *The Daily Oklahoman.*

with Harlow August 17, 1970, Harlow defended Nixon's policies toward minorities, "A good part of the black community is reacting to imagery instead of actuality. . . The Philadelphia Plan to open construction jobs to blacks was undertaken and achieved over a very heavy opposition." Harlow continued, "In the field of school desegregation, always an area of interest, our record is solid, responsible and rapid advance, despite unending criticism from both sides of the issue. During the last year there has been more progress in fairly executing the law than any time in the entire 16 years since the Supreme Court desegregation decision."12

George Shultz remembered a 1970 trip Nixon and key staff members made to New Orleans, Louisiana, to meet with black and white education leaders seeking to make smooth the desegregation. Returning to Washington aboard *Air Force One*, the President asked Harlow, "the only real southerner in the group with any real instinct for the South," how the desegregation situation was going.

Harlow lectured Nixon, Shultz, and Moynihan for several minutes about why he thought racial conflict would be more vicious in the North than in the South, "In the South," Harlow theorized, "we live with the Negro side-by-side in the homes and bring up our children together. So on a human scale we're close to them, they are our friends. In the South we love the Negro as a human being but we hate the Negro as a race." He explained, "In the North, it's the other way around. People in the North are always talking about how they love the Negro race, but they have no experience with the Negro as a human being. Basically, the North can't get along with Negroes as human beings. So that's going to mean that in the North you're really going to have trouble."13

Harlow has been referred to as Nixon's "hatchet-man" in deciding who should be invited into the Oval Office to discuss certain issues or problems. Harlow was usually the man sitting next to Nixon, "whispering in the good king's ear," explaining why certain people were present at that particular meeting. When someone Nixon did not trust was in attendance, Harlow played the part of the tough guy, quietly explaining to the aide that he or she really had nothing to contribute to the conversation. Sometimes Harlow justified the presence of certain participants in Oval Office meetings, saying to the President, "He should be in here. You need to listen to him. He has something very important to tell you."[14]

If an aide failed to speak up when Harlow knew he had important information for the President, the diminutive Oklahoma-born power-broker chastised the aide in the hallway on the way back to the West Wing, scolding, "We didn't bring you in here to waste the President's time. What are these comments you had, these feelings?"[15]

Harlow was a peacemaker and arbitrator in battles of high-powered egos in the Nixon White House. When Kissinger, Laird, Secretary of Commerce Peter G. Peterson, Haldeman, Ehrlichman, or a dozen other major players in world politics sparred in high-level meetings, it was Harlow who said, "Let's calm things down."[16]

Mike McKevitt respected Harlow greatly, calling him "a feisty little rooster who wouldn't take anything from anybody." McKevitt had his own spin on President Harry Truman's familiar saying, "You want a friend in Washington, buy a dog." McKevitt's version was, "I don't need a dog because Bryce Harlow is my friend."[17]

When questioned by the press in 1970 about Nixon's stepped-up criticism of Congress, Harlow responded, "Well, if Congress is fairly chargeable with having frustrated the President's efforts to do what he promised the country he would do, I suspect he will talk about that with the American people. Time is running out while such administration programs as the crime-control package just sits there. The President has asked in a nice way; he has then asked in a pressing way, and maybe finally he'll have to ask in a very indignant way."[18]

Newsweek applauded Harlow's efforts on behalf of the administration in a July, 1970, feature article. Calling Harlow, "the most experienced man in government, forever being called into the Oval Office by the President to seek his opinion on a wide variety of issues." *Newsweek* blamed the President himself for lack of success in Congress, charging, "Harlow's biggest problem is Mr. Nixon's lack of a firm hand at the controls, his extraordinary tendency to dither."[19]

Harlow was thrown into the middle of a dispute in 1970 between Attorney General Mitchell and Health, Education, and Welfare (HEW) Secretary Finch over racial policies. Leon Panetta of California, a top aide to Finch, and later a California Democratic congressman and President Bill Clinton's Chief of Staff, became a symbol for Nixon of all that was wrong at HEW, including what Nixon considered over-enforcement of desegregation deadlines imposed on Southern school districts. Harlow began conveying to Nixon complaints he heard on Capitol Hill from powerful Southern committee chairman. Nixon was angry and demanded that Finch force Panetta to resign. Panetta left, telling the press that Harlow, Ehrlichman, and Haldeman opposed civil rights for minorities and were out to get him personally.[20]

President Nixon's concerns turned to his own Cabinet in May, 1970, after Secretary of the Interior Walter Hickel charged that the President lacked appropriate concern for dissenting young people protesting the Vietnam War. It was the beginning of the end for Hickel. Nixon assigned Harlow the task to gently tell Hickel that he should quit his Cabinet post and go home to Alaska to run for governor. On November 7, Nixon convened a high-level, post-election bull session with Harlow, Haldeman, HEW Secretary Finch, Attorney General Mitchell, Colson, Office of Economic Opportunity Director Donald Rumsfeld, and Ehrlichman at Key Biscayne, Florida.

Nixon surprised his small elite audience when he announced he wanted to replace Hickel, Housing and Urban Development Secretary George Romney, and Treasury Secretary David Kennedy. Nixon wanted Rogers Morton to replace Hickel and tabbed Harlow to replace Morton as Republican National Chairman. It was news to Harlow, who promptly rejected the honor. As part of wholesale Cabinet changes, Nixon soon fired Hickel, Romney, and Kennedy.

A strategy session in Nixon's library at Key Biscayne, Florida, following the 1970 election. Left to right, Nixon, Donald Rumsfeld, Attorney General John Mitchell, John Ehrlichman, Chuck Colson, Harlow, and Robert Finch, back to camera. It was at that meeting that Nixon offered the job of Republican National Chairman to Harlow. Harlow quickly said, "No, thank you." Courtesy The National Archives.

Earlier, in July, 1970, the President had looked for a meaningful role for Vice President Agnew, who he believed had become too outspoken to trust on most assignments. Nixon chose Agnew to carry the administration responsibility for campaigning nationally for Republican candidates in the 1970 mid-term election. Some candidates, fearing that Agnew's remarks would turn off black and Jewish constituents, sent word that Agnew was not welcome. When Ohio Sen-

ator Robert Taft said publicly that Agnew was not welcome in his state, Nixon asked Harlow to call Taft and protest, to tell him that was no way to talk about the Vice President. Harlow, always an obedient servant, called Taft. Even though Harlow's protest was mild, Taft hung up on Harlow.[21]

Nixon, afraid to turn Agnew loose alone on the American people, asked Harlow to take charge of Agnew's campaign efforts. It was an assignment Harlow cherished. He was the only White House staff member Agnew trusted. And Harlow enjoyed being around Agnew, calling him the "most enjoyable political figure I've ever met, always playing pranks and never taking himself too seriously."[22]

The Vice President trusted Harlow's speechwriting abilities. Often, when his own staff drafted a major speech, Agnew asked Harlow to look it over and make suggestions. Some give Harlow the credit for Agnew using catch-phrases to get his point across.[23]

The Agnew assignment was perfect for Harlow in another way. He had told Nixon he was leaving in November to return to Procter & Gamble. And because Congress was in recess for the election campaign, Harlow's duties on Capitol Hill were diminished.

To help him oversee the Agnew campaign, Harlow drafted three other Nixon aides, Pat Buchanan, who described Harlow as "a most decent man, the best politics had to offer,"[24] Martin Anderson, and William Safire. All were skilled speechwriters. Harlow told Safire, "Brother Safire, I have always considered you *primus inter pares* of the speechwriters," using the Latin for "first among equals." Safire responded, "I appreciate that Counselor, but that's what Buchanan says you just told him." Harlow, never shaken by such a turn of events, said, "I consider you both *primus inter pares.* Yours is the opportunity to volunteer for a refreshing and one might even say exhilarating political experience, that of assisting our Vice President as he carries the banner of truth to the far reaches of the land, which the President cannot do because he is burdened by the affairs of state. Let me emphasize it would be entirely voluntary. You may, if your prefer, continue along your humdrum path."[25]

Bowing to Harlow's good-humored invitation, Safire and the remaining invitees accepted their temporary assignment. On September 9, the President himself presided over an Agnew campaign planning session in the Oval Office. For some strange reason Agnew was not invited to attend. Harlow opened the meeting with a briefing on the states that Agnew would visit on the first swing, Illinois, Wyoming, California, Nevada, New Mexico, and Michigan.

Nixon, animated and decisive, dominated the discussion for two hours, warning to keep Agnew away from network specials and play toward the wire services and local television coverage.[26]

Harlow and his team of crack writers, and Harlow aide, Dick Burress, boarded the campaign plane with the Vice President and began a tour of America. Harlow decided the subject of speeches, from an eleven-page, single-spaced memo of speech ideas from Agnew. Then Buchanan, Safire, and Anderson began the meticulous job of drafting comments for the Vice President to make at campaign stops in different parts of the country.

Buchanan wrote for Agnew a speech designed to criticize the reelection efforts of United States Senator Charles Goodell, who in Nixon and Agnew's eyes, had turned from his conservative ways. Buchanan's speech contained a line that accused Goodell of becoming the "Christine Jorgensen of the Republican Party," referring to the famous sex-change celebrity. When the speech was reviewed by the President, the line was stricken. Nixon said, "We've got troubles with the guy but the Vice President can't use this kind of royal rhetoric."[27]

The rhetoric was shelved, but Agnew had seen the speech and remembered the line as the campaign plane flew on to destinations around the country. The Vice President invited his campaign speechwriters to stop off in New Orleans for the weekend. But Harlow flew home to Washington, not seeing the need to stay with the Vice President in New Orleans since no official campaign appearances or speeches were scheduled. Agnew and Buchanan were speaking with a reporter from a New Orleans newspaper when the Vice President was asked about Senator Goodell. Agnew blurted out, "He's the Christine Jorgensen of the Republican Party."[28]

By the time Harlow's plane arrived at Washington's National Airport, the Agnew quote had hit the Associated Press wire. Nixon tracked Harlow down immediately and said, "I thought I told you to keep an eye on those two."[29] Harlow took the next plane back to New Orleans and reassumed his watch over the campaign and its mutterings.

Harlow and his speechwriters actually enjoyed working for Agnew. They were accustomed to writing for Nixon, "with his tightly controlled methods and speeches based on crowd-stirring one liners."[30] On the other hand, Agnew was easier-going, far less intense than Nixon. Safire later wrote, "Formal in his appearance, always combed and well turned out, Agnew could be warmly informal with the men he worked with. I will not soon forget the sight of the tired Vice President of the United States, two o'clock in the morning after a long day's campaigning, swapping dirty jokes with Bob Hope over the telephone and laughing until tears rolled down his cheeks."[31]

The Agnew blitz worked. At every stop he lashed out at radical liberals in the Senate who blocked Nixon's legislative agenda. The Vice President said the Democrats must be blamed for everything, from campus protests to drugs and the general breakdown of law and order. Agnew's campaigning was so well received that the President put out a press release saying he was proud of Agnew's campaigning ability. Nixon himself joined Agnew on the campaign trail during the last weeks before election day. Republicans made a net gain of two in the Senate, far short of the number needed to gain control. The news was worse in the House, where Democrats picked up nine seats to further cushion their majority.

For some time, bickering among White House staffers had grated on Harlow's nerves. He saw two distinct camps within the White House. Haldeman and Ehrlichman were the leaders of the so-called "Downtown Staff." Harlow and Timmons led the "Hill Staff." On numerous occasions, the two factions sparred during meetings with the President, often expressing totally opposing viewpoints. Some would say the disparity of opinion gave the President options, others would say the dissension only worsened Nixon's isolation from a broad range of opinion on domestic and international subjects.

Frustrated over the dissension and desiring to get back to the company that had treated him so well, Harlow made plans to leave the White House in December, 1970, to return to his post as Director of Governmental Relations for Procter & Gamble. But Harlow had one last important task to complete.

Before exiting the White House, Harlow was asked by the President again to take the post of Republican National Chairman. As before, Harlow calmly said "no." Harlow was boxing up his personal papers for the move to the P&G office when 47-year-old freshman Kansas United States Senator Robert Dole came to his White House office with a fresh idea.[32]

Dole wanted to do more to influence the direction of the Republican party. He proposed, and Harlow seconded, that Dole could serve as head of the national GOP and at the same time do a good job for his constituents in Kansas. Dole told Harlow that he wanted to defend Nixon's programs from a broader platform than the floor of the United States Senate.[33] Harlow immediately began the process of convincing Nixon that Dole was the right man to lead the party.

Authors Evans and Novak laid out the landscape that faced Nixon: "In the listless search for a successor to [GOP Chairman Rogers] Morton, Nixon had shown by his own momentary preferences that he had no clear idea whether he wanted a front-man making stump speeches (Morton) or a nonpolemical technician [Ray Bliss] at the National Committee. Harlow would have been both. Kleppe [United States Representative from North Dakota] would have bee neither, Dole was orator but not technician.[34]

Harlow had one last fight with Haldeman over Dole's selection as Republican National Chairman. Haldeman said Dole was "too independent, too irreverent"[35] for the job. When Dole was told that he would not be GOP Chairman, he urgently called Harlow.

Dole, who served the country well for decades in the Senate

and carried the GOP banner as the party's presidential nominee in 1996, described the tense moments that followed, "In desperation I reached out to Bryce Harlow and I remember him coming to the Republican National Committee about midnight in pouring rain, came from home, as I recall. For the next three or four hours we worked everything out and got the situation back on track."[36]

In a few days Dole was named Republican National Chairman. Dole attributed his successful pursuit of the job to Harlow, "It was largely through Bryce's efforts of negotiating back and forth with some of the Nixon White House."[37] Dole said Harlow was "a man of integrity and principle who cared about the government and cared about the people who worked for the government."[38]

The Road to Watergate

WATERGATE COULD NOT HAVE HAPPENED HAD NIXON
CONFIDED MORE IN HARLOW.

DR. HENRY KISSINGER

This book is not an attempt to explain or define Watergate. More has been written on that subject than almost any other political scandal in history. However, a biography of Bryce Harlow cannot be complete without a brief discussion of the familiar faces, names, and actions of the men of Watergate, some of whom Harlow had brought into the White House.

After Harlow left the White House in 1970, he settled once again into the routine of representing Procter & Gamble and its interests before the Congress and the federal bureaucracy in Washington. He did not completely turn his interests away from Republican politics and was asked to help write the GOP platform in 1972. Harlow was called upon by his old friend, Congressman John Rhodes of Arizona, chairman of the Republican Platform Committee, to polish the final draft of the platform before the GOP National Convention. President Nixon still occasionally called Harlow for advice on sensitive dealings with the Congress.

Harlow had little difficulty shifting his focus from the White House to his representation of one of the nation's largest companies. His integrity was so well known, and respected, in all corners of the world of Washington politics, his going back and forth from the White House to the private sector was seldom criticized. Historians are not likely to find one credible person who questioned Harlow's motives. In fact, once when Harlow had returned to the White House, a fellow lobbyist asked for his advice on a legislative matter. Harlow looked his good friend in the eye and said, "A month ago, I could give you an answer. But now, I'm on the other side and can't talk about it."[1] Not even in the privacy of his own home, with a dear friend, would Harlow breach his own rules.

Lamar Alexander recalled a sterling example of Harlow's highest possible ethics, "Harlow was looking forward in 1970 to taking a short vacation in August about the time the President would take a vacation. Bryce and Betty were going down to Mexico with some old friends who had nothing to do with government. He concluded that going to their home would not create any problems whatsoever." Alexander continued, "However, a few weeks before they were to leave, the friend called Bryce and apparently asked him for something, some very small, incidental thing. As a result of that call, Bryce called him back in about and a week and told him that the President's plans had changed and that he and Betty would not be able to come to Mexico." Alexander reflected, "He didn't embarrass his friend, but he made absolutely certain, that because his friend had called with some minor favor, Bryce could not accept even being a houseguest for a few days. He almost single-handedly gave lobbyists a good name."[2]

Harlow recognized the increasing complexity of the interplay between corporate America, Congress, and the executive branch of the federal government. He told his fellow lobbyists, "You gentlemen of the business community better get organized."[3] Harlow encouraged the formation of coalitions with representatives of companies and special interest groups to guide promising legislation that was favorable to the business climate and vigorously work for the defeat of the hundreds of "crazy" pieces of legislation introduced each session of Congress.

Harlow met regularly with other lobbyists such as John Motley and James D. "Mike" McKevitt of the National Federation of Independent Business; Emmett W. Hines, Jr., of Armstrong World Industries; Wayne Smithey of Ford Motor Company; Al Borland of General Motors; Bob Conner of Chrysler; and Gene Hardy of the National Association of Manufacturers. The group met every two or three weeks when Congress was in session to facilitate communication between business representatives and congressional leadership. Staff members from the House and Senate Republican leadership often met with Harlow and other business representatives at the Carlton Club, a small suite on the 10th floor of the Carlton Hotel.[4]

The business coalitions met to plan advertising and letter writing campaigns to reach the grassroots of the country on important issues such as labor law reform and consumer protection. Time and time again, the coalitions successfully beat back attempts to further strangle American business with overburdensome labor, products safety, or environmental protection legislation.

Harlow's advice to young corporate representatives normally stuck with them. Don V. Cogman, now president and chief operating officer of Burson-Marsteller, the world's largest public relations firm, recalls Harlow's words of wisdom, "To succeed in Washington, you need to believe in one simple credo, 'If you give a damn, you can make a difference."[5]

Even though Harlow continued his top-level job representing Procter & Gamble in Washington, he was called back to public service on occasion. In June, 1972, House Minority Leader Gerald Ford picked Harlow to coordinate his staff and the staff of Majority Leader Hale Boggs of Louisiana on a fact-finding trip to China. Ford chose Harlow for the strategic role because he knew that he and Boggs both admired and respected Harlow greatly. Ford was happy with his choice of Harlow, "Bryce, as usual, was the manifestation of good judgement, respect, and he again lived up to all the expectation."[6]

The Boggs-Ford entourage visited the People's Republic of China for ten days at the invitation of the quasi-governmental Chinese People's Institute of Foreign Affairs and with the encouragement of President Nixon. The mission had two principal objectives: first, to learn as much as possible about China, its leaders, its people, its economy; second, to contribute to better relations between the United States and China.

Harlow, center, inspects plants in a Chinese greenhouse as House Minority Leader Gerald Ford, right, adjusts a movie camera to record the historic visit. Courtesy Gerald R. Ford Library.

With the ancient wall of China in the background, the Gerald Ford-Hale Boggs entourage poses in 1972. Harlow is fifth from the right. Courtesy Gerald R. Ford Library.

After the Congressional trip to China, Harlow and Boggs' aide Gene Theroux authored a comprehensive report entitled "Impressions of the New China." In the document, Boggs and Ford concluded, "The world has little to fear from China... But time will not stand still for China. No matter how weak she may be today relative to other nations, China is a land of vast human and natural resources. If she can maintain political stability, if she can upgrade her agriculture and industry, if she can remain free from outside interference—what will China be like in another two or three short decades?" The report said the answer was obvious, "If she manages to achieve as she aspires, China in the next half century can emerge a self-sufficient power of a billion people, a nation whose agricultural output can provide for her population, whose industrial capacity can be enormous, whose military capability can be very substantial, with a people united in devotion and obedience to the State."7

A few months after the trip to China, Congressman Boggs died and his wife, Lindy, was elected to his Louisiana district's seat in the House of Representatives. Harlow became Mrs. Boggs' mentor and guided her through the intricacies encountered as a member of the House Banking and Currency Committee. Lindy Boggs, appointed by President Bill Clinton as United States Ambassador to the Holy See, remembered Harlow's "remarkable dexterity at diplomacy" and called him "a special national treasure."8

While Harlow was in China, in June, 1972, burglars with connections to Nixon's White House staff broke into the Democratic National Committee at the Watergate Hotel office complex in downtown Washington.

At first the administration tried to pass off the break-in as a third-rate burglary. But the dogged investigative reporting of Bob Woodward and Carl Bernstein of the *Washington Post* uncovered the extent of the conspiracy and the degree of White House complicity.

Nixon's personal involvement in the cover-up of the Watergate break-in was not known to voters in November, 1972. In a landslide, Americans re-elected Nixon and Agnew to serve a second term as leaders of the United States and the free world. With the re-election came a sense of a "mandate" from the people. Harlow told an interviewer many years later that the 1972 Nixon landslide gave too much power to the administration and the added power led to corruption. Harlow mused that "If it hadn't been Watergate, it would have been something much worse."9

In December, 1972, Harlow was frightened of the way Nixon allowed Haldeman and Ehrlichman to build a wall around him.

Harlow secretly wished that Nixon would call and ask for his help. Harlow saw the inner group around the President as "high on power."[10]

After the 1972 election, Ehrlichman replaced Moynihan as Nixon's chief domestic adviser, further expanding Haldeman's grip on everyday operations of the White House. Only Henry Kissinger's office was not completely controlled by Haldeman. Chuck Colson's influence with Nixon grew. When Harlow had hired him in 1969, he told staff members, "I warn you, we've got a tiger on our hands; this Colson will chew some people up."[11]

Republican National Chairman Robert Dole was also a casualty of the second Nixon term. Shortly after the election, Nixon began the push to have former Texas Congressman George Bush take over the reins of the GOP. Dole again turned to Harlow for help. Harlow could not save Dole's job but negotiated for Dole a face-saving transition and promises from Nixon.

The American delegation was received by Chinese Premier Chou En-Lai. The powerful Chinese leader is flanked by Congressman Hale Boggs, left, and House Minority Leader Gerald Ford, right. Boggs' wife, Lindy, later a member of Congress and American Ambassador to the Vatican, is fourth from the left, front. Betty Ford is third from the right, front. Harlow stands behind Lindy Boggs. Courtesy Gerald R. Ford Library.

After a meeting with the President, Attorney General John Mitchell, and Colson, Harlow wrote Dole with a list of concessions he had garnered for Dole. Nixon promised to help Dole in his 1974 Senate re-election campaign with both money and personal appearances. Dole would be selected for an overseas mission "for visibility purposes."[12] Dole's apartment in the Watergate Hotel would be taken care of by the Republican National Committee for another nine months. And Dole would be allowed to hold a press conference to announce his own successor and to indicate that he, Dole, had recommended George Bush to Nixon.[13] The deal put together by Harlow allowed the transition between Dole and Bush as Chairman of the GOP to be smooth and unventful.

As the storm clouds of Watergate grew darker over Washington, Harlow was greatly concerned about his friend, the President. It was still a closely-held secret, and still unknown to Harlow, that Nixon may have been involved in the cover-up. Harlow still believed in Nixon and wanted somehow to help Nixon restore the public's confidence in his leadership.

Watergate was, in the view of many writers of the era, a direct result of the complexity of President Nixon's staff, and Nixon's dark side. The young White House staffers who had come out of Nixon's California campaigns were light on federal government experience. People like Harlow, Melvin Laird, William Rogers, Herb Klein, Arthur Burns, Robert Finch, Maurice Stans, Daniel Patrick Moynihan, George Shultz, and Caspar Weinberger were men of integrity, their well-seasoned advice serving as a leavening influence for Nixon.

Dr. Henry Kissinger has written about the Nixon staff, and Harlow's influence. "Harlow was a man not of soaring imagination but of encompassing prudence. He knew what the traffic would bear in Washington, but, more important, he understood what restraints must not be tested if democracy is to thrive." Kissinger continued, "He had a deep sense for the Presidency, its power, its majesty, and the awful responsibility it imposes. His fundamental loyalty to a President was bonded by his personal integrity, his reverence for our institutions, and a sense of duty to the nation."[14]

President Gerald Ford later reflected on Harlow's role in the Nixon White House during Watergate. "Nixon had a very limited group, Haldeman, Ehrlichman, and Colson. They were the real insiders and unfortunately, in my opinion, they gave President Nixon bad advice." Ford explained, "Bryce was very close personally to Dick Nixon, but he was not a part of that little coterie. Nixon would have been a lot better off if he had relied on Harlow than those other three."[15]

Before Harlow had left the White House in 1970, and before the terrible tragedy of Watergate, Kissinger saw Nixon paying more attention to the advice of Colson, Haldeman, and Ehrlichman. It was Harlow's integrity and his respect for justice and the rights of others that caused his advice and counsel to be shunned. Kissinger wrote, "With such a philosophy, Bryce found himself pushed to the sidelines by eager young votaries who were crudely assertive when it was not really necessary and craven when their careers were unexpectedly jeopardized."[16]

In April, 1973, two administration officials, John Dean and Jeb Magruder, implicated Haldeman and Ehrlichman in the cover-up of the White House involvement in Watergate. The nation was stunned. Nixon was undecided what he action he must take against Haldeman and Ehrlichman. The public demanded he do something. His options ranged from forcing the two aides to take a protracted leave of absence to firing them outright.

Nixon was in Florida and called Harlow by telephone and asked for his advice. It was not a time for small talk. Harlow got right to the point and told the President, "If Haldeman, Dean, and Ehrlichman have undertaken actions which will not float in the public domain, they must leave quickly—they are like a big barnacle on the ship of state, and there is too much at stake to hang on for personal reasons."[17]

At the President's request, Haldeman and Ehrlichman resigned on April 30, 1973. Nixon appointed Brigadier General Alexander Meigs Haig, Jr., to replace Haldeman as Chief of Staff. Haig, a native of Pennsylvania, compiled an impressive record that included service as a combat officer in Korea and Vietnam, a staff officer at the Pentagon and at West Point. He had served as military adviser to presidential aide Kissinger and moved to the White House from his post as Vice Chief of Staff of the Army.

Nixon desperately wanted to gain back the momentum he enjoyed after the 1972 election. He remained popular in national polls, but there was a lingering doubt in the backs of the minds of many about Nixon's involvement in Watergate. The President again looked to his old comrade Harlow for help. In May, Congressman John Rhodes suggested to Nixon that he needed to have people around him he could trust, people like Harlow.

Washington insiders speculated that Harlow might be asked to resume his duties as a close adviser to Nixon. Longtime *Daily Oklahoman* Washington correspondent Allan Cromley wrote on May 30, "When the Watergate scandal began to reach epic proportions, people supposedly in the know expected Harlow to be called back to clean up the mess. Harlow wants no part of it, but most government-watchers agree that he has had more White House experience in two Republican administrations than anyone else in the country. Better yet, he has no visible scars."[18]

George Shultz recalled why Nixon needed Harlow back at the White House, saying, "Under circumstances like that [Watergate], somebody who is trusted makes all the difference. He can go to Congress and tell them something and they believe it. Bryce was the wise man that you always went to if you had a problem. He didn't presume to tell you things that were outside his area of expertise. He could give you a sense, he had a wonderful seat-of-the-pants judgment about people and dealing with people."[19]

The heavyweights of Congress, leaders such as House Speaker Carl Albert of Oklahoma and House Minority Leader Gerald Ford of Michigan and Senators Hugh Scott of Pennsylvania and Mike Mansfield of Montana asked for a meeting with Harlow and former Nixon Defense Secretary Melvin Laird. The congressional leaders brought along a dozen or so other members of Congress for the meeting held in the basement recreation room of Laird's home. The message from congressional Democrats and Republicans alike was direct, "Laird, you and Bryce have got to go back to the White House. Things are going to pot over there and you two have got to go back and get them on track."[20] After the meeting, Laird told Harlow he would only go back to the White House if Harlow would also.

The President summoned Harlow and Laird to Camp David, the presidential retreat in the Maryland mountains, on two different occasions, to try to convince the two former top aides to return to the crippled White House. Harlow and Laird, along with the rest of the country, did not fully understand all the difficulties facing the administration. The existence of the Watergate tapes had not been revealed. The President's personal support of the massive cover-up was still not known.

Harlow, thinking that Nixon could survive the mess of Watergate, was considering, with Laird, accepting Nixon's invitation to return to the White House on the condition, however, that Nixon was not implicated personally. Harlow and Laird looked the President directly in the eye, and asked, "Mr. President, did you have anything to do with the break-in, or the cover-up?" Without hesitation, Nixon answered, "Absolutely not." With that absolute assurance, and only with it, Harlow and Laird agreed to return to the Nixon White House June 11 as Counselors to the President.[21]

Harlow returned home and broke the news to Betty. His sense of duty and personal loyalty to Nixon, and his conviction that the future of the presidency and the republic might depend upon his service, overrode his concerns about leaving his secure position as lobbyist for Procter & Gamble.

Harlow and his trusted secretary Sally Studebaker again boxed up their personal files and moved back into the West Wing of the White House. Nixon also made other changes intended to win back the confidence of the American people. He appointed William Colby Director of the Central Intelligence Agency and James Schleslinger as Secretary of Defense, and hired Fred Buzhardt, General Counsel of the Department of Defense, to handle the continuing Watergate investigation.

Nixon, feeling confident with Harlow and the other respected members of his old team in place, wrote, "We had taken some hard blows, but slowly we were gathering strength and beginning to climb back on our feet again."[22]

The *Chicago Tribune* reported on June 11, "President Nixon brought Bryce Harlow, 56, an old and trusted associate, back to the White House today as he continued to make repairs to a Presidential staff ripped apart by the Watergate scandal. Harlow's job may be impossible."[23]

Pat Buchanan saw Harlow's return to the White House as Harlow not having an agenda but having Nixon as "a client, who he had to keep out of trouble."[24] Buchanan said, "Bryce had to make sure that Nixon was in the proper framework. Bryce looked out for pitfalls. . . and potholes and gave Nixon the benefit of his [Harlow's] experience in Washington. . . Bryce made sure the President did not walk into some unnecessary ambush."[25]

Harlow friends, such as Robert Bennett, warned Harlow privately how serious of an impact the Watergate burglary would have on the Nixon presidency. Harlow incorrectly believed the controversy would melt away from its position in the headlines after a few weeks. However, a lunch with Bennett at Washington's downtown Metropolitan Club, changed Harlow's thinking. Bennett predicted that the press would not let go of Watergate and that it might bring down the President.[26]

Harlow listened carefully to Bennett. Harlow was so concerned that he immediately went back to the White House and assembled the entire senior staff. Harlow told the staff that he had just had lunch with a seasoned Washington observer who had convinced him that there was more to Watergate than he had previously supposed. Harlow said it was "absolutely essential that anyone connected with Watergate in any way be identified and, if there was even a hint of illegal activities, terminated."[27]

Harlow Returns to the White House

HARLOW CLAIMED HE WENT BACK TO THE WHITE HOUSE A
THIRD TIME BECAUSE HE WANTED A THIRD CHAIR, THE
TRADITIONAL GIFT FOR DEPARTING CABINET MEMBERS, BECAUSE
HE HAD THREE CHILDREN. THERE WAS NO WAY FOR HIM TO
WRITE A WILL DIVIDING TWO CHAIRS THREE WAYS.

EMMETT W. HINES, JR.

Harlow began his third tour of duty at the White House during one of the most precarious times of the American presidency. Watergate had become a bottomless pit. The morale of the White House staff was sinking seriously. Harlow tried to sell Congress on legislative programs proposed by Nixon, but even his best friends on Capitol Hill told Harlow the President was powerless to overcome the growing concern among congressional leaders that the Nixon presidency was drawing to a close.

The Senate Select Committee on Presidential Campaign Activities, informally called the Ervin Committee, after its chairman, Senator Sam J. Ervin, Jr., Democrat of North Carolina, dogged Nixon with a stepped-up investigation of White House involvement in the Watergate affair. Harlow spent countless hours behind the scenes asking Ervin Committee members to tread easily and deliberately. Harlow received so many phone calls during the

Ervin Committee investigation that Donald Rumsfeld remembers one day Harlow scooped up hundreds of un-returned call slips from his desk and deposited them in a nearby trash can. Even the veteran Harlow, accustomed to great pressures at the highest levels of government, was adversely affected by the pressures of Watergate.[1]

Just 12 days after Harlow returned to his White House post, he was told by Nixon aide Alexander Butterfield of the existence of the infamous Watergate tapes. Harlow was shocked and saddened. He left his office and walked down the hall in the West Wing of the White House. As he rounded a corner, there stood his old friend, Republican National Chairman, and later Vice President and President, George Bush. In hushed tones Harlow told Bush about the tapes. Bush recalled the moment, "As a man of honor he told me that the taping could well bring down the President. He was sick about the fact that people, without their consent, had been taped. So was I."[2]

Melvin Laird said Harlow's instincts were right and that "Butterfield didn't know what he was doing, but told about the tapes when he testified before the Congressional Committee. Bryce and I already knew about the tapes and knew we had been lied to. Such a great disappointment to Bryce and I don't think he ever got over that as far as President Nixon was concerned. As a matter of fact, Bryce wasn't one of those who went up to see Nixon very often after that. He decided he couldn't be trusted. To be lied to like that was a great disappointment to both of us."[3]

Americans were glued to their television sets in the long, hot summer of 1973, as witness after witness paraded before the Ervin Committee. "Watergate" had become a household word. Nixon's approval rating plummeted from 68 percent in May to 27 percent by November.

Harlow and Laird, unable to carry out their normal White House duties because of the gloom of Watergate that hung heavy over Washington, told the President they felt isolated from him. Nixon later explained why he avoided the topic of Watergate with Harlow and Laird, "There were two reasons that I did not like to discuss the subject with them. First, I believed that it was important for as many people on the staff as possible to stay away from Watergate; second, it was simply a painful subject for me to discuss with anyone."[4]

As if Watergate was not enough, the Nixon administration was crippled further in August, 1973, when it was publicly revealed that Vice President Spiro Agnew was under investigation by the United States Attorney's office in Baltimore, Maryland, on charges of tax fraud, extortion, bribery, and tax evasion. Actually, the White House had received periodic reports from the Justice Department for several months, hinting that serious allegations were being made against the Vice President. Agnew, the son of a Greek-born immigrant, had served as Baltimore County Executive and as Governor of Maryland before accepting the second spot on the 1968 GOP ticket with Nixon.

The allegations against Agnew hit Harlow hard. The two men had maintained a close relationship for many years. In his book, *Go Quietly. . . or else,* Agnew said of Harlow, "He was one of the few men in the White House whom I felt I knew well. . . was regarded as one of the wisest men in the Republican party. He was also in a small inner group of people who had privately aligned themselves with me for the future."[5]

Agnew's secret committee, of which Harlow was the most prominent member, planned to wait for the right moment to announce Agnew's intentions of seeking the 1976 GOP nomination after Nixon served out his two terms. Harlow believed that Agnew had the intelligence and insight to succeed Nixon as President.[6]

Agnew's fate was in the hands of United States Attorney General Elliot L. Richardson who had accumulated testimony of engineers and contractors who were prepared to testify that cash donations were made to Agnew in exchange for state building contracts when Agnew was Governor of Maryland.

On August 6, the White House was informed that *The Wall Street Journal* would break the story the following day detailing the magnitude of the charges against Agnew. Nixon, not wanting to deal directly with the Vice President, flew to Camp David and summoned Harlow and Chief of Staff Alexander Haig to the Maryland retreat. Nixon was convinced that Agnew must resign and sent Harlow and Haig back to Washington for a 9:00 P.M. meeting with Agnew.

Agnew, still waiting for an appointment with Nixon at Camp David, described Harlow and Haig as "serious and glum, and extremely ill at ease."[7] Harlow informed Agnew that there would be no meeting with the President, that he and Haig were sent to deliver the message that Agnew's indictment on information provided by Attorney General Richardson was inevitable. Harlow told Agnew, "This is a national crisis. Congress will undoubtedly act. You will be impeached."[8]

Agnew was incensed that Harlow and Haig, rather than the President himself, were in his office, asking him to resign as Vice President. Agnew began pacing the floor and adamantly refused to resign. Seething with rage, frustration, and despair, the Vice President ushered Harlow and Haig out of his office, later recalling his feelings, "I could not imagine that they could think I would resign without even talking to the President and having at least a chance to defend myself. Harlow knew better than that. I was disappointed in him, because I had a very great affection for him, and I still do. When I was in Washington in 1978 and found out he was critically ill in the hospital, I sent him a handwritten note, saying 'the past is the past,' and I wished him a speedy recovery."[9]

Agnew bitterly concluded that he was no longer part of the Nixon team. But the Vice President would not accept the reality that he must resign, later writing, "Although Haig and Harlow claimed to speak for Richard Nixon in demanding that I resign at once, I clung to the belief that the President himself would help me when he heard my side of the story in reply to the version peddled to him so persuasively by Elliot Richardson."[10]

Agnew hung on. In September, he found an unexpected ally in United States Senator Barry Goldwater of Arizona who was angered at Nixon's handling of the Agnew affair, concluding that the President had "cut Agnew loose among the wolves."[11] Goldwater phoned his concerns to Harlow at the White House. Fearing that

Goldwater might publicly come to Agnew's defense, President Nixon sent Harlow and White House Counsel Fred Buzhardt on the evening plane to Arizona where Goldwater had flown home, "tired and depressed" over the whole incident.[12]

When Goldwater arrived as his Phoenix, Arizona, home, he received a message that Harlow and Buzhardt were on their way and would arrive at his home within the hour. Small talk was short when the two presidential emissaries presented themselves at Goldwater's front door. Harlow told Goldwater that Attorney General Richardson was prepared to drop bribery charges against Agnew if the Vice President would plead guilty to a single charge of federal income tax evasion. Harlow showed Goldwater some of the affidavits and documents that substantiated the charges against Agnew. Goldwater did not receive the news well. He later wrote, "This was shameful. The White House was threatening to allow Agnew's prosecution unless he handled the matter their way—resignation in disgrace... I was sick of this dirty business, so I spoke to the pair in plain political terms."[13]

Goldwater warned Harlow and Buzhardt that White House treatment of a conservative like Agnew would divide the Republican party. The meeting ended with Goldwater shouting, "I don't give a damn if Agnew is as guilty as John Dillinger, he has the right of every American to be presumed innocent unless proved guilty."[14]

Agnew was defiant. With the help of Harlow, and Congressman Gerald Ford who actually set up the meeting, Agnew met with House Speaker Carl Albert, House Judiciary Committee Chairman Peter Rodino of New Jersey, and Congressman Tip O'Neill of Massachusetts to ask for a full impeachment inquiry. Agnew vehemently denied he had taken any money after assuming the office of Vice President and said the charges were part of a concerted Democratic effort to sink him.[15] The next day Speaker Albert called Nixon with a flat-out rejection of Agnew's request for a full inquiry. Nixon, having been briefed on the seriousness of the charges against Agnew, asked Harlow to convince him that he must resign for the good of the country, and that of his family.

Nixon refused to see Agnew personally, insisting that Agnew deal through Harlow. Agnew was angry, later writing, "Without even an opportunity to be heard in my own defense, I was to be jettisoned, a political weight too heavy to allow the presidential plane, now laboring on its last engine, to remain airborne."[16]

On October 9, Agnew walked into the Oval Office and submitted his resignation as Vice President. The following day he walked into a federal courtroom in Baltimore and pleaded no contest to one count of federal income tax evasion. He was sentenced to three years' probation and a $10,000 fine.

Years later, in an interview in *The New Republic*, Harlow called Agnew "a product of a political system which is different from what it is in most states." Harlow said, "The use of corporate money in campaigns and the use of campaign money in peculiar ways has occurred in Maryland for many years. I think Agnew was startled to find that there was a morality problem involved in it."[17] Harlow concluded that Agnew believed he was victimized by an ex post facto morality that did not exist at the time of the offenses.

During the Agnew controversy, Watergate continued to simmer. The partial release of the White House tapes was becoming a major concern for Nixon. By October, 1973, the President realized that the appointment of a special prosecutor, Archibald Cox, to probe the White House involvement in the Watergate break-in, was a mistake. Nixon wanted Attorney General Richardson to fire Cox and return the investigation back to the Justice Department. The President sent Harlow to meet with Richardson and his top aides to secure the firing of Cox. Richardson rebuffed the attempt to axe Cox and warned that any such action would be seen by the American people as more cover-up of an already festering sore.

A temporary compromise between the White House and the Attorney General was reached. Cox would cease his attempts to subpoena additional White House tapes, a fishing expedition that had begun in July, creating a constitutional battle over what a President must turn over to investigating authorities.

Harlow spent the evening of October 19 calling Cabinet members to explain the tentative compromise over the further release of tapes. Tired from hours on the telephone, Harlow dialed a wrong number and mistakenly called Attorney General Richardson. Even though Harlow quickly apologized, Richardson went into a rage, and complained, in the heat of a terribly stressful situation, that he had never been treated so shabbily.[18] Harlow slipped into Haig's office and told the Chief of Staff how upset Richardson was. Haig telephoned the Attorney General, who apologized, told Haig that he was very tired and had had a drink and that things were looking better to him."[19]

When Cox refused to obey the directive to limit his subpoena of additional tapes, Nixon demanded Richardson fire Cox. On October 20, the Saturday Night Massacre occurred. Attorney General Richardson and his top assistant, William Ruckelshaus, resigned. The third-ranking official in the Justice Department, Solicitor General Robert Bork, fired Special Prosecutor Cox. The press accused Nixon of acting like a madman. By October 23, there were 21 resolutions for Nixon's impeachment floating in various stages on Capitol Hill. On November 15, the House voted to begin the process of impeachment.

Pat Buchanan and Diane Sawyer were assigned the task of comparing the transcripts of several of the Watergate tapes with the official testimony of John Dean before the Senate Watergate Committee. Buchanan and Sawyer prepared an analysis of the tapes, pointing out numerous descrepancies which they thought would call Dean's credibility into question. Both Buchanan and Sawyer wanted to release the tapes and their analysis but Harlow rejected the idea. Harlow, fearing the public's reaction to the string of curse words contained on the Nixon tapes, told Buchanan, "We can not have the President of the United States talking like that."[20] Harlow successfuly held up the release of the Watergate tapes, at least for awhile.

Harlow and his wife Betty were invited by the President and First Lady Pat Nixon to the White House for an intimate small dinner a few days before Christmas, 1973. It was evident to all that Watergate was taking its toll on Nixon and his official family. In attendance at the White House dinner were the Harlows, Pat

Rare smiles during the height of Watergate in July, 1973. Left to right, Harlow, Melvin Laird, and George Shultz, leave the Bethesda, Maryland, Naval Hospital after conferring with President Nixon who was hospitalized with viral pneumonia. Courtesy *The Daily Oklahoman.*

and Shelley Buchanan, Rose Mary Woods, Barry Goldwater, presidential speechwriter Raymond Price, Mary Brooks, an old Nixon friend who was Director of the United States Mint, and David and Julie Eisenhower.

Those who have written about the small White House gathering paint a picture of a relaxed, convivial evening, laced with the stories of a desperate President working his tiny, influential audience. Gathered in the yellow oval sitting room in the second-floor family quarters of the White House, the group of Nixon's closest advisers and friends, talked of Watergate, and its effect upon America. In *The Final Days,* Bob Woodward and Carl Bernstein prominently wrote of the dinner. But Ray Price, present for every conversation of the night, challenges Woodward's and Bernstein's

Harlow and President Nixon in the Oval Office, July, 1973, discussing the festering Watergate investigation. Until Harlow discovered the existence of the Watergate tapes, he believed strongly that Nixon would survive the Ervin Committee investigation. Courtesy *The Daily Oklahoman.*

description of Nixon as drunk, rambling, and incoherent.[21]

Nixon recognized how divisive and destructive Watergate had become, "I suddenly realized how deeply its acid had eaten into the nation's grain. . . how badly frayed the nerves of the American people had become."[22]

With the sound of a comfortable Christmas fire coming from the sitting room fireplace, Nixon moved from one dinner guest to another, changing from one topic to another. Goldwater remembered, "I had never seen Nixon talk so much, yet so erratically, as if he were a tape with unexpected blank sections."[23]

Nixon discussed Congress with Harlow and the upcoming State of the Union speech with Price. As the group sat down for dinner, Nixon turned to Goldwater and asked, "How do I stand,

Members of the Watergate Committee confer in July, 1973. Left to right, Chairman Sam Ervin, Jr.; Committee Chief Counsel Samuel Dash; Connecticut Senator Lowell P. Weicker, Jr.; Tennessee Senator Howard Baker; and Committee Deputy Counsel Rufus Edmisten. Courtesy *The Daily Oklahoman.*

One of Harlow's artistic doodles, drawn during a 1972 conference at a Washington, D.C., hotel. Courtesy Don A. Goodall.

Barry?" Even though the President had not mentioned Watergate, the table fell silent, knowing what Nixon was fishing for. Goldwater later wrote, "Silence, not a single word from anyone. Julie looked at her plate. Price and Buchanan seemed to be staring into the distance. Harlow gazed at me without expression. Rose Mary Woods toyed with her salad. Nixon peered into the bottom of his wine glass."[24]

Senator Goldwater, never known for glossing over an answer to any question, said, "Mr. President, let's talk about this matter as family and friends in the spirit of Christmas. Let's open our hearts. Let us solve all this together and put it behind us, for the good of the nation."[25]

After an eternity of 15 or 20 seconds of silence, Nixon changed the subject, talking about a recent family vacation and asking Harlow to offer his views on the energy issue. As Harlow began slowly to talk about energy, Nixon cut him off and began an open attack on liberals in the media.[26]

Goldwater, in his book entitled *Goldwater,* wrote that he asked himself if he was witnessing a slow-motion collapse of Nixon's mental balance. Goldwater said he phoned Harlow the following day and bluntly asked Harlow about the President's behavior. Goldwater said Harlow told him Nixon had been drunk before and during the dinner.

After the President bade his guests farewell, Price and Harlow walked together toward the West Wing. Feeling the gravity of the evening they had witnessed and the overwhelming expectations of the next few months, Price grinned at Harlow and said, "Well, Bryce, I guess we've both been had." Harlow replied, "I guess we have."[27]

The Beginning of the End

BRYCE STOPPED ME IN THE HALL TO TELL ME ABOUT
THE NOW FAMOUS OR INFAMOUS [WATERGATE] TAPES.
HE WAS SICK. SO WAS I.

PRESIDENT GEORGE BUSH

By January, 1974, Harlow considered himself on overtime at the White House. He had been trying for months to return to Procter & Gamble. However, his involvement in the selection of a new Vice President to replace Spiro Agnew forced him to stay on awhile longer.

After Agnew resigned Harlow told Nixon it was time for him to leave his government post and return to his private sector job. However, Nixon convinced Harlow to stay on and help in the selection of a new Vice President. Nixon could not have known what an incredible impact Harlow would have in the next few weeks on such a momentous decision to select a Vice President who within a year would ascend to the Presidency.

Several members of Congress used Harlow to gain access to Nixon to discuss the picking of a new Vice President. Democratic and Republican congressional leaders came to the White House to tell Nixon of their concerns. The Democrats were apprehensive because the sudden elevation of a Republican would surely put that person at the head of the pack of candidates running for the GOP presidential nomination in 1976. Democrats urged Nixon to appoint only a caretaker Vice President, someone who was not interested in running for President three years hence. Senator

Mike Mansfield suggested Kentucky Senator John Sherman Cooper and former Secretary of State William Rogers. The press had bantered about the names of John Connally, Nelson Rockefeller, and Ronald Reagan. However, Democrats promised strong opposition to any of the three.[1]

Nixon asked 400 Republican leaders around the nation to list their recommendations. Reagan and Rockefeller were virtually tied for first place; Connally was third; and Ford, fourth, even though responses from members of Congress had Ford first.

Nixon's first choice was Connally, the former Governor of Texas who was well-known nationally for having been wounded at the time President John F. Kennedy was assassinated in Dallas in November, 1963. As Nixon moved closer to announcing Connally as his choice, Harlow and Melvin Laird worked feverishly in support of their choice, House Minority Leader Gerald Ford of Michigan. Harlow and Laird liked Connally but were afraid of the backlash from Republicans who still had not accepted Connally's switch from the Democratic to the Republican party. Harlow told Nixon that Connally could not be confirmed by the Senate.

On the morning Nixon prepared to announce Connally's nomination, Laird and Harlow, in the words of Laird "put out a full-court press and got all our friends on the Hill and so on and arranged meetings in Nixon's office at 5:00 P.M. the next day."[2]

The following day congressional leaders paraded into the Oval Office and confirmed Harlow's prognostication, Connally could not be confirmed. Nixon considered Reagan and Rockefeller, concluding that nominating either would split the Republican Party and result in a bitter partisan fight.[3] Much to the delight of Harlow and Laird, Nixon turned to Ford. Harlow and Laird called Ford at home and informed him that Nixon would be calling, and offering him the chance to become Vice President. Both told Ford, "Don't you dare turn it down."[4]

The next evening, October 12, 1973, Nixon announced to the nation the selection of his new Vice President. Laird later recalled, "Ford would never have been President if Bryce and I were not in the White House."[5]

Harlow again told his closest friends he was ready to leave the White House. This time, it was Vice President Ford who asked Harlow to stay on longer to help him get his feet on the ground in his new job. Always a slave to public service, Harlow bowed to Ford's request and put off again his expected move to Procter & Gamble.

In December, 1973, still another problem arose in the Nixon presidency. Nixon's income tax deduction for giving his presidential papers to the National Archives was questioned by newspapers and Nixon detractors. Harlow suggested that Nixon should submit his tax returns for examination by Joint Congressional Committee on Internal Revenue Taxation, chaired by Congressman Wilbur Mills of Arkansas. Nixon's friend, prominent tax attorney Kenneth Gemmill, agreed with Harlow that the Joint Committee was the proper forum in which to resolve the dispute over the challenged deduction.

Harlow had suggested to Nixon that in ordinary times the Joint Committee would be a fair forum. But these were not ordinary times, and soon it was apparent that Chairman Mills was opposed to Nixon. Mills told reporters that Nixon should resign because of dismay over his taxes.[6] Harlow's weekly reports to the President on the status of the income tax investigation grew "increasingly bleak."[7] The Joint Committee staff, most unfavorable to the President, drafted a report that rejected Nixon's presidential paper deduction and even suggested that Nixon reimburse the government for airfare for his wife and children if they accompanied him on *Air Force One*. Republicans on the Joint Committee promised Harlow that the matter would be turned over to the Internal Revenue Service. But, bowing to pressure, all Republicans refused to overturn the staff recommendations that gutted Nixon's arguments in support of his tax returns. Harlow saw the tax situation as just another chink in the Nixon armor.

In November, 1973, the White House staff was concerned over the public announcement that an 18-and-a-half-minute gap existed in the Watergate tapes. New Watergate Special Prosecutor Leon Jaworski stepped up his efforts to gain access to all the Nixon tapes. Nixon asked Harlow and Press Secretary Ron Ziegler to review the tapes and summaries of the conversations prepared by Pat Buchanan. Nixon was still optimistic that the tapes would somehow prove that John Dean lied and that he, Nixon, had told the truth about his alleged complicity in the cover-up. Harlow did not share Nixon's optimism. Nixon later recalled, "Harlow in particular thought that the tapes would be deadly because the conversations on them were just too realistically political for public consumption."[8] Buchanan wanted to release the transcripts of the tapes to the public. Harlow said no. Nixon, relying on Harlow's assessment of how the public and Congress would react, decided to not voluntarily release the transcripts.

The year 1974 was a disaster for Nixon. On January 4, Nixon hired attorney James St. Clair to head his Watergate defense strategy. Melvin Laird left the White House February 1 and only a personal plea from Nixon kept Harlow on after the Laird exodus. The *Christian Science Monitor* reported that Nixon had "leaned on Harlow," telling him that it was of utmost importance that Harlow help Nixon get several legislative programs underway, particularly election reform.[9]

On March 1, a federal grand jury in Washington indicted Haldeman, Ehrlichman, Mitchell, Colson, and three others for their part in the cover-up of the Watergate burglary. Nixon was named as an unindicted co-conspirator, even though that information was kept secret for the time being.

When the House Judiciary Committee subpoenaed 42 more tapes on April 11, Harlow knew the final unraveling of the Nixon presidency had begun. When he learned about the latest subpoena, Harlow walked into his White House office and told Sally Studebaker, "Set up an impeachment file."[10] Without further conversation, Harlow went into his office, closed the door, and looked out the window, quietly contemplating the national crisis that would follow in the next few months. He decided that afternoon that he could do nothing else to save the Nixon legacy and looked forward to quickly move back to Procter & Gamble.

On April 12, Harlow dictated, and Sally typed, a resignation letter. In the letter Harlow, now 57 years old, wrote that he had tried to quit three times before and promised that he would be available to Nixon in private life. The *Washington Post* said Harlow's resignation ended speculation in the corridors of Washington that Harlow would become Republican National Chairman. When Nixon received Harlow's letter of resignation, he responded in a handwritten note that he was "immensely sorry" and felt "a very special sense of loss."[11]

On July 5, Nixon wrote in his personal diary:

> I remember Harlow saying almost a year ago, this issue has no legs to it. He may be right, may have been right, then, but so much as been added on, the personal taxes and all that sort of thing, so many doubts have been raised that one wonders what the situation is now. I think of myself worrying as I have from time to time, what was going to happen next, and you get that sinking feeling in the bottom of your stomach and sometimes there are nights that are sleepless. . . Our only course of action is to keep fighting right through to the last and not to die a thousand deaths in the meantime.[12]

On July 12 Harlow attended a White House ceremony at which Nixon signed the Congressional Budget and Impoundment Control Act of 1974, a comprehensive piece of legislation engineered by Harlow to force Congress to keep the federal budget at agreed-upon levels. After the ceremony, Harlow told Nixon, "Boss, you've got it won," an obviously incorrect assessment of the President's standing with the House impeachment process. Vice President Ford echoed Harlow's sentiment, "Don't worry Mr. President. You've got this beat with a solid 50-vote margin in the House."[13]

Nixon's problems worsened on July 24 when the United States Supreme Court ruled 8-0 that the President must turn over 64 tapes sought by Special Counsel Jaworski. One particular tape, of conversations of June 23, 1972, heavily implicated Nixon in the cover-up of Watergate criminal activity. On July 27, the House Judiciary Committee passed its first article of impeachment, charging the President with obstruction of justice in attempting to cover up Watergate. Two days later a second article of impeachment was approved. The third and final article was approved the following day.

On August 5, the White House released transcripts of the three taped conversations of June 23, 1972. Nixon met with John Dean and discussed paying off Howard Hunt, one of those implicated in the burglary. On the tape, in a meeting with Dean, Haldeman, and Mitchell, Nixon said, "I don't give a shit what happens. I want you all to stonewall it. Let [the accused burglars] plead the Fifth Amendment, cover up, or anything else, if it saves the plan. That's the whole point. . . We're going to protect our people if we can."[14] Nixon, recognizing his days in the Presidency were limited, asked speechwriter Ray Price to draft a resignation speech.

White House Chief of Staff Haig visited Vice President Ford shortly after the release of the tape that implicated Nixon in the cover-up. Haig said, "Are you ready, Mr. Vice President, to assume the Presidency in a short period of time?"[15] Ford assured Haig he was ready, if Nixon either resigned or was impeached.

Haig briefed Ford on the new damning evidence against Nixon and laid out the possible scenarios of Nixon leaving office, either as an impeached President or a President resigning in exchange for a promise from the new President for a pardon. Haig insisted the idea of a pardon was not his, but he was duty-bound to convey the idea to Ford.

Ford and his staff recognized that the mere mention of a possible pardon of Nixon was a time bomb. Ford had to talk to someone he trusted. The former President wrote of the incident in his 1979 book *A Time To Heal:*

> To whom could I turn? Almost instantly, Bryce Harlow came to mind. A short, solemn-faced Washington business executive who had served as adviser to six Presidents, he was a man of total integrity. Possessed of infinite tact. . . he also had more common sense and political perception than anyone I knew. I was sure I could rely upon him totally, and I told [aide Robert] Hartmann to arrange a meeting as soon as possible.[16]

After being briefed by Ford on the conversation with Haig, Harlow's explicit opinion was that the issue of a pardon should never have been mentioned, and that Ford should quickly make it clear to Haig that he did not agree to anything. Harlow told Ford, "It is inconceivable that [Haig] was not carrying out a mission for the President, with precise instructions, and that it is the President who wants to hear your recommendations and test reaction to the pardon question. But the President knows he must be able to swear under oath that he never discussed this with you and that you must be able to swear that you never discussed it with him."[17] The Vice President accepted Harlow's counsel and called Haig and told him not to misunderstand their conversation, there was no promise of a pardon for a resignation.[18]

On August 6 Harlow was invited to a clandestine meeting at the home of William G. Whyte, a vice president of United States Steel and close friend of the Vice President. It was a meeting anticipating the transfer of power from Nixon to Ford. The younger members of the transition team listened carefully at Harlow's advice on how to smoothly move into the White House and continue, unabated, the affairs of state. Ford had suggested Harlow attend the meeting along with Secretary of the Interior Rogers Morton and former Congressman John W. Byrnes of Wisconsin, all veterans of Washington politics.[19]

On August 8, Nixon met with his Cabinet and many close friends, including Harlow, to tell them of his decision to resign. The emotional level in the room was unbelievable. Many were crying. Nixon restrained tears until he heard his old friend, Congressman Les Arends, sobbing. Nixon broke into tears as he said goodbye. The crowd jammed around him so tightly the President could not move his chair to get up. That task was performed by Bill Timmons.

Shortly thereafter, Nixon told the American people that the burden of Watergate was too much for him, his family, and for the country, and that he would resign the following day. Dr. Henry Kissinger waited for Nixon in the corridor after the speech, "Mr. President, after most of your major speeches in this office we have walked together back to your house. I would be honored to walk with you again tonight."20

Nixon remembered, "As we walked past the dark Rose Garden, Kissinger's voice was low and sad. He said that he thought that historically this would rank as one of the great speeches and that history would judge me one of the great Presidents. I turned to him and said, 'That depends, Henry, on who writes the history.' "21

The following morning, Haig performed one of his final tasks as White House Chief of Staff for Nixon. He knocked on the door of the Oval Office and said, "This is something that will have to be done, Mr. President, and I thought you would rather do it now." Haig took a sheet of paper and put it on the desk in front of Nixon, who read the single sentence and signed it:

I hereby resign the Office of President of the United States.

Former President Nixon bids goodbye to members of his staff as he boards a helicopter outside the White House on August 9, 1974. Courtesy *The Daily Oklahoman.*

HARLOW, THE PRIVATE CITIZEN

BRYCE EMERGED UNSCATHED AND WITH HIS REPUTATION INTACT
EVEN THOUGH THE SAD PERIOD OF WATERGATE RUINED SO
MANY PROFESSIONAL LIVES AND SHOOK THE FAITH OF THE
COUNTRY IN POLITICAL INSTITUTIONS.

W. DEVIER PIERSON

Even though Harlow was a private citizen and top lobbyist, President Ford continued to call upon the veteran for advice and counsel. He leaned heavily upon Harlow in the first week of his presidency to assess the qualifications of potential candidates for Vice President.

Harlow began with a list of sixteen and pared it down to five. He considered the national stature, executive experience, and ability of the men to broaden Ford's political base, and then assigned them points and ranked them numerically. In the Harlow evaluation, Republican National Chairman, and former Texas Congressman and United Nations Ambassador George Bush led all contenders. Harlow described Bush as "strongest across the board."[1] Some Ford aides argued, however, that Bush was not fitted for the rough challenges of the Oval Office.

Second on Harlow's list was Rogers Morton, a former GOP National Chairman, although there was doubt about his age and health. House Minority Leader John Rhodes was third and Tennessee United States Senator Bill Brock fourth, assessed by Harlow as "generally strong and especially useful and attractive to youth."[2]

The fifth name on Harlow's list was Nelson Rockefeller, former Governor of New York, and a longtime national Republican leader. Harlow considered Rockefeller, "professionally the best qualified by far with the added strengths of (a) proving the President's self-confidence by bringing in a towering number two, (b) making available superb manpower resources to staff the Administration and (c) broadening the Ford political base."[3]

Harlow pointed out Rockefeller's drawbacks, his age, 66, his unpopularity among Republican conservatives, and the possible discomfort Rockefeller might feel serving as the number two man for someone else.

In a detailed memo to President Ford, Harlow narrowed his Vice-Presidential list to Bush and Rockefeller, adding, "For party harmony, plainly it should be Bush. But this would be construed primarily as a partisan act, foretelling a Presidential hesitancy to move boldly in the face of known controversy." Harlow saw the selection of Rockefeller as being received heartily by the media normally most hostile to Republicans. Harlow suggested, "It would encourage estranged groups to return to the party and would signal that the new President will not be the captive of any political faction."[4]

After all the pages of analysis, Harlow concluded that Rockefeller was the best choice because a Ford-Rockefeller ticket in 1976 would be "an extremely formidable combination against any opponents the Democrats could offer."[5]

Some of Ford's staff members thought Rockefeller might be too strong a Vice President, and possibly overshadow the President. However, Ford stuck to Harlow's list, and the sound Harlow reasoning, and announced his selection of Rockefeller as Vice President within days.

President Ford has said there are several reasons why he trusted Harlow so much. "His judgment was his best sales pitch. His word was his bond. He was blessed with a sense of high integrity. His influence ran deep with leaders of both political parties. He really believed that our economic system was sound and particularly as it operated under democratic society. I say democratic, with a small "d." He thororoughly believed in free enterprise, democratic capitalism."[6]

In September, 1974, Ford struggled with the idea to pardon former President Nixon. He called for Harlow's advice and the counsel of the men who made up his Cabinet and inner staff. The President knew that granting Nixon a pardon would have severe political fallout. However, Ford saw an elongated Nixon trial as a national tragedy that would overshadow anything he accomplished as President. In his memoirs, Ford wrote, "No other issue could compete with the drama of a former President trying to stay out of jail. It would be virtually impossible for me to direct public attention to anything else. Passions on both sides would be aroused. A period of such prolonged vituperation and recrimination would be disastrous for the nation. America needed recovery, not revenge. The hate had to be drained and the healing begun."[7]

Within weeks, details were worked out for Ford to fully pardon Nixon for any crimes he committed from January 20, 1969 to August 9, 1974. Ford announced the pardon and criticism came quickly from all sorts of people, friends, foes, members of Congress, and even privately from old advisers such as Laird and Harlow.

Ford's transition team had suggested the new President convene a "kitchen-cabinet," a group of trusted advisers outside the government to periodically advise Ford. Harlow, Melvin Laird, David Packard, John Byrnes, Bill Whyte, and former Pennsylvania Governor William Scranton made up the "kitchen-cabinet" that informally met with the President on a monthly basis.

At one of the first meetings of the kitchen cabinet, the economy was the issue. Harlow warned that time was running out and that Ford must do something to reverse the decline of the American economy. Ford agreed and asked his trusted advisers to work with his staff to develop specific recommendations of economy-boosting moves.

Harlow worked with Donald Rumsfeld and Robert Hartmann to draft ideas for Ford to use in an address to a joint session of Congress on October 8, 1974. A 10 percent investment tax credit and a cessation of government controls that decreased productivity were the cornerstones of Ford's proposal to Congress. "Inflation," said Ford, "our public enemy number one, will, unless whipped, destroy our country, our homes, our liberties, our property and finally our national pride as surely as will any well-armed wartime enemy."[8]

Ford cherished his times with his kitchen cabinet, writing, "At least once every six weeks they would troop into the Cabinet Room, roll up their shirtsleeves and tell me what they thought of the job I was doing as President. They were free to praise or criticize. When things were getting tough, they gave me encouragement and said the Administration was pursuing the right course." Ford reflected, "When things were picking up, they kept me from getting carried away with myself. Sure, the polls look good, they'd say, but don't get overly optimistic. And they reminded me I still had this or that problem to solve." Ford analyzed his advisors, "Laird was the most 'political' member of the group. Scranton the most liberal on social issues, Harlow and Whyte the most fiscally responsible. And they gave me blunt advice when I needed it most."[9]

Rumsfeld later revealed his opinion of Harlow's bigger-than-life acceptance by Presidents, saying, "He was so unimpressed with himself, uninflated, balanced, and well-rooted. People who get to the White House frequently have sizable egos and being there doesn't do much to moderate that tendency. Having a person around like Bryce who had such enormous talents and such superb relationships in the town, and yet whose demeanor was one that was calm and thoughtful and balanced, was helpful to other people."[10]

In October, 1975, Harlow and other kitchen cabinet members met with Ford whose Gallup poll numbers had leveled off at 47 percent despite a turnaround in the economy and some limited successes in foreign policy. Harlow's opinion was that public divisions within the Administration were creating the impression that Ford was not fully in command. Harlow opined that the feud between Secretary of State Kissinger and Defense Secretary James

Schlesinger, who had embarrassed the President more than once with leaks to the press, was responsible for the public's view of Ford's control of his own Cabinet.

Ford moved firmly and quickly and replaced Schlesinger with Donald Rumsfeld who had served with distinction in Congress, as director of the Office of Economic Opportunity, head of the Cost of Living Council, and as Ambassador to NATO. For the first 15 months of the Ford Administration, Rumsfeld had been the senior member of Ford's White House staff.

Harlow played a prominent role as a Ford adviser at the 1976 GOP convention in Kansas City. Harlow's former aide, Bill Timmons, served as Ford's convention manager and relied heavily upon his old boss for advice.

Ford was opposed for the Republican nomination by popular California Governor Ronald Reagan. However, when Reagan announced he would name Pennsylvania Senator Richard Schweiker, a liberal Republican, as his running mate, delegates began switching to Ford, securing the nomination of the sitting President before the first gavel of the convention.

After winning the nomination, Ford went about the business of selecting a running mate to replace Vice President Rockefeller who chose not to stand for election, after GOP experts told him he was a liability to the ticket because of the Republican Party's move to the right, leaving the more liberal Rockefeller behind.

Harlow again was asked to gather around the table with Laird, Rockefeller, Texas Senator John Tower and others to select a running mate for Ford. After long meetings nominating and eliminating contenders, Kansas Senator Robert Dole was chosen.

The political savvy of Harlow was magnificently demonstrated during the last night of the 1976 GOP convention. President Ford had snatched the nomination from Ronald Reagan who sat in a skybox high above the convention floor. Reagan and his aides heard a quiet knock of the skybox door. A Secret Service agent announced it was Bryce Harlow at the door. Harlow, in his quiet, unobtrusive manner, told Governor Reagan it would be terrible if Reagan left the convention hall without speaking.

Reagan's aides huddled to discuss the offer. As Senator Robert Dole completed his speech, Harlow turned back to Reagan's staff and said, "Reagan has to speak to this convention. Those delegates down there have picked two candidates. Now they want to hear from Reagan. If he doesn't, it will split the Republican party in two." Reagan assistant Michael Deaver said Reagan should speak only if he was asked to do so by the President.

Harlow knew his mission and immediately went to the convention floor to talk to Senator Dole. When he returned to the skybox, Harlow gathered in a tight circle with Reagan and his top aides. "Bent over like a quarterback calling signals in a football game, Harlow said, 'It's all set. As soon as President Ford is through speaking and the demonstration begins, Senator Dole will

Facing: President Gerald Ford during a 1975 official visit to Oklahoma. Left to right, United States Senator Dewey Bartlett, United States Senator Henry Bellmon, Governor David Boren, the First Lady, the President, and *The Daily Oklahoman* publisher Edward L. Gaylord. Courtesy *The Daily Oklahoman*.

go up to him on the platform and tell him that Reagan is willing to come down if he will ask him over the microphone."[11]

Harlow returned to the convention floor and alerted the Secret Service that Reagan might be coming to the platform. Ford finished his speech, accepted the cheers of the thousands of delegates, and looked up toward Reagan's skybox as the spotlights followed his lead. Ford raised his long arms high over his head and "beckoned to Reagan with a wide, sweeping thrusts and said in pantomine, 'Come on down'."[12]

As Reagan left the skybox to join Ford on the platform, Richard Whalen, one of Reagan's campaign advisers, said quietly, "Ford has just given the future of the party to Reagan."[13]

When the Ford-Dole team was defeated by former Georgia Governor Jimmy Carter and Minnesota Senator Walter Mondale in the November, 1976 general election, Harlow was understandably profoundly disappointed.

The Harlows, Bryce and Betty, took part in a final tribute to Gerald and Betty Ford two nights before President Carter was inaugurated. The Harlows, Kissingers, Lairds and other couples who were close to the Fords, planned, with the President's knowledge, a surprise for the First Lady. Returning from a dinner engagement, the President and First Lady arrived at the White House and took the family elevator to the first floor. All was quiet with only a few lights shining on the Marine band at the bottom of the staircase. However, Mrs. Ford was not suspicious because she had been told the band was in the White House to have photos taken.

Even after leaving the Nixon White House and resuming his post as Vice President of Procter & Gamble, Harlow's advice was frequently sought by President Ford as a member of Ford's "kitchen cabinet." Courtesy *The Daily Oklahoman*.

The President said to his First Lady, "As long as we're here, why don't we have a last dance?" The First Lady agreed and requested the band play "Thanks for the Memory." As the Fords glided onto the floor, the Harlows, Kissingers, and dozens of other couples joined them, "beaming with delight." The First Lady had her back to the crowd and was totally unaware of their presence until someone tapped her on the shoulder. With a gasp of surprise and big tears rolling down her face, Mrs. Ford giggled as everyone crowded around, hugging and kissing her. The President said, "Seeing her so happy was one of the greatest joys of my life."[14]

In 1977, Harlow was named to the Oklahoma Hall of Fame, sponsored by the Oklahoma Heritage Association. He was introduced at the induction ceremony by Dr. Henry Kissinger, who said, "One of the most revealing things about Bryce Harlow is that he served an amazing number of the leaders of our nation: Two Presidents officially and four Presidents unofficially, two great military leaders, and congressional leaders almost too numerous to mention. His 11 years of service in the White House as a key Presidential advisor are matched by few others in the history of that institution."[15]

Many of Harlow's Washington comrades made the trek to Oklahoma to watch the aging warrior receive his home state's highest award. Harlow, with his wit and inordinate ability to use weird combinations of English words, later thanked his friend Emmett W. Hines, Jr., Director of Government Relations for the Armstrong Cork Company, writing, "So a special thanks for your very special fervor and favor, amigo—and an ardent hope y'all found at least a modicum of enjoyment while cavorting in the Southwest paradise of Harlow and Clyde Wheeler. Your coming was far greater distinction than any State can confer, and my eyes brim, my lips quiver, my throat grows tight as I think of it. Never before has your doing so much done so much. Maudlinly, Bryce."[16]

An Active Retirement

YOU COULD TAKE HARLOW'S WORD TO THE BANK.

MARK SHIELDS

After leaving the White House for the last time, Harlow resumed his corporate representation duties as a vice president of Procter & Gamble. With a straight face, Harlow could squeeze the names of ten P & G products into a single sentence. He often told audiences, "Bear in my mind the Cascade of resources that buoy my talk, Joy and Zest and Thrill, wish a Dash of Bold as I Crest the Washington Tide by Pampering the great, all the while remaining Mr. Clean."

Harlow was the dean of corporate lobbyists in Washington. His counsel was highly respected and many young lobbyists looked to Harlow for guidance in how to deal with the sprawling federal government.

Frank Jones, corporate representative for the Aluminum Company of America (ALCOA), knew Harlow from age 11 when he served as a page in the House of Representatives. Jones said of Harlow, "He was a giant in the lobbying business because of integrity and love of country. Anyone who gets into our business and wants to follow in his footsteps and emulate his virtues, would be well-advised to keep those two things in mind at all times because Bryce was never without either."[1]

Dr. Henry Kissinger called Harlow creative, writing, "His real contribution was in business statesmanship in placing business into the context of the political system while retaining its freedom of economic decision."[2]

Former presidential counselor and Washington lawyer Clark Clifford was an admirer of Harlow's methods of lobbying. He said, "Harlow was exceedingly careful about the manner in which he used his government service and his government standing. All the time he was here I never remember hearing the slightest suggestion of criticism that he had used contacts that he had made in government in an inappropriate manner."[3]

Clifford said Harlow knew the meaning of commitment, "When you had an agreement with Harlow, you could forget about it because you knew it was going to be done. If he took on an assignment, he completed it."[4] Thomas "Tip" O'Neill, former Speaker of the House, called Harlow a "high-minded, open-front type of individual who was extremely candid." O'Neill believed that "when you talked to Bryce Harlow, you knew you were getting it straight from the shoulder. That is how he built his reputation in Washington."[5]

As many as two dozen corporate representatives regularly met Harlow for breakfast or lunch. Emmett W. Hines, Jr., recalled one lunch when Harlow barked at two young aides in President Jimmy Carter's White House business liaison office. One of the immature assistants spouted off about how he could apply certain pressures

A Harlow doodle drawn during an October 27, 1977 meeting of a group lobbying against the proposed Consumer Protection Agency. Courtesy Sally Harlow.

on government agencies if requested to do so. Harlow pointed his finger at the Carter aide, "Young man, don't you ever dare do that. Don't you risk your President doing anything like that. Everybody around this table can get what they need from government by going through the proper channels. And don't you ever, ever forget that."[6]

Harlow and Hines teamed up to defeat legislation that would create a super consumer protection federal agency in 1977. Hines had founded, and chaired for seven years, the Consumer Issues Working Group (CIWG), a strong coalition of as many as 400 businesses and special interest groups. Time magazine recognized the clout of the CIWG, "Strategy is crafted by a 20-member steering committee headed by Emmett W. Hines, Jr., Armstrong Cork's Washington representative, with assistance from Bryce Harlow, Procter & Gamble's shrewd lobbyist and onetime legislative aide to Presidents Eisenhower and Nixon."[7]

One of Harlow's assistants during his last year at Procter & Gamble was Jane Fawcett-Hoover, who in 1999 occupied Harlow's old job as chief lobbyist for P&G. Fawcett-Hoover cherished the short time she sat at master Harlow's feet, "Bryce said to me when I came to work for him that a person has two things in Washington, his credibility and his integrity. No matter how much you get paid, if you lose either one or both of those qualities, you can never regain the confidence of people you work with. He told me that above all else, you need to protect these attributes."[8]

At his desk at the Procter & Gamble Washington office, Harlow forged alliances with other company representatives and officials of trade associations to battle against Congressional plans to create a super consumer watchdog agency. Harlow always opposed the creation of a super consumer affairs agency because, in his opinion, such an agency would only add additional levels of bureaucracy to an already over-regulated marketplace.

Harlow retired from Procter & Gamble on June 30, 1978, but was retained as an occasional consultant. He was replaced by Mike Manatos as the giant company's chief lobbyist in Washington. Harlow had hired and trained Manatos, a political advisor to both

Presidents Kennedy and Johnson after serving four different senators from his home state of Wyoming.

Shortly after Harlow retired, the *Baltimore Sun* honored him in an editorial. "There is no law that bears his name, no grand design for restructuring social services or national defense that history will credit to him. Yet he was the 'insider's insider' in Washington, who by virtue of his personality, knowledge, skill and tireless effort formed a bridge between executive and legislative."[9]

President Gerald R. Ford hand-wrote a letter to Harlow upon his retirement. Its contents are laudatory and historic:

Dear Bryce:

It will be difficult to believe that the nation's capital won't have Bryce Harlow around to keep it on an even-keel. With your retirement the Nation will be the loser. No one, during my nearly 30 years in Washington, did more than you to help others, Democrat or Republican, Senators or Congressmen, Presidents, or others. I was the beneficiary of your friendship, your wise counsel and your loyalty. I will be forever grateful.

Betty and I have so many wonderful memories of our friendship with Betty and Bryce. Such beautiful relationships make all the heartaches and disappointments so insignificant. We thank you both for making our lives better in so many ways.

Each of your countless friends could write a book about how much good you have done for our country. No one could write a line of criticism. You leave Washington with one of the most enviable records of thoughtful, constructive and effective action.

We do hope you will take it easy and thoroughly enjoy your well earned retirement. Betty and I will be thinking of you, praying for your good health and hoping we can get together. If you come west, the door is open. We would love to have the Harlows spend some time with us.

We love you both.

Gerald Ford[10]

Betty Ford wrote across the bottom of the letter, "Jerry certainly said it all."[11]

Asthmatic bronchitis, a cousin to emphysema, gradually wore Harlow down. Almost 40 years of heavy smoking took their toll on Harlow's lungs. He first began having symptoms of breathing difficulty in June, 1977, and quit smoking shortly thereafter, recognizing, "I had already killed myself by then."[12]

Harlow was hospitalized for treatment of his bronchitis in January, 1979. One of first visitors was former President Nixon, in town to attend a state dinner for the Vice Premier of China at the White House, his first visit to his former home since the 1974 resignation. After the 30-minute visit, Harlow told a reporter, "Nixon still has an incredibly penetrating and encyclopedic mind. His intellect shoots out flames about a foot long. He is forceful and exciting."[13] Harlow, his body weakened by disease, retained his powerful mind and incredible grasp of the English language.

Harlow and his wife Betty retired to a meticulously landscaped four-acre paradise along the Potomac River in Harpers Ferry, West Virginia, 90 miles upriver from Washington. He called the riverfront home "Riparian Idle Idyll." Harlow had purchased the small house from California Congressman Bob Wilson years before, in 1972, and remodeled and enlarged the dwelling shortly before retirement.

The Harpers Ferry house was five miles upstream from where Robert E. Lee crossed the river enroute to the battles of Antietam and Gettysburg in the Civil War. It was a peaceful setting where Harlow sat on his flagstone patio only 100 yards across a well-kept lawn from the Potomac.

Even though bronchitis, and ultimately emphysema, slowed Harlow, he was anything but inactive. The phone was his constant companion. *The Daily Oklahoman* reporter Allan Cromley visited Harlow in 1979 and wrote, "On the table beside him is the ever-present telephone which claims his attention frequently. He can carry the phone into the adjacent sun room and other parts of the house, using a 30-foot extension which connects him with the outside world like an umbilical cord." The story continued, "Harlow is apt to get a call on any given day from most any famous Republican you can name: Nixon, Ford, Ronald Reagan, Bob Dole, and staff members for virtually all the other prospective GOP presidential candidates."[14]

Harlow, slowed by emphysema, kept the 100 yards between his home and the Potomac River meticulously manicured. Courtesy *The Daily Oklahoman.*

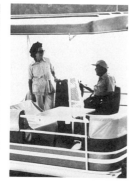

Far right: Harlow and wife Betty on their pontoon boat, anchored on the Potomac River behind their home. Harlow called the vessel his "martini boat," used to entertain the countless friends and public officials who visited Harpers Ferry for the Harlows' friendship and counsel. Mike McKevitt recalls the precious moments listening to the wisdom of Harlow surrounded by old friends and congressional-battle comrades such as Emmett Hines, Jr.; Wayne Smithey; Walter Hasty, Jr.; Al Borland; and Bob Connor. Courtesy *The Daily Oklahoman.*

Harlow and his phone were constant companions on his patio at Harpers Ferry. Even in retirement, he kept in contact with both present and future Republican aspirants. Courtesy *The Daily Oklahoman.*

In a glowing account of Harlow's retirement routine, Cromley wrote, "Harlow has volumes in his head, and in material accessible to him, that may never be written. Instead, he will talk to Republican powers, advise Procter & Gamble about the government, and observe the wildlife around his home. Recently he saw, just outside his dining room window, a prothonotary warbler, the rare bird that was made famous in those Alger Hiss hearings of the early 1950's. . . He now has time to reminisce with those who have had their day in the sun and advise those who are seeking theirs. So he dotes on this three children and nine grandchildren, who live in the Washington, D.C. area. . . and sends Betty to Charles Town every day for the newspapers."[15]

The Harlows entertain guests in 1979. From Bryce Harlow, with hands raised, clockwise, Bill Whyte, Betty Harlow, Don Goodall, Peggy Whyte, Rodney Markley, Grace Goodall, Terry Rice, and Annabel Markley. Courtesy Bill Whyte.

Harlow enjoyed occasional conversations with GOP presidential nominee Ronald Reagan in the summer of 1980. In fact, Reagan requested Harlow review an economic policy package before it was unveiled in September, 1980. Harlow liked the program, which announced as its objectives cutting individual and business tax rates, slowing the growth of domestic spending, increasing defense spending, and balancing the federal budget as quickly as possible.[16]

Sally Studebaker was Betty's best friend and visited the Harlows at Harpers Ferry almost every weekend. While Harlow was tied up on the telephone or reading some Republican hopeful's position paper, Sally and Betty talked or went shopping in nearby villages. Betty's retirement was anything but boring. She was active in local and regional chapters of Kappa Alpha Theta, was a member of a local bridge club and a bowling team, and organist at the Bethesda United Methodist Church near Harpers Ferry.

In retirement, Harlow was still a world-class teacher, not only of politics, but of history. Mike McKevitt, a past president of the Arlington National Cemetery Historical Society, and vice president of the United States Capitol Historical Society, spent days with Harlow walking through the Civil War battlefields around Harpers Ferry. Recalling one such trip, McKevitt said, "I remember him just vividly walking me through the corn rows and describing the whole battle. He was the kind of person who could almost read the mind of somebody already deceased. I think that was part of his military exposure to Marshall and Eisenhower. He would say, 'They made a horrible mistake,' demonstrating with his right hand out and little fingers and hands shaking and quivering, 'The North just blew it, It was pathetic.' "[17]

McKevitt and other close Harlow friends would bait Harlow into telling stories about the Civil War with an off-handed comment such as, "Bryce, what about Robert E. Lee, can you tell us some stories tonight?"[18]

Harlow's public service was never limited just to his official public jobs. Over the years he served faithfully as Chairman, Advisory Committee on Program Priorities, American Enterprise Institute for Public Policy Research; Counselor, Meridian House Foundation; President, Oklahoma State Society; member of the Consumer Affairs and Public Relations committees of the United States Chamber of Commerce; and on the advisory boards of the Capitol Hill Club, Business-Government Relations Council, Hoover Institution on War, Revolution and Peace, International Management and Development Institute, Space Applications Board of the Assembly of Engineering, Robert A. Taft Institute of Government, University of Oklahoma College of Business Administration, United States Capitol Historical Society, Woodrow Wilson International Center for Scholars at the Smithsonian Institution, and Atlantic Council of the United States.

Harlow took great pride in the success of former employees. He looked forward to many of them calling for his advice on major decisions in their lives. David J. Elliott took leave of absence from Procter & Gamble to become President Carter's Deputy Assistant Secretary of Commerce for Congressional Affairs. Elliott would not take the job until he received the okay from Harlow, who warned him, "You will be considered a Democrat for the rest of your life, but go ahead. It should be good experience for you. There are things you'll learn working inside the Administration that you'll never learn just being a lobbyist." Harlow was his "telephone counselor," sometimes daily guiding Elliott through the congressional maze.[19] Elliott attributed to Harlow two famous phrases: "There is no limit to how much you can accomplish in Washington if you don't care who gets the credit," and "There are two things into which you should not inquire closely, one is the making of sausage and the other is the making of law."[20]

From his Harpers Ferry patio, Harlow still talked occasionally with Nixon, telling a newspaper reporter, "He's like a human cork. Push him under the water and he just pops back up."[21]

Top Reagan aides called on Harlow for advice on a variety of subjects. James A. Baker, III, Reagan's Chief of Staff, said, "When Harlow spoke, we all listened. . . He frequently helped us out with advice—most often solicited, but occasionally unsolicited. I never remember an instance where that advice was not excellent, nor an instance where we did not try to follow it."[22]

One bit of "unsolicited" advice for the Reagan White House spilled out in a Mark Shields column in June, 1981. Harlow had warned Reagan's staff to be aware of the perception that the Administration did not care about the "little people." Shields wrote, "[T]hat's what the Harlow antennae are beginning to pick up, and if that perception grows, it could be, he [Harlow] knows, the political kiss of death. . . Like his [Harlow's] word, which you could take to the bank, his judgment is still very reliable."[23]

On June 3, 1981, more than 200 of Harlow's best friends and colleagues gathered to honor him at a dinner at the Capital Hilton Hotel. It was called the Bryce Harlow Recognition Dinner, a $100-a-plate affair. It was a night to remember.

The program was laced with both serious and not so serious comments by stalwarts of the world of Washington corporate representatives. Conoco's Terry Rice gave the invocation. The Master of Ceremonies was Emmett Hines, Jr., of Armstrong World Industries, Inc.

The first speaker was Jesse Smith, for many years the top lobbyist for Armstrong World Industries, Inc. and one of the "few men gainfully employed as a corporate representative when Bryce hit town." Smith told the audience, "Bryce has used his talents, he has helped write history at the deepest level. We are all better for it. I feel blessed for having known him."[24]

The next speaker was Clyde A. Wheeler, Jr., a fellow Oklahoman who served with Harlow on the Eisenhower staff and worked as corporate representative for Sun Company, Inc. Wheeler lauded his old boss and admired mentor, "What Will Rogers did for our ability to laugh at our problems, Bryce has done for our ability to believe that we can solve our problems. . . Bryce is a man of common opinion with uncommon ability. . . I think I will always remember him best for having a telephone hanging from his ear all the time. Callbacks were about as thick as the D.C. telephone book. His enthusiasm was contagious and it was fun to work for him."[25]

Sally Studebaker, Harlow's secretary for most of his Eisenhower years, and all 17 years at Procter & Gamble, said, "He worked the daylights out of me with his normal 10- to 12-hour days, and made me enjoy it. Somehow he managed to have every crisis happen during the holiday period and we had to summon members of Congress back to Washington. He completely ruined my golf game."[26]

Bill Whyte, who headed United States Steel Corporation's government relations office in Washington for 15 years, kept the audience laughing with stories of Harlow losing his White House bathroom to Kissinger and Harlow's part in the formation of the Business Round Table. Whyte said, "He was one hell of a bridge between government and American industry."[27]

Harlow had tears in his eyes as he watched a film that chronicled his life. Then he rose slowly, hampered by lungs that failed to provide him the stamina he once enjoyed. With a glimmer in his eye, Harlow began, "Most of you realize that I may be unable to finish these remarks because of a busted carburetor. Don't let that spook, fluster, or flutter you. Someone will do it if I can't. We arranged that so no one would get away without hearing every last pearly, rapturous and unforgettable Harlowism, for which you put up a bundle tonight."[28]

BRYCE N. HARLOW RECOGNITION DINNER

Capital Hilton Hotel
Washington, D.C.
June 3, 1981

The program for the June 3, 1981 Bryce Harlow Recognition Dinner was graced by one of Harlow's famous doodles. Courtesy Bryce Harlow Foundation.

Sally Studebaker Harlow collected Harlow's doodles in her many years of his service as his personal secretary. On April 10, 1970, a White House discussion was held on President Nixon's decision to send American troops to Cambodia. Harlow helped shape the speech that Nixon delivered to the nation 10 days later and his thoughts came out in the doodles at bottom right. At top left is his scribbling as Nixon imposed wage-price controls on August 16, 1971. At bottom left, Harlow's thoughts came out in geometric designs in July, 1979, during a conversation with Thomas S. Gates, Jr., Secretary of Defense in the Nixon Administration. The top center drawing was Harlow's first after being appointed presidential counselor, and top right was his idea of a proposal to reorganize government. Courtesy Sally Harlow.

Harlow accepted the accolades of his friends with the same inimitable style for which he had become known. He remarked, "Several times this evening, I felt like the distraught damsel who put her bra on backward and found that it fit better... To all of you, we Harlows genuflect, we make obeisance, we humble ourselves, we prostrate ourselves, and, yes, figuratively, at least, but don't test us, we buss your pedal extremities, or such other physiological protuberances as might serve to manifest reverential appreciation of your generosity."[29] It was Harlow's way of simply saying, "Thanks," to his friends.

After the dinner, Harlow wrote Hines, "I have tried every which way to find the thoughts and words to salute your Harlow Sublimation Orgy. None will do. You wrought a miracle."[30] To Bill Whyte, Harlow wrote, "There has gotta be a retaliatory gizmo of some kind... Your willingness to share in it the way you did blew a little mist in my eyes... I am slackjawed about it, sir, plus agape."[31]

The 1981 appreciation dinner was the springboard for the creation of the Bryce Harlow Foundation. Profits from the dinner became seed money for the foundation that was incorporated in 1982 as a non-profit organization. The stated mission of the Bryce Harlow Foundation is "to enhance the national interest by promoting better understanding and cooperation between business and government and to establish, conduct, and otherwise advance education programs designed to improve and professionalize business-government relations."[32]

Since 1982 hundreds of Washington politicians and corporate representatives have gathered annually to salute Harlow and raise money to fund three major programs of the foundation.

The Bryce Harlow Foundation Scholarship Program provides scholarships to congressional and executive branch staff and government workers interested in pursuing a career in business-government relations through part-time graduate level studies at George Washington University and American University. Sixteen scholars are funded yearly. The program is unique because funds for graduate level, part-time students are almost nonexistent.

The Bryce Harlow Educational Forum is made up a series of information discussions with Washington representatives of major corporations who meet with undergraduate or graduate students and faculties around the country. The discussions are designed to give participants an opportunity to evaluate corporate business policies and the practice of business-government relations.

The Bryce Harlow Award is given annually to a member of the business, government, journalism, academic or other profession who has contributed significantly to the advancement of business-government relations and who embodies Harlow's qualities of integrity and dedication. Among the more notable recipients of the Bryce Harlow Award are former United States Senator Howard Baker, former United States Senator and University of Oklahoma president David L. Boren, former Defense Secretary Richard Cheney, former United States trade representative Carla Hills, and former United States Senator and Republican presidential nominee Robert Dole.

The original Board of Directors of the Bryce Harlow Foundation consisted of Robert D. Buehler; Allan D. Cors; Joseph J. Ely; Walter A. Hasty, Jr.; Emmett W. Hines, Jr.; Frank P. Jones, Jr.; Melvin R. Laird; Edward A. McCabe; Theron J. Rice; John F. Ryan; Jerome D. Schaller; J. Richard Sewell; Wayne H. Smithey; and Clyde A. Wheeler, Jr. Christine LaRocco was the Foundation's Executive Director in 2000.

Two facts underscore the significance of the tribute paid to Harlow in the creation of the Foundation that bears his name. Edward McCabe wrote, "First, nothing of this magnitude had ever before been undertaken to honor a retired Washington corporate lobbyist and to encourage emulation of the qualities that distinguished him and his work. Second, all founding directors were Bryce's peers—and all but two were Washington representatives of major American corporations, each engaged in the same general range of activities Bryce handled so well for Procter & Gamble. An oustanding tribute to Bryce from those who knew him best."33

John Harper was the first recipient of the Bryce Harlow Award in 1983. Left to right, Emmett W. Hines, Jr., Harper, Vice President George Bush, and Harlow. Courtesy Emmett W. Hines, Jr.

In October, 1981, President Reagan chose Harlow to receive the Presidential Medal of Freedom, the nation's highest civilian honor. Harlow, the first person chosen by Reagan for the prestigious award, was honored at the White House in an elaborate ceremony October 9, 1981. Reagan called Harlow "an American patriot, in the truest sense of the word." Harlow was deeply touched by the recognition and responded to the President's glowing remarks with a simple "thank you."

PEOPLE WOULD BELIEVE HARLOW WHEN THEY WOULDN'T
BELIEVE ANYONE ELSE.

HOWARD BAKER

Harlow was once more at the center of national attention in June, 1982, when the United States Supreme Court rendered a far-reaching decision on the issue of immunity for presidential assistants.

Harlow, former President Nixon, and Nixon aide Alexander Butterfield were sued by Air Force budget analyst A. Ernest Fitzgerald who was demoted from his Pentagon job in 1969 after publicly criticizing cost overruns in the Air Force's C-5A transport plane. It was Harlow's first involvement in court litigation.

Fitzgerald claimed that Harlow and the other defendants conspired to reorganize the Air Force so that his job as a civilian was eliminated. The $3.5 million dollar lawsuit immediately became a constitutional test of what immunity from such lawsuits the President and presidential counselors should enjoy.

Harlow, Nixon, and Butterfield all appeared at depositions as the case wound it way through the lower courts to an ultimate date with the highest court in the land. The basis of Fitzgerald's claim against Harlow was rested in four conversations Harlow had with Air Force Secretary Robert Seamans. However, there was never any evidence deduced that pointed to anything other than normal conversations between Seamans and Harlow about congressional reaction to a sweeping overhaul of the Pentagon. In fact, in one of the conversations, Harlow warned Secretary Seamans that "the timing was wrong" for firing Fitzgerald because members of Congress were expressing support for the whistleblower.[1]

In briefs filed in the case, Harlow, Butterfield, and Nixon told the Supreme Court that immunity from civil suit was essential for the conduct of the public business. Harlow was represented by Elliot Richardson, who wrote, "It is hard to conceive of a case having any weaker factual foundation. If the Court rules in Fitzgerald's favor, senior advisers in every administration will never be able to escape the inevitable risks and burdens of trial, and they will always live and govern in fear of financial ruin."[2]

Harlow responded to reporters' questions about the suit, "White House aides should be totally immune from civil suits because, if you're in the White House, you're the president's instrument, his alter ego."[3]

Harlow also took issue with Fitzgerald's use of a Nixon quote from the White House tapes. Fitzgerald's legal pleadings alleged that Nixon said, "Bryce was all for canning him [Fitzgerald]." However, the entire transcript painted a wholly different story. Nixon said, "Bryce was all for canning him, wasn't he?" Nixon's press secretary Ron Ziegler replied, "No, I think Bryce may have been the other way."[4]

On June 24, 1982, the Supreme Court announced its 8-1 decision. A sweeping opinion written by Associate Justice Lewis Powell, Jr., recognized absolute immunity from civil suit for a President for his official actions, but refused to grant blanket immunity for presidential aides, instead rewriting the qualified immunity doctrine.[5]

Justice Powell, in refusing to approve absolute immunity for presidential aides, wrote, "The resolution of immunity questions inherently requires a balance between the evils inevitable in any available alternative. In situations of abuse of office, an action for damages may offer the only realistic avenue for vindication of constitutional guarantees."[6]

The only dissent in the Harlow decision came from Chief Justice Warren Burger, who noted that aides to members of Congress enjoyed absolute immunity from civil suit. The Chief Justice wrote, "How can we conceivably hold that a President of the United States, who represents a vastly larger constituency that does any Member of Congress, should not have 'alter egos' with comparable immunity? To perform the constitutional duties assigned to the Executive would be literally impossible, in view of the complexities of the modern process... without the help of aides and assistants."[7]

In clearly defining what it meant by "qualified immunity," the Supreme Court decision in the Harlow case was seen as giving lower courts more freedom in dismissing outright frivolous claims against presidential aides without the expense of a trial.

Facing possible dismissal by a lower court of his case against Harlow and Butterfield, Fitzgerald dismissed the lawsuit in February, 1983. Harlow was happy with the decision and observed that the unusual lawsuit might benefit future administrations, "Prospective Presidents and aides may not now shy away from their jobs because of the fear of lawsuits."[8]

Betty Harlow died of lung cancer on November 3, 1982, at the home of her daughter, Trudy, in Arlington, Virginia. She had noticed a mole on her lip a half-year before. A physician conducted tests on the growth and found it cancerous. Betty was 64 and was survived by her husband, three children, ten grandchildren, and her sister, Mrs. Leonard H. Savage, and her brother, J. P. Larimore of Oklahoma City.

Memorial services for Betty were held at the Rock Springs Congregational Church in Arlington, Virginia. The church was packed with friends and admirers. Senior Reagan White House staff members, including Michael Deaver, Ed Meese, and James Baker, and a large contingent from the White House Legislative Affairs office attended the funeral. Betty was buried on the Harlow property at Harpers Ferry, in a final resting place between the garden and a spring-fed pond.

Harlow's health slowed his pace further. Never far from a portable oxygen tank for the times when breathing became difficult, Harlow spent most of his time in an apartment in the Crystal City Apartments in Crystal City, Virginia, across the Potomac from Washington. His daughters kept his apartment clean and he spent quality time with all his children and his ten grandchildren.

In the same apartment complex lived Sally Studebaker, who still worked at Procter & Gamble, and occasionally brought Harlow mail and messages from friends at P & G. One evening in December, 1982, as Sally brought by the day's mail, Harlow invited his longtime secretary in for dinner, a couple of pot pies Harlow quickly stuck in the oven.

Harlow caught Sally completely off guard. He started slowly, "Now, I want to say something to you and I don't want you to interrupt me. We have known each other for a long time and we have a lot of the same interests and everything and I think you and I ought to get hitched."9

Sally was speechless. She opened her mouth but nothing came out. A thousand conflicting ideas raced through her mind. So many of their friends thought of "Bryce and Betty," yet Sally and the Harlows knew many of the same people. Betty had been her best friend.

Sally did not give Harlow an immediate answer. She thought about the proposal day and night while spending the Christmas holiday at the home of her brother, Roger Studebaker, and his wife in Bethany, Oklahoma. She was quiet during the holidays, thinking, "Two different worlds, his world and my world. . . but we know each other pretty well."10

When Sally returned from Oklahoma, Harlow asked her out for dinner at a hotel near their apartments. She looked the elder statesman in the eye and said, "Well, I guess it will work out." For the time being, the agreement was a secret.

When Harlow announced his intentions to his children, they were joyous. Sally had been considered a member of the family for most of their lives. Sally retired from her job at Procter & Gamble July 1, 1983. Harlow hosted a retirement party for her at Harpers Ferry and invited her associates and friends, and Harlow's children and grandchildren.

After Sally opened gifts from others at the party, Harlow approached her and said, "Sally would you stand up, please? I have a present for you too. Give me a kiss." He pulled out an engagement ring and placed it on Sally's finger. The crowd cheered.

Sally and Harlow were married at the Rock Springs Congregational Church less than a month later, on July 28, 1983. Before the wedding, Harlow quipped, "For 27 years Sally has been taking dictation from me. Now, the situation will be reversed."[11]

Harlow and Sally divided their time between the Crystal City apartment and Harpers Ferry until 1984, when they permanently moved to Harpers Ferry. Harlow needed oxygen more frequently and utilized an electric scooter or wheelchair to whisk him around malls on shopping trips with Sally.

Harlow and Sally Studebaker exchange flowers on their wedding day, July 28, 1983. Courtesy Sally Studebaker Harlow.

Chuck Colson visited Harlow on a day when Harlow was thinking about the future. He told Colson, "I'm going to die." Colson asked Harlow, "Bryce, where do you stand with the Lord?" Assured that Harlow had everything right with his maker, Colson turned to other subjects. He recalled how when he was released from prison after Watergate, Harlow was the first person he visited. Colson thanked Harlow for his generous financial support of his prison ministry.[12]

Harlow knew the end of his life was near. He told Lamar Alexander that he had no regrets, but wished he could have lived two lives, one in Washington, and one in his beloved home state of Oklahoma. Harlow told Alexander that he had always wondered what his life would have been in Oklahoma had he resisted the 1952 call from Eisenhower.[13]

In January, 1987, it grew increasingly difficult for Harlow to breathe. He and Sally were sitting at the table in the kitchen when Harlow picked up the phone and told his doctor that he thought he needed to come to the hospital. Sally made arrangements for an ambulance to take him directly to the hospital. She called the children and a few close friends.

Three days later, on February 17, 1987, at age 70, Harlow died. His remains were cremated, and after a memorial service at the Westmoreland Church in Bethesda, Maryland, were buried next to Betty in their private burial site at Harpers Ferry, where a third name, Sally Studebaker Harlow, had been added to the headstone. The headstone faced south, toward Washington, where Harlow served so many, so long.

At the memorial service on February 21, Edward McCabe served as spokesman for the family and made arrangements for a surprise visitor to the funeral, former President Nixon, who had called Sally and asked if she minded him coming to honor his old friend.

Nixon slipped in the back door of the waiting room behind the church and visited with Sally and the family for about 15 minutes. He approached Sally with a request, "If it would be all right with you, I would be honored to escort you into the church."[14] With no fanfare, no bands playing, no crowds waving, the former President and Sally, followed by the Harlow children and grandchildren, walked down the aisle to the front pews of the church to say goodbye to a fallen American hero and patriot.

Sidney Lovett, the former pastor of the Rock Spring Congregational Church, and longtime friend of Harlow, eulogized Harlow as "one of God's selfless stewards of our nation's soul." Lovett told the Harlow grandchildren, "If you want to become acquainted with your grandfather and your grandmother, look around you to see the sacred monuments of this country and look around you to the wealth of our freedom."15

The church was filled with life-long friends and admirers of Harlow. But, as Edward McCabe, said, "There was yet another service to come—a final, closing service—classic in its simplicity and powerful in its poignancy and its symbolism. Vintage Harlow!"16

The final service McCabe spoke of occurred at the Harlow home at Harpers Ferry after the conclusion of the memorial service. Reverend Lovett, a few family friends, and the Harlow family, including Harlow's ten grandchildren, assembled in a half circle on the lawn between the house and the Potomoc River, facing Harlow's headstone.

Lovett gathered Harlow's grandchildren around the headstone. Holding Harlow's ashes in a small plastic container, Lovett talked to the grandchildren about life and death and eternity. Using a small gardening tool, he "raked up a patch of soil, gently spread the ashes, and then covered them over with the new soil."17

Family and friends retired to the house for refreshments. As McCabe and others prepared to leave an hour later, a soft, white, and gentle snow had begun falling. McCabe said he will never forget the sight. "At least a half-inch had already accumulated, blanketing the entire scene. The ashes and the newly raked earth by the headstone were no longer visible. They were snug beneath their new white robes. All was quiet, not a sound to be heard. A deep hush had settled over the river and the whole valley... Visibly, our friend had left us with our memories. In the late afternoon stillness, it seemed we now fully and finally realized that—with the same elegant dignity which marked his great life—Bryce Harlow had quietly gone home to Glory!"[18]

Official Washington lauded Harlow in his death. President Reagan called Harlow "an insightful architect of public policy whose contributions have strengthened our democracy's political process."[19] Stephen Hess of the Brookings Institution said "He was worthy of trust. He reported each side accurately to the other. He made no cutting comments in drawing rooms or gossip columns." Dr. Henry Kissinger spoke of his admiration for Harlow's reverence to American institutions, "He had a deep sense for the Presidency, its power, its majesty, and the awful responsibility it imposes."

Clyde A. Wheeler, Jr., who successfully lobbied for Sunray DX Oil Company, and later Sun Oil Company, after serving on Harlow's White House team, said Harlow's reputation would endure far beyond the end of his natural life, "This place will miss Bryce Harlow."[20]

Congressman Robert Michel reflected on his 30 years of knowing Harlow, "I cannot think of another individual for whom there was such genuine bipartisan respect. Bryce was the very soul of integrity, a gentleman of ready wit and deep understanding, at home here on the Hill and in the White House."[21]

Kansas Senator Robert Dole remembered Harlow as "a quiet man who spent a lifetime in service to his country. . . who understood that the good of the country always came first."[22]

When news of Harlow's death arrived in the chambers of the United States Senate on February 17, Harlow's dear friend, and fellow Oklahoman, Senator Daniel Patrick Moynihan, asked his colleagues for time to reflect upon the life of Harlow. Without a prepared script, simply from the heart, Moynihan spoke slowly and deliberately, "I have seen him in the cabinets that we served in together. And in circumstances of great privacy, great strain, great drama and trauma. I never heard him utter a dishonorable or mean thought. He had very simple notions about the presidency. He served best when he served most openly. . . We are today very much left to ourselves, but largely because of his time with us, we know better our duties and perhaps can better perform them."[23]

The Daily Oklahoman, published in the city of Harlow's birth, carried an editorial on February 19, 1987, entitled "A Master Bridge Builder:"

> Although no public works projects bears his name, Bryce Harlow will be remembered as one of the ablest bridge builders in American political history.
>
> His career as a behind-the-scenes adviser serves as a blueprint for modern-day government relations. The methods he developed to span the gap between the executive and legislative branches of government, and later to bring government and business closer together, have stood the test of time.
>
> Others got the credit for his successes, Presidents Eisenhower, Nixon, and Ford, and that didn't bother him. In a political world of giant egos, the diminutive Oklahoman was content to work in the shadow because he was a practical, highly principled, problem solver who devoted his energies and skills to making the American system of government work...
>
> His reputation as a power broker with the highest integrity will stand as a lasting tribute.[24]

To honor Harlow's memory, The Bryce Harlow Institute on Business and Government Affairs was created by The Fund for American Studies at Georgetown University in 1990. The Harlow Institute has brought together some of the best and brightest students from around the world to study and learn Harlow's craft.

The lasting legacy of Bryce Harlow is probably, except for his fine children and grandchildren, the more than 200 former employees and associates who call him their mentor. Among that group is former *U.S. News and World Report* editor David Gergen, who said, "Harlow was one of those trustworthy political figures who brought much good sense to our politics over the years."[25]

University of Oklahoma President David L. Boren called Harlow one of the most patriotic citizens he ever knew, "He loved his country and was a steward of our great institutions of government. While he was an ardent Republican, his greatest concern was 'Will this strengthen the country? Will it strengthen the office of the President? Will it cause Congress to function better? Is it good for the country in the long run?' He always had his eye on the history book—a sense of history."[26]

When House Minority Leader Robert Michel introduced Senator Howard Baker as the 1992 recipient of the Bryce Harlow Award, Michel tried to define the Harlow legacy, "How does one define his gift? We might call it the Harlow touch. His view was that: Raising the level of your voice does not raise the level of discussion. Listening with care is better than talking in 'sound-bites' and thinking in slogans. Achieving peaks of uncommon progress can be reached by paths of common courtesy. Having his gift means being a knowledgable professional and being darned proud of it. It also means being serious without being somber; being tough without being mean; being shrewd without being devious; and being witty without being malicious."[27]

Harlow's own words, from a speech in his native Oklahoma in 1961, sum up the philosophy that governed his life:

> If informed, responsible citizens. . . will devote an increasing share of their organizational skills and ability to influencing public affairs, then America's liberty and America's future will be secure.

AN UNACCOUNTABLE GUSH OF CANDOR COMPELS ME TO
CONFESS THAT I AM AS HERAPHRODITIC POLITICALLY AS I HAVE
BEEN OCCUPATIONALLY.

BRYCE HARLOW

Even though Bryce Harlow has been absent from his station on planet earth for more than a decade, his words live on. Any attempt to explain to future generations the value of the Harlow's life and contributions would be sorely deficient without samples of his incredible ability to use both common and uncommon words of the English language to express himself in a refreshing and unique way. Here are some examples:

ON POLITICS

Politics is a potpourri of unpredictabilities, ambiguities and opacities created in prejudice, preconceptions, biases and phobias, the whole of it rendered suspect by rhetorical guile, deception, hypocrisy, and sly selectivity in the use of the truth.

When I began ricocheting around the White House I was six feet four inches tall. As you can see, I got out just in time.

It can be a heady wine if one forgets that it's really the job, not the temporary occupant of the job, that is important.

Old soldiers may fade away, but erstwhile bureaucrats vaporize instantly once their names are stricken from the Federal payroll.

The White House is the universe of American politics. It's where it all comes together, and therefore it should be the most universal place in the whole operation of the government. Oddly, it becomes the most parochial place because of the way the White House functions and because of the steel fences around the White House manned by police to keep people out.

ON BUSINESS LOBBYING

All of us in the room are individually and collectively hopeless, helpless, futile, down the tube and kaput if we try and do our Congressional businesses the next two years as we have done it with sporadic success in the past. It's awfully hard to sing bass when you've just been made a soprano—which is to say our old ways won't hack it anymore.

ON BUSINESS

Business is a very important element of preserving liberty in this country. And what is more a manifestation of personal liberty and freedom than private enterprise? And so you look across the country at countless thousands of activities going on under the name of private enterprise and you're talking about the heartbeat of liberty in this democratic system.

What concerns the business community concerns the United States, and vice versa. I think Emerson once said we are like a raft in a democracy, everybody sits on it and their tail assemblies get wet and uncomfortable, but they never sink. That's contrasted with the dictatorship which is like the Titanic that runs into an iceberg and sinks. We are seared by the disparate nature of our society and business, labor, agriculture, and other major elements of it.

ON RICHARD NIXON

Nixon understood the Congress intimately. He needed liaison people like he needed two heads. I came in to set up the legislative system which Nixon had been comfortable with when he served as Vice President under Eisenhower. A major part of my job under Nixon was to meet with the congressional crowd for him. He simply would not concede that a majority of the congressmen were competent to deal with the rigors of managing the nation's affairs. He has smart enough to play their game. He took the members places and gave them things in order to put them in the glow of the presidential spotlight. Typically, such efforts resulted in their support for a very brief period of time.

ON RICHARD NIXON'S STAFF

President Nixon did not like to have much staff around him, and yet he developed the largest staff in the history of the White House. That is paradoxical. He did not see many of them, ever. And this staff burgeoned under Bob Haldeman. The reason for it was that the President moved the management of the government into the White House, and Haldeman had to create the various offices competent to do this. And so there was endless, endless growth of the White House staff.

ON GERALD FORD

Gerald Ford knew the Congress with the greatest of intimacy. He was a splendid behind the scenes operator. He knew all the techniques for measuring congressmen and their likely responses. He was very familiar with which buttons would need pushing in a particular situation. I think the most important benefit from his congressional experience was the fact that he possessed the implicit knowledge of who could be trusted and who could not be trusted. He was also very familiar with the role congressional leadership could play at the White House because he had been attending those meetings when he was Minority Leader.

ON THE JOB OF A CONGRESSMAN

All of us who have been around the process very long realize that politics is not a hobby, it's a business. The bottom line is not profit and loss, it's votes. A Congressman's profit is more votes than a competitor can get. That puts him in the black. So whatever contributes to his getting a profit in the next election instead of a deficit, which is fatal, is a motivator for him. A lot of people sneer at this and say it creates only weathervane, thoughtless robots, but that's the way our system is.

A WEEKEND INVITATION TO FRIENDS

If y'all find a dull weekend coming with really nothing worth doing and the blahs taking over—just grab the phone, call the Harlows and say you're coming up to let Nature clear it up. We'll have a quiet sit on the patio, listen to the birds, blink slowly, say something occasionally if need be, turn in early and y'all get up farm style next morning all reconstituted.

Everything hurts, and what doesn't doesn't work.

The gleam in my eye is sun on my bifocals.

I feel like the night after but haven't been anyplace.

I get winded playing checkers.

I decide to procrastinate but can't get around to it.

I know all the answers but no-one asks me the questions.

I look forward to a dull evening.

I sit in a rocking chair and can't get it going.

My knees buckle and my belt won't.

I burn the midnight oil until nine o'clock.

My back goes out more than I do.

I sink my teeth in a steak and they stay there.

I start on my favorite war story but am asked instead to talk about San Juan Hill.

Silence is my only form of repartee that gets respect.

I sit and my belly rumbles, stand and my knees creak, talk and my teeth click, eat and I
> dribble on the tablecloth.

A dash to the restroom costs me all the 7 o'clock news and two commercials.

I consult my preacher more and my Congressman less.

AFTER THE 1981
BRYCE HARLOW
RECOGNITION DINNER

To be sure, the gurgly and bubbly flowed apace at the June 3 Harlowfry, but even so those who came and stayed may recollect that Fryee Harlow oratorically sloshed everyone in a Niagara of gratitude....From ages past it has come down that the surest way to test and prove a friendship is to appeal for instant labial extraction of the poison when one's derriere has been pierced by reptilian fang...

So with overflowing and palpitating heart I again drench you, even marinate you, with appreciation. Unhappily I have neither viper nor asp with which to put our bond to the ultimate test, but nonetheless I thank you for standing so tall and being so very special in the Harlow pantheon of friends.

AT THE 1983 HARLOW
FOUNDATION DINNER

Good government is our free system requires quality representation of their varied constituencies by elected officials and also by the countless fractional groups and activities that together make up the body politic. Competitive enterprise is the nation's dynamo, and the bridging, informing, adjusting, analyzing, interpreting, persuading and dissuading done by corporate reps in behalf of their publics with the people who serve a different public mix in the governmental sphere is crucial to the efficiency and vitality of the total system. The better the interchange, the more extensive and sophisticated the private and public representation, and the more these activities can be made to undergird the public's interests, the stronger and more stable and secure our system will be.

A LETTER TO BRAD OELMAN
FROM HARPERS FERRY

In recent times by vista hardly corresponds to what you guys see down there in Washington. When you see Lowell Weicker, I see a wild turkey—our equivalent. When you see Reagan down there, I see an eagle, an osprey, a redshouldered hawk. When you see Tip O'Neill, I see an old crow marching pompously and always volubly around my front yard.

Bob Dole is my pileated woodpecker, racy, darting here and there, and banging the hell out of things in rat-a-tat-tat style. John Dingell is my vulture always ready to pounce for investigative carrion. Ed Meese, a Great Blue Heron stalking about soberly and in stately fashion. Rehnquist, a barred owl and Shultz a barn owl. All you guys, my former colleaguers, are a passel of goldfinches flashing and swooping and looking like a million bucks and giving forth that irresistible tinkle of the coin of the realm, always in flight, continually chirruping, and forever up to your kiesters in stinging nettles. With these marvelous creatures my daily companions and preoccupation you had better dismiss if not discount by thoughts on your concerns down there. Indeed, I just might get down to talking about skunks and reptiles and the little cowbird who sneaks her eggs into other birds' nests, just as we corporate reps like to do—hooking our amendments on someone else's that has a better chance to pass.

Godspeed to you and the brethren. Tell them that when they see Laxalt, I see a bushwhacker; and, obviously, when anyone sees Harlow, he sees a magpie!

TO THE OKLAHOMA CITY MEN'S DINNER CLUB IN 1977

I give you fair warning. I'm here to talk on whatever comes to mind. For you that's a come-on, and for me a license to meander. It's like a kimono, touches little but covers everything.

There's a good reason why pinning Harlow down is like trying to nail a custard pie to the wall. It's because I have wallowed in and out of the public trough for so long.

An unaccountable gush of candor compels me to confess that I am as heraphroditic politically as I have been occupationally. I was born and raised here in a Democratic family, and may the Lord forgive me and co-sinner Ronald Reagan, I openly lived as a Democrat in my early years.

The problem seems to have been that people with inadequate public experience were in positions of major governmental power and were using that power in political ways. There was a dangerous mix. My basic notion is that what went the "wrongest" was forcing campaign activities into the government, instead of keeping it in a political committee.

The so-called Watergate episode essentially reaffirmed an old truth—that eternal vigilance remains the price of liberty in this country. The presidential bloat which started in the New Deal days and swelled until the early 1970's came to threaten the constitutional checks and balance system. Now we know once again, from the Watergate years and before, that the possibility for abuse and distortion in public service, and the seductivity of power for its own sake, are never securely protected against.

To me, Watergate is more of an evolutionary event that an isolated tragedy. Some administration just had to be toed in sooner or later. That had to wait, however, until the political ambiance of Washington allowed it. Not until a journalistic-Congressional complex coalesced in the 1970's did a power larger than the Presidency develop. Had it developed pre-Nixon, an equivalent of Watergate would have come earlier. Had it been only the press or only the Congress outraged in Nixon's time, the corralling of the Presidency would have been deferred still longer.

I think the country will disserve itself if it fails to understand that basically, far more than any one President, it was the Presidency that had become grotesque after four decades of imperializing. If we rivet on that truth, we will stay vigilant against similar or worse transgressions in the future.

It may reassure you to know that your ubiquitous, indefigable, ebullient and dauntless Dr. Hoxie has not brought me here as your scholastic peer. Rather, I come as a pragmatic political engineer— one with a lifetime of building bridges across the yawning constitutional chasm fashioned by our power-fearing Fathers to keep the Congress and the President at a safe distance from one another in the interest of human liberty.

Mine is, as you know, an inexact science, and I have to admit it is on occasion frustrating and disheartening, for despite all these years of applied research, the many bridges I have lofted to uncheck the checks and imbalance the balances, so that the whole government might smoothly articulate toward agreed goals, have proved one after the other to be impermanent. As best I can ascertain, the only reason my license to build was not revoked long ago is that no other practitioner of this exotic science seems to have better techniques or more durable materials than those which have been available to me.

ON HIS SUCCESS

I am so grateful that a little incompetent, indefinite person from the prairies as I was, was allowed by divinity to come into Washington, spent 50 years consorting with such magnificent people. I am grateful for that. I do not understand it, don't know why and how it happened. I have hobnobbed with the Presidents and the people who run our government and our country. All of it without design, without plan, without purpose, and without expectation.

ON POLITICS

Politics is a very funny business. It's one of the very few activities left where your word is your bond. You don't have to sign a document. You give your word as a politician. What difference does it make? It makes all the difference in the world in how you do business in Washington. If you are lobbying for a business in Washington and are found short from the standpoint of integrity, you are ruined instantly. There is no recovery possible.

Suppose you get into a meeting with some of these great pachyderms stomping around and up comes an issue they are arguing about. You are in complete opposition to their idea when the chairman says, "All right boys, is this all agreed to?" What do you do? Do you have the guts to say, "Mr. chairman, not me?" It hurts to do that. But it hurts far worse to keep your mouth shut and have people believe you supported the idea. Silence in politics gives consent.

ON SPECIAL INTERESTS

The ultimate special interest in America is the individual. When you organize a hundred individuals, that's the special interest of a group of people who agree on something. Shouldn't they tell the government what they want? Of course they should. We have a representative Republic.

CORPORATE REPRESENTATION

BY BRYCE HARLOW

The role of corporate representation in Washington—in, that is, what has come to be known rather grandly as the policy-making process—has never been widely understood. As the reader may suspect, I have a few thoughts on the subject (and on any number of other subjects as well, but they will have to await another occasion). I cannot hope with a single essay to treat all the details or to dispel all the myths and simplisms about corporate representation that have emerged over the years. But there may be value in presenting a few highlights, and there is certainly no harm in trying to dispel some of the illusions.

My starting point is a very simple proposition that just happens to run counter to much of what one reads these days: Business is not a malign influence—something evil called a special interest that harms the public interest. Think about it: Business is an indispensable pillar of our prosperity, of our strength as a nation, of our capacity to provide opportunities for mobility in our society and for the fulfillment of individual potentials. In short, business is at the heart of America's well-being.

It follows, I believe, that corporate representation is a profession worthy of talented people. Those who are effective and principled advocates of the interests of their companies and of the business community as a whole help government arrive at better-informed and, therefore, potentially better decisions. Good representatives of good businesses contribute a great deal to good government.

I do not use the word "profession" lightly. One of the points I most want to convey is that corporate representation in Washington is becoming, and needs to be, highly professionalized-that it involves and requires a multiplicity of skills, knowledge, and sensibilities as well as an unassailable character. Any corporation large enough to have need of Washington representation is likely to be beset by a confusing array of complex and sensitive policy concerns within the Jurisdiction of a daunting jumble of government agencies and congressional committees. A Washington representative whose expertise is limited to a refined understanding of social small talk and various techniques of self-ingratiation is not likely to do well or last long in this maelstrom of issues, institutions, and powerful national figures.

And make no mistake about it: What happens in Washington is often so critical for corporations that they simply cannot risk reliance on amateurs to fend for them.

Corporations have learned this the hard way. The increase over the past two decades in the federal government's regulatory and legislative activities has been paralleled by a rapid growth in the number and quality of corporate representatives deployed in Washington—and in the number of trade associations and other business groups that have found it prudent to move their headquarters to the capitol city.

So just what is it that the many corporate representatives now in Washington do to earn their keep? And what qualities and habits of work are needed to be a successful practitioner of the art and science of corporate representation? Being a methodical fellow, I will address the first question first.

THE JOB OF A CORPORATE REPRESENTATIVE

Much of a Washington representative's time is spent in intelligence-gathering—anticipating, monitoring, and interpreting policy developments of possible or future concern to his company. The remainder is spent trying to affect those developments deemed by the company to be of particular importance.

In 1961, when I opened Procter & Gamble's Washington office, corporate representatives along the banks of the Potomac were not nearly as numerous as they are now. Indeed, until Procter took its gamble on me, it had never had a full-time Washington representative. At the outset, my tiny outpost was charged with keeping close tabs on events unfolding in Congress and the executive branch-and with helping Procter's top people decide which matters required their attention and presence. As the office evolved and expanded, we began to do as well as look -to become players as well as observers.

The task of tracking all of the developments that Procter had a significant stake in was itself quite a challenge. We drew upon personal contacts, association intelligence, trade journals, magazines, the wire services, newspapers, congressional reports, and so on. No small amount of our awareness, I should add, was obtained from specialists back in the firm's home offices who spotted in professional reports of various sorts mentions of this or that governmental occurrence too arcane to be noted in conventional Washington sources. Having been apprised of such nuggets of fact or rumor, we in Washington would then set about verifying their authenticity and ascertaining their significance.

The matters that we had to oversee ranged the federal spectrum; such was the breadth of the company's activities and concerns. We kept our eyes trained on the Federal Trade Commission, the Environmental Protection Agency, the Federal Communications Commission, the Securities and Exchange Commission, and a generous assortment of cabinet departments, including Labor, Commerce, Treasury, HEW, Agriculture, State, and Defense.

In the meantime, up on Capitol Hill a roiling, contentious, and unpredictable organism called the Congress consumed a great deal of our time and attention as well. There were dozens of congressional committees and scores of subcommittees to be mindful of, and at any one time a goodly proportion of them, we found, were considering or preparing to consider bills of immense significance to our company—or conducting investigations of potentially similar consequence. In addition, we had to watch a large proportion of the 535 individual members of Congress—each rough, tough, and independent; each reporting only to his Maker and his constituency (and not necessarily in that order); each quite capable of a sudden, unexpected assault on the company for good reason, bad reason, or no reason at all.

As must be obvious, there was so much activity to be overseen that not all of it could be kept under constant scrutiny. Our priorities were set by the firm's management, according to the relative importance of particular matters to the company as a whole.

Where the corporation's interests were critically affected, we did more than report; we acted. Our efforts typically involved out-and-out lobbying of members of Congress and their staff members or jawboning senior officials of the executive branch. Oftentimes, we would conduct our advocacy jointly with other companies, either on an ad hoc basis or through a trade association. We were frequently buttressed by the personal participation of company leaders and experts, flying in from Cincinnati or elsewhere when the going got too rough.

The importance of coordination in attempting to formulate a viable policy on governmental matters cannot be overstated. One aspect of this is coordination of activities within a firm. A Washington office must be able to work freely, unhampered by intermediate layers or channels, with its company's top officers, its technical experts, its advertising and press relations people, and its field personnel to achieve maximum impact. If key people within the corporation are not working together toward an agreed-upon objective—or, worse yet, if they are pulling in different directions—the prospects for success can be considerably diminished.

There is another type of coordination, noted above, that is also vital—coordination among companies with similar interests in an issue. It usually takes a good deal of cajolery—and sometimes requires some top-level discipline—to create a united front out of anarchy, but the time and angst involved are well worth investing. The hard truth is that when business really tries, when it is fully unified and raring to go, it never loses a big battle in Washington.

What follows is a list of some of the characteristics that are in my judgment needed to be a good—that is to say, an effective—corporate representative in Washington. The list could be expanded, but I doubt that it could be contracted; these are qualities that I think are just plain crucial.

1. INTEGRITY

The coin of lobbying, as of politics, is trust. One's word is one's bond. Habitual truth-telling and square dealing are of paramount importance in this profession. If a corporate representative lies, misrepresents, or even lets a misapprehension stand uncorrected—or if he cuts his corners too slyly—he is very quickly dead and gone, never to be resurrected or even mourned.

2. A WILLINGNESS TO WORK HARD

Representation of any major company, done right and well, is invariably a grinding, around-the-clock task. It may look simple and easy to people on the outside, but those doing it know that it is a tough, devouring job that leaves precious little time for goofing off.

3. ADAPTABILITY TO CHANGE

The environment in which corporate representatives operate is agonizingly mutable. The formal and informal rules of the game undergo frequent and sometimes subtle modifications; problems and issues are in constant flux; and public perceptions and attitudes flutter about wildly. And, lest we forget, key participants in the policy process turn over with alarming celerity. No sooner does a ranking official profess to see merit in a company's position than that official resigns, dies, gets transferred or fired, or is beaten in an election. The whole painstaking process of education and persuasion then has to be started from scratch with the official's successor. A corporate representative who cannot roll with such unpredictabilities will soon start shoveling smoke, become futile, and vanish from sight and mind.

4. HUMILITY AND PERSPECTIVE

A Washington representative needs to recognize and accept the fact that whatever it is that he represents is much more important to the political animals in town than his own personality and atmospherics. A good politician looks right through a corporate representative to the power package behind the beseecher; he wants to know, and is busy calculating as the representative makes his pitch, how the representative's company and its employees might help or hurt him in his never-ending fight for political survival. If a company can neither help nor hurt, its representative's persuasive powers would have to be as irresistible as Jean Harlow's once were for him to prosper.

5. AN UNDERSTANDING OF THE PROCESSES OF GOVERNMENT

A corporate representative needs to have a clear fix on how the government actually works—how the pieces fit together, how things get done. The best way—though not the only way—to learn the finer points of the mechanics is to work inside the apparatus for a while. The real tricks of the government trade are not written down; they have to be absorbed through experience. Many an amateur in this business has committed harikarl without even being aware of it, by violating an unwritten rule of conduct or behavior.

The issues that a corporate representative must deal with are often highly technical; minute changes in legislative language or in numbers can be crucial; and nuances can be telling. It is important that a corporate representative be able to comprehend, communicate, and manipulate the seemingly small matters that can oftentimes have very substantial effects on corporate competitiveness and profitability—and that he not be hesitant to solicit expert help from his company or elsewhere when that becomes essential.

A FEW FINAL WORDS

Corporate representation is sometimes dangerous, often frustrating, and always time-consuming and difficult. It calls for an unceasing effort to educate and Motivate current and potential allies—and to discourage and befuddle foes. It requires the coordination of personal visits, telephone calls, and letters from top management; the flexing of political muscle in the home districts of particularly recalcitrant members of Congress; the fine-tuning of press relations and advertising; and, throughout, a dogged determination to prevail. That may sound tedious and vexing and grim. But for the right person, corporate representation can also be fascinating, challenging, immensely satisfying, and—on balance, most of the time—fun.

A Royal Heritage

1 Rex Harlow. *Oklahoma Leaders.*
(Oklahoma City: Harlow Publishing
Company, 1928).
2 *The Daily Oklahoman* (Oklahoma
City, Oklahoma), January 5, 1936.
3 *The Chronicles of Oklahoma,* Volume 40, No. 3, p. 342.
4 Dott Carrier Baker wrote an interesting biographical sketch of Harlow
in a Garfield County history. Her story was based on personal interviews
with students of Northwestern Academy and the wife of Victor E. Harlow,
Jr.
5 Rex Harlow. *Oklahoma Leaders.* p.
221
6 Interview, Jonathan Clair Harlow,
August 24, 1970, Oral History Collection, Oklahoma Historical Society,
Oklahoma City, Oklahoma.
7 *The Daily Oklahoman,* January 20,
1968.
8 *Ibid.,* November 8, 1969.

On the Job Training

1 Lynch, Kevin. *Bryce Harlow* (Washington, D.C.: The Fund for American
Studies, 1998).
2 *The Washingtonian,* April, 1985,
p.168-170.
3 Harlow speech to a Naval Reserve
unit, April 21, 1965. Bryce Harlow
File, Dwight D. Eisenhower Library,
Abilene, Kansas, hereinafter referred
to as Eisenhower Library.
4 *Ibid.*
5 Lynch, *Bryce Harlow.*
6 Harlow speech, April 21, 1965.

Eisenhower Library.
7 *Ibid.*
8 *Ibid.*
9 *Ibid.*
10 *Ibid.*
11 James M. Smallwood. *Urban
Builder, the Life and Times of Stanley
Draper.* (Norman: University of Oklahoma Press, 1977.), p. 41.
12 Roy P. Stewart. *Born Grown* (Oklahoma City: Fidelity Bank, 1974.),
p. 213.
13 *Current Biography.* 1947, p. 429.
14 Harlow speech, April 21, 1965.
Eisenhower Library.
15 *Ibid..*
16 Interview, Bryce N. Harlow, February 27, 1967, Columbia University
Oral History Collection, New York,
New York, hereinafter referred to as
Columbia interview.
17 *Ibid.*
18 *Ibid.*
19 *New York Times* (New York, New
York), December 16, 1968.

Back to Washington

1 *Current Biography,* 1942, p. 856.
2 Columbia interview.
3 *The Washingtonian,* April, 1965, p.
180.
4 Colombia interview.
5 Robert A. Caro. *The Years of Lyndon
Johnson* (New York: Knopf, 1982), p.
341.
6 *Ibid.*
7 Harlow speech, April 21, 1965.
Eisenhower Library.
8 *Ibid.*
9 *Ibid.*
10 Letter from William H. Darden to
authors, May 19, 1998. Archives,

Bryce Harlow Collection, Oklahoma
Heritage Association, Oklahoma City,
Oklahoma. Hereinafter cited as BHC.
11 *Ibid.*
12 Interview, Edward McCabe, May
6, 1998. BHC.
13 *Ibid.*
14 Interview, Trudy Harlow Dervan,
November 5, 1998. BHC.

The Call of the White House

1 Dwight D. Eisenhower. *Mandate
for Change.* (Garden City, New York:
Doubleday and Company, 1963), p.
19.
2 *Ibid.*, p. 87.
3 *Current Biography* 1951, p. 3.
4 Eisenhower, *Mandate for Change,* p.
116.
5 Columbia interview.
6 *Ibid.*

A Different World

1 Columbia interview.
2 *The Washingtonian,* April, 1985, p.
170.
3 Interview, Bryce Larimore "Larry"
Harlow, March 12, 1998. BHC.
4 *Ibid.*
5 *Current Biography,* 1969, p. 215.
6 Columbia interview.
7 *Ibid.*
8 *Ibid.*
9 Dwight D. Eisenhower, *Mandate
for Change,* p. 493.
10 Letter, Edward McCabe to authors, January 1, 1999. BHC.
11 Harlow speech, April 21, 1965.
Eisenhower Library.
12 Letter from Allan Cromley to authors, January 21, 1999. BHC.

13 *Ibid..*
14 Eisenhower Library.
15 *Ibid.*
16 *Ibid.*
17 *Ibid.*
18 *Ibid.*

Anatomy of a State of the Union
Address

1 Columbia interview.
2 *Ibid.*
3 *Ibid.*
4 *Ibid.*
5 Henry Cabot Lodge, Jr. to Harlow,
December 18, 1953. Eisenhower Library.
6 Harlow to General Persons, December 28, 1953. Eisenhower Library.
7 Harlow to Cabinet officers, December 31, 1953. Eisenhower Library.
8 Eisenhower Library.
9 *Ibid.*
10 Eisenhower, *Mandate for Change,*
p. 287.
11 Columbia interview.

Chief Speechwriter

1 Martin Anderson, *Revolution, The
Reagan Legacy* (Stanford: Hoover Institution Press, 1970), p. 254
2 *Ibid.*
3 *Ibid.*, p. 255.
4 Interview, Melvin Laird, May 15,
1998. BHC.
5 Lynch, *Bryce Harlow,* p. 16.
6 William Bragg Ewald, Jr., *Eisenhower the President: Crucial Days, 1951-
1960.* (Englewood Cliffs, New Jersey:
Prentice-Hall Inc., 1981), p. 145.
7 *Ibid.*
8 *Ibid.*, p. 148.

9 *Ibid.*, p. 149.
10 *Ibid.*, p. 150.
11 *Ibid.*
12 *Ibid.*
13 *Ibid.*, p. 151.
14 Interview, Edward McCabe.
15 Ewald, *Eisenhower the President,* p. 153.
16 Lynch, *Bryce Harlow,* p. 18.
17 Milt Hill to Harlow, April, 1954. Eisenhower Library.
18 *Ibid.*
19 *Current Biography,* 1946, p. 173.
20 Harlow file, Eisenhower Library.

McCarthyism and Beyond

1 Eisenhower, *Mandate for Change,* p. 321.
2 *Ibid.*
3 Ewald, *Eisenhower the President,* p. 124.
4 *Ibid.*, p. 125.
5 Harlow file, Eisenhower Library.
6 *Ibid.*
7 Harlow to Josephy McCarthy, September 2, 1955. Eisenhower Library.
8 Earle D. Chesney to Harlow. Eisenhower Library.
9 John Eisenhower to Harlow, August 10, 1954. Eisenhower Library.
10 *Ibid.*
11 John Foster Dulles to Harlow, August 4, 1954. Eisenhower Library.
12 *Ibid.*
13 Harlow file, Eisenhower Library.
14 Eisenhower, *Mandate for Change,* pp. 375-378.
15 Harlow to Lamar Alexander, April 16, 1985. BHC.
16 *Ibid.*
17 *Ibid.*
18 *Ibid.*
19 *Ibid.*

The Power Game

1 Columbia interview.
2 *Washington Post* (Washington, D.C.), June 9, 1981.
3 *Ibid.*
4 Hedrick Smith. *The Power Game* (New York: Ballantine Books, 1989), p. xvi.
5 *Ibid.*, p. 10.
6 Ewald, *Eisenhower as President,* p. 151.
7 *Ibid.*, p. 152.
8 *Ibid.*, p. 154.
9 Columbia interview.
10 Ewald, *Eisenhower as President,* p. 154.
11 *Ibid.*, p. 156.
12 *Ibid.*
13 *Ibid.*, p. 158.
14 *Ibid.*, p. 159.
15 Interview, Clyde A. Wheeler, Jr., December 12, 1998. BHC.
16 *Ibid.*
17 Edward McCabe to authors, January 1, 1999. BHC.
18 *Ibid.*

Family Matters

1 *The Daily Oklahoman,* October 18, 1959.
2 Interview, Trudy Durvan, November 5, 1998, BHC.
3 *Ibid.*
4 *The Daily Oklahoman,* November 6, 1982.
5 Interview, Margery Gindling "Peggy" Harlow, December 14, 1998. BHC.
6 *Ibid.*
7 *Ibid.*
8 *Ibid.*
9 *Ibid.*

10 Interview, Trudy Durvan.
11 *Ibid.*
12 *Ibid.*
13 *Ibid.*
14 Interview, Peggy Harlow.
15 Interview, Larry Harlow.
16 *Ibid.*
17 *Ibid.*
18 *Ibid.*
19 *Ibid.*
20 Bryce Harlow to Larry Harlow, April 24, 1973. BHC.
21 Interview, Larry Harlow.
22 *Ibid.*

The 1956 Campaign

1 Sherman Adams. *Firsthand Report, The Story of the Eisenhower Administration.* (New York: Harper and Brothers, 1961) p. 278.
2 *Ibid.,* pp. 280-281.
3 Tom Wicker, *One of Us* (New York: Random House, 1991), p. 196.
4 *U.S. News and World Report,* October 5, 1956, p. 84.
5 Interview, Sally Studebaker Harlow, June 19, 1998. BHC.
6 *Ibid.*
7 *Ibid.*
8 *Ibid.*
9 Harlow file, Eisenhower Library.

A Second Term

1 Columbia interview.
2 *Ibid.*
3 *Ibid.*
4 *Ibid.*
5 Interview, Howard Baker, December 19, 1997. BHC.
6 Harlow file, Eisenhower Library.
7 *Ibid.*

8 *Ibid.*
9 Eisenhower to Senator Richard B. Russell. Eisenhower Library.
10 Harlow to Eisenhower, October 1, 1957. Eisenhower Library.
11 Brownell to Harlow, September 28, 1957. Eisenhower Library.
12 Interview, Larry Harlow.
13 Interview, James D. McKevitt, May 27, 1998. BHC.
14 Eisenhower to Harlow, December 30, 1957. Eisenhower Library.

Help for Oklahoma

1 Jerrie Cobb, *Woman Into Space* (Englewood Cliffs, New Jersey: Prentice and Hall, Inc., 1963), pp. 116-117.
2 *The Daily Oklahoman,* May 26, 1957.
3 Jack Leach to Harlow, May 27, 1957. Eisenhower Library.
4 Harlow to Jack Leach, May 28, 1957. Eisenhower Library.
5 Eisenhower to Bud Wilkinson, October 13, 1957. Eisenhower Library.
6 Dwight D. Eisenhower, *Waging Peace* (Garden City, New York: Doubleday and Company, 1965), p. 225.
7 W.G. Dudgeon to Harlow, February 6, 1958. Eisenhower Library.
8 Hobart *Democrat Chief* (Hobart, Oklahoma), January 30, 1958.
9 *Ibid.*
10 James C. Milligan and L. David Norris, *Raymond Gary: The Man on the Second Floor,* (Oklahoma City: Western Heritage Books, 1988), pp. 98-101.
11 *Ibid.*
12 *Ibid.*

White House Reorganization

1 Adams, *Firsthand Report,* pp. 442-43.

2 Edward McCabe to authors, January 1, 1999. BHC.

3 Interview, Clyde A. Wheeler, Jr.

4 *Ibid.*

5 John S. D. Eisenhower, *Strictly Personal* (Garden City, New York: Doubleday and Company, Inc., 1974), pp. 223-26.

6 *Ibid.,* p. 225.

7 *Ibid.,* p. 228.

8 Harlow file. Eisenhower Library.

9 Eisenhower to Harlow, April 18, 1958. Eisenhower Library.

10 Andrew J. Goodpaster to authors, May 21, 1998. Eisenhower Library.

11 *The Daily Oklahoman,* April 13, 1958.

12 Harlow to Eisenhower, May 5, 1958. Eisenhower Library.

13 *Ibid.*

14 Harlow to Eisenhower, April 10, 1958. Eisenhower Library.

15 Goodpaster to authors, May 21, 1998. BHC.

16 Interview, Clyde A. Wheeler, Jr.

17 Interview, Henry Bellmon, December 14, 1998, BHC.

18 Edward McCabe to authors, January 1, 1999. BHC.

19 *Ibid.*

20 Interview, David L. Boren, December 16, 1998, BHC.

21 *Ibid.*

22 *Ibid.*

Procter & Gamble

1 Oscar Schisgall, *Eyes on Tomorrow, The Evolution of Procter & Gamble* (New York: Doubleday and Company, 1981), an excellent history of Procter & Gamble, p. 119.

2 1998-99 Procter & Gamble fact sheet. BHC.

3 *Ibid.,* pp. 123-125.

4 *Ibid.,* p. 190.

5 *Ibid.,* p. 202.

6 Harlow speech at a Procter & Gamble dinner, December 7, 1977. BHC.

7 Interview, David J. Elliott, June 18, 1998. BHC.

8 *Ibid.*

9 Letter from Emmett W. Hines, Jr. to authors, January 1, 1999. BHC.

10 Harlow speech, April 21, 1965. Eisenhower Library.

11 Harlow speech, December 7, 1977. BHC.

12 "Corporate Representation," an essay on lobbying written by Harlow. BHC.

13 Harlow speech, December 7, 1977. BHC.

14 Interview, David L. Boren.

15 *Ibid.*

16 Interview, Jane Fawcett-Hoover, June 4, 1998, BHC.

17 Schisgall, *Eyes on Tomorrow,* p. 259.

18 *American League of Lobbyists News,* March, 1987, p. 3.

19 Business-Government Relations Council brochure. BHC.

20 Emmett W. Hines, Jr., to authors, January 1, 1999. BHC.

21 Bryce Harlow to Emmett W. Hines, Jr.. BHC.

Ike's Man in Washington

1 Eisenhower, *Waging Peace,* pp. 652-653.

2 Harlow to Eisenhower, February 25, 1961. Eisenhower Library.

3 *Ibid.*

4 *Ibid.*

5 Eisenhower to Harlow, February 23, 1961. Eisenhower Library.

6 Harlow to Eisenhower, March 1, 1961. Eisenhower Library.

7 Eisenhower to Harlow, February 23, 1961. Eisenhower Library.

8 Eisenhower to Harlow, March 2, 1961. Eisenhower Library.

9 *Ibid.*

10 Interview, Clyde A. Wheeler, Jr.

11 Eisenhower to Harlow, March 21, 1961. Eisenhower Library.

12 Harlow to Eisenhower, September 5, 1961. Eisenhower Library.

13 *Oklahoma Journal* (Midwest City, Oklahoma), November 17, 1968.

14 Harlow to Eisenhower, February 20, 1961. Eisenhower Library.

15 Harlow to Eisenhower, March 15, 1961. Eisenhower Library.

16 Harlow to Ann Whitman, September 24, 1962. Eisenhower Library.

17 Harlow to Eisenhower, August 23, 1962. Eisenhower Library.

18 Raymond K. Price, Jr. *With Nixon* (New York: Viking Press, 1977), p. 52

19 Harlow to Eisenhower, March 3, 1966. Eisenhower Library.

The Nixon Connection

1 Wicker, *One of Us,* p. 51.

2 Richard Nixon, *In The Arena* (New York: Simon and Schuster, 1990), 282.

3 *Ibid.*, pp. 247-48.

4 Richard Nixon, *The Memoirs of Richard Nixon* (New York: Grosset and Dunlap, 1978) p. 307, here-inafter referred to as Nixon Memoirs.

5 *Ibid.*

6 *Ibid.*

7 Interview, Howard Baker, December 19, 1997, BHC.

8 Allan Cromley to authors, January 21, 1999. BHC.

9 William Safire, *Before The Fall* (Garden City, New York: Doubleday and Company, Inc., 1975), pp. 80-81.

10 Harlow interview by James Reichley, November 3, 1977, Gerald R. Ford Library.

11 *Ibid.*

12 *Ibid.*

13 Nixon Memoirs, p. 326.

14 *Ibid.*

15 *Ibid.*, p. 327.

16 *Ibid.*, p. 333.

Nixon's Inner Circle

1 *New York Times,* November 13, 1968.

2 *Ibid.*

3 *The Evening Star* (Washington, D.C.), November 13, 1968.

4 Interview, Peggy Harlow.

5 Robert Bennett to authors, February 5, 1999, BHC.

6 *Ibid.*

7 Interview, Peggy Harlow.

8 Andrew J. Goodpaster to authors, May 21, 1998. BHC.

9 Wicker, *One of Us,* p. 399.

10 *Ibid.*

11 *Washington Star,* November 16, 1968.

12 *Ibid.*

13 *Oklahoma Journal,* November 17, 1968.

14 *Chicago Tribune* (Chicago, Illi-

nois), February 24, 1969.
15 Wicker, *One of Us,* p. 399.
16 Safire, *Before the Fall,* p. 113.
17 The *New York Times Magazine*
(New York, New York), August 3,
1969.
18 *Ibid.*
19 Safire, *Before the Fall,* p. 114.
20 *Ibid.*, p. 115.
21 Interview, Pat Buchanan, January
23, 1999, BHC.
22 *Ibid.*
23 W. DeVier Pierson to authors, July
27, 1998. BHC.
24 *Ibid.*
25 Wicker, *One of Us,* p. 403.
26 The *New York Times Magazine,*
August 3, 1969.
27 *Ibid.*
28 *Ibid.*
29 *Oklahoma Journal,* March 16,
1970.
30 Interview, Pat Buchanan.
31 *The Washingtonian,* April, 1985.
32 *Ibid.*
33 *Ibid.*
34 *Ibid.*
35 *Ibid.*
36 Interview, Lamar Alexander, April
30, 1998, BHC.
37 Lyn Nofziger to authors, October
15, 1998. Some of Nofziger's comments are from an unpublished man-
uscript written about his service in
the Nixon White House and provided
to the authors. BHC.
38 *The Washington Post* (Washinton,
D.C.), December 6, 1971.
39 Interview, Charles W. Colson,
February 3, 1998, BHC.
40 *Ibid.*
41 *Ibid.*
42 Dan Rather and Gary Paul Gates,

The Palace Guard (New York: Harper
and Row, 1974), p. 213.
43 *Ibid.*
44 *Ibid.*
45 *Ibid.*
46 Lyn Nofziger to authors, October
15, 1998, BHC.
47 Interview, Lamar Alexander.
48 James Reichley interview with
Harlow, November 3, 1977, Gerald
R. Ford Library.
49 *Ibid.*
50 Interview, George P. Shultz, January 22, 1998, BHC.
51 *Ibid.*
52 *Ibid.*

Congressional Battles

1 Interview, Lamar Alexander.
2 Wicker, *One of Us,* p. 404.
3 W. DeVier Pierson to the authors,
July 27, 1998, BHC.
4 Wicker, *One of Us,* p. 405.
5 *Congressional Record,* November 20,
1979, S17149.
6 Emmett W. Hines, Jr., to authors,
January 1, 1999, BHC.
7 Robert Bennett to authors, January
30, 1999, BHC.
8 *Ibid.*
9 Nixon Memoirs, p. 416.
10 *Ibid.*, p. 418.
11 Stephen Ambrose, *The Triumph of
a Politican* (New York: Simon and
Schuster, 1989), p. 290.
12 *Ibid.*
13 Interview, Charles W. Colson.
14 *Ibid.*
15 Nixon Memoirs, p. 418.
16 Jonathan C. Rose to authors, February 10, 1999, BHC.
17 *Ibid.*

18 *Ibid.*

19 Ambrose, *The Triumph of a Politician,* p. 292.

20 *Ibid.*

21 *Ibid.*

22 *Newsweek,* July 14, 1969.

23 *Ibid.*

24 *Ibid.*

25 *Ibid.*

26 Rowland Evans, Jr., and Robert D. Novak, *Nixon in the White House: The Frustration of Power* (New York, Random House, 1971), p. 105.

27 *Ibid.*

28 *Ibid.*

29 *Ibid.,* p. 113.

30 *Ibid.,* p. 109.

31 *Ibid.,* pp. 109-110.

32 Lyn Nofziger to authors, June 15, 1999, BHC.

33 Chief Justice William H. Rehnquist to authors, January 6, 1999, BHC.

34 John Ehrlichman, *Witness to Power* (New York: Simon and Schuster, 1982), p. 118.

35 *Ibid.,* p. 126.

36 *Ibid..*

37 Interview, Peggy Harlow.

38 Jeb Stuart Magruder, *An American Life* (New York: Atheneum, 1974), pp. 111-12.

39 *Ibid.,* p. 112.

40 Wicker, *One of Us,* p. 652.

Cabinet Rank

1 *The Daily Oklahoman,* November 5, 1969.

2 White House news release, November 4, 1969. The Nixon Project, National Archives, Washington, D.C.

3 Lynch, *Bryce Harlow,* p. 23.

4 Evans and Novak, *Nixon in the White House,* p. 117.

5 Lynch, *Bryce Harlow,* p. 20.

6 Interview, Edward McCabe.

7 Interview, Pat Buchanan.

8 Interview, Lamar Alexander.

9 *Ibid.*

10 Interview, Emmett W. Hines, Jr., April 17, 1998, BHC.

11 *Ibid.*

12 *U.S. News and World Report,* August 17, 1970.

13 Interview, George Shultz.

14 Interview, James D. McKevitt.

15 *Ibid.*

16 *Ibid.*

17 *Ibid.*

18 *Newsweek,* July 23, 1970.

19 *Ibid.*

20 Ehrlichman, *Witness to Power,* p. 227.

21 *Ibid.,* p. 103.

22 *The New Republic,* April, 1981.

23 Interview, Peggy Harlow.

24 Patrick J. Buchanan to authors, December 21, 1998, BHC.

25 William Safire, *Before the Fall,* p. 317.

26 *Ibid.,* p. 318.

27 Interview, Pat Buchanan.

28 *Ibid.*

29 *Ibid.*

30 Safire, *Before the Fall,* p. 325.

31 *Ibid.*

32 Evans and Novak, *Nixon in the White House,* p. 363.

33 *Ibid.*

34 *Ibid.,* p. 364.

35 Interview, Senator Robert Dole, January 21, 1999, BHC.

36 *Ibid.*

37 *Ibid.*

38 *Ibid.*

The Road to Watergate

1 Interview, David Elliott, June 18, 1998, BHC.
2 Interview, Lamar Alexander.
3 Interview, James D. McKevitt.
4 Emmett W. Hines, Jr., to authors, January 1, 1999, BHC.
5 Don V. Cogman to authors, November 23, 1998, BHC.
6 Interview, President Gerald R. Ford, December 12, 1997, BHC.
7 Joint Report to the United States House of Representatives, House Document No. 92-337, 1972. Government Printing Office, Washington, D.C., pp. 7-11.
8 Corrine Lindy Boggs to authors, March 1, 1999, BHC.
9 Reichly interview with Harlow, Gerald R. Ford Library.
10 *Ibid.*
11 Jeb Stuart Magruder, *An American Life* (New York: Athenum Press,1974), p. 64.
12 Harlow to Robert Dole, December 19, 1972, BHC.
13 *Ibid.*
14 Henry Kissinger, *Years of Upheaval* (Boston: Little, Brown and Co., 1982) pp. 92-93.
15 Interview, Gerald R. Ford.
16 Kissinger, *Years of Upheaval*, p. 93.
17 Nixon Memoirs, p. 840.
18 *The Daily Oklahoman*, May 30, 1973.
19 Interview, George Shultz.
20 Interview, Melvin Laird.
21 *Ibid.*
22 Nixon Memoirs, p. 857.
23 *Chicago Tribune,* June 11, 1973.
24 Interview, Pat Buchanan.
25 *Ibid.*
26 Robert Bennett to authors, Feb. 22, 1999, BHC.
27 *Ibid.*

Harlow Returns to the White House

1 Interview, Donald Rumsfeld, June 8, 1998, BHC.
2 President George Bush to authors, May 26, 1998, BHC.
3 Interview, Melvin Laird.
4 Nixon Memoirs, p. 909.
5 Spiro T. Agnew, *Go Quietly...or else* (New York: William Morrow and Company, Inc., 1980), p. 102.
6 *Ibid.*
7 *Ibid.*
8 *Ibid.*, p. 103.
9 *Ibid.*, p. 104.
10 *Ibid.*, p. 105.
11 Barry M. Goldwater, *Goldwater* (New York: Doubleday, 1988), p. 264.
12 *Ibid.*
13 *Ibid.*, p. 265.
14 Agnew, *Go Quietly...or else,* p. 151.
15 Nixon Memoirs, p. 917.
16 Agnew, *Go Quietly...or else,* p. 101.
17 *The New Republic.* BHC.
18 Nixon Memoirs, p. 932.
19 *Ibid.*
20 Interview, Pat Buchanan.
21 Raymond K. Price, Jr., *With Nixon,* p. 95.
22 Nixon Memoirs, p. 935.
23 Barry Goldwater, *Goldwater,* p. 267.
24 *Ibid.*, p. 268.
25 *Ibid.*, p. 269.
26 *Ibid.*
27 Price, *With Nixon,* p. 95.

The Beginning of the End

1 Nixon Memoirs, p. 925.
2 Interview, Melvin Laird.
3 Nixon Memoirs, p. 926.
4 Interview, Melvin Laird.
5 *Ibid.*.
6 Nixon Memoirs, p. 959.
7 *Ibid.*
8 *Ibid.*, p. 968.
9 *The Christian Science Monitor* (Boston, Massachusetts), February 28, 1974.
10 Interview, Sally Harlow.
11 *The Washington Post,* April 13, 1974.
12 Nixon Memoirs, p. 1040.
13 *Ibid.*, p. 1042.
14 *The Washington Post,* August 6, 1974.
15 Gerald R. Ford, *A Time to Heal* (New York: Harper and Row, 1979), p. 3.
16 *Ibid.*, p. 11.
17 Stephen Ambrose, *Nixon: Ruin and Recovery* (New York: Simon and Schuster, 1991), p. 408.
18 Interview, Gerald R. Ford.
19 Bob Woodward and Carl Bernstein, *The Final Days* (New York: Touchstone, 1976), p. 400.
20 Nixon Memoirs, p. 1084.
21 *Ibid.*

Harlow, the Private Citizen

1 Ford, A Time to Heal, p. 142.
2 *Ibid.*, p.143.
3 *Ibid.*
4 Harlow to President Ford. Gerald R. Ford Library.
5 *Ibid.*

6 Interview, Gerald R. Ford.
7 Ford, *A Time to Heal,* p. 161.
8 *Ibid.*, p. 195.
9 *Ibid.*, p. 261.
10 Interview, Donald Rumsfeld.
11 Anderson, *Revolution: The Reagan Legacy,* p. 65-69.
12 *Ibid.*
13 *Ibid.*, p. 69.
14 Ford, *A Time to Heal,* pp. 440-41.
15 Kissinger speech at Oklahoma Hall of Fame banquet, November, 1977, BHC.
16 Harlow to Emmett W. Hines, Jr., November 30, 1977, BHC.

An Active Retirement

1 Comments from corporation representation video produced by Gramercy Broadcast Center, New York, "The Harlow Legacy." BHC.
2 *Ibid.*
3 *Ibid.*
4 *Ibid.*
5 *Ibid.*
6 Interview, Emmett Hines, Jr.
7 Time magazine (New York, New York), July 4, 1977.
8 Interview, Jane Fawcett-Hoover.
9 Baltimore Sun (Baltimore, Maryland), July 5, 1978.
10 Gerald R. Ford to Harlow, June 23, 1975, BHC.
11 *Ibid.*
12 *The Daily Oklahoman,* September 30, 1979.
13 *Ibid.*, January 31, 1979.
14 *Ibid.*, September 30, 1979.
15 *Ibid.*
16 Martin Anderson, *Revolution, The Reagan Legacy,* p. 124.

17 Interview, James D. McKevitt.

18 *Ibid.*

19 Interview, David J. Elliott.

20 *Ibid.*

21 *The Cincinnati Inquirer* (Cincinnati, Ohio), May 7, 1978.

22 James A. Baker, III to authors, June 3, 1998, BHC.

23 *Boston Globe* (Boston, Massachusetts), June 6, 1981.

24 Written transcript of speeches presented at the Bryce Harlow Recognition Dinner, June 3, 1981, BHC.

25 *Ibid.*

26 *Ibid.*

27 *Ibid.*

28 *Ibid.*

29 *Ibid.*

30 Harlow to Emmett Hines, Jr., June 14, 1981, BHC.

31 Harlow to Bill Whyte, June 14, 1981, BHC.

32 Bryce Harlow Foundation pamphlet. BHC.

33 Edward McCabe to authors, January 1, 1999, BHC.

11 *The Daily Oklahoman*, July 20, 1983.

12 Interview, Charles W. Colson.

13 Interview, Lamar Alexander.

14 Edward W. McCabe interview.

15 Congressional Record, March 10, 1987.

16 Edward McCabe to authors, January 1, 1999, BHC.

17 *Ibid.*

18 *Ibid.*

19 *The Daily Oklahoman*, February 19, 1987.

20 *Ibid.*, February 18, 1987.

21 *The Washington Post,* February 19, 1987.

22 *Congressional Record,* February 17, 1987.

23 *Ibid.*

24 *The Daily Oklahoman*, February 19, 1987.

25 *The Washington Post,* February 19, 1987.

26 Interview, David L. Boren.

27 Robert H. Michel to authors, December 30, 1998, BHC.

His Final Years

1 *The Daily Oklahoman*, November 29, 1981.

2 *Ibid.*, June 23, 1981.

3 *Ibid.*, November 29, 1981.

4 *Ibid.*

5 Harlow v. Fitzgerald, 457 U.S. 800, 102 S.Ct. 2727 (1982).

6 *Ibid.*, at p. 816.

7 *Ibid.*, at p. 825.

8 *The Daily Oklahoman*, February 20, 1983.

9 Interview, Sally Harlow.

10 *Ibid.*

BIBLIOGRAPHY

COLLECTIONS

Bryce Harlow Collection (BHC), Oklahoma Heritage Association, Oklahoma City, Oklahoma.
Bryce Harlow File, Dwight D. Eisenhower Library. Abilene, Kansas.
Bryce Harlow File, Gerald R. Ford Library. Ann Arbor, Michigan.
Bryce Harlow File, The Nixon Project. National Archives. Washington, D.C.
Bryce Harlow File, Richard M. Nixon Library. Yorba Linda, California.
Oral History Collection, Oklahoma Historical Society. Oklahoma City, Oklahoma.
Oklahoma Hall of Fame Archives. Oklahoma Heritage Association. Oklahoma City, Oklahoma.
Columbia University Oral History Collection, New York, New York.
George C. Marshall Foundation, Washington, D.C.

NEWSPAPERS

Baltimore Sun. Baltimore, Maryland.
Boston Globe. Boston, Massachusetts.
The Daily Oklahoman. Oklahoma City, Oklahoma.
Chicago Tribune. Chicago, Illinois.
Christian Science Monitor. Boston, Massachusetts.
The Cincinnati Inquirer. Cincinnati, Ohio.
The Oklahoma Journal. Midwest City, Oklahoma.
Oklahoma City Times. Oklahoma City, Oklahoma.
New York Times. New York, New York.
Harlow's Weekly. Oklahoma City, Oklahoma.
Hobart Democrat Chief. Hobart, Oklahoma.
Washington Post. Washington, D.C.
Washington Star. Washington, D.C.
The Evening Star. Washington, D.C.

BOOKS

Adams, Sherman. *Firsthand Report, The Story of the Eisenhower Administration*. New York: Harper and Brothers, 1961.
Agnew, Spiro T. *Go Quietly. . . or else*. New York: William Morrow and Company, Inc., 1980.
Ambrose, Stephen. *The Triumph of a Politician*. New York: Simon and Schuster, 1989.
_____. *Nixon: Ruin and Recovery*. New York: Simon and Schuster, 1991.
Anderson, Martin. *Revolution, The Reagan Legacy*. Stanford: Hoover Institution Press, 1970.
Caro, Robert A. *The Years of Lyndon Johnson*. New York: Knopf, 1982.
Cobb, Jerrie. *Woman Into Space*. Englewood Cliffs, New Jersey: Prentice and Hall Inc., 1963.
Dean, John. *Blind Ambition*. New York: Simon and Schuster, 1976.
Eisenhower, Dwight D. *Mandate for Change*. Garden City, New York: Doubleday and Company, 1963.
_____. *Waging Peace*. New York: Doubleday and Company, 1965.

Eisenhower, John S. D. *Strictly Personal.* Garden City, New York: Doubleday and Company, 1974.

Ehrlichman, John. *Witness to Power.* New York: Simon and Schuster, 1982.

Evans, Rowland, Jr. and Robert D. Novak. *Nixon in the White House: The Frustration of Power.* New York: Random House, 1971.

Ewald, William Bragg, Jr. *Eisenhower the President: Crucial Days, 1951-1960.* Englewood Cliffs, New Jersey: Prentice-Hall Inc., 1981.

Ford, Gerald R. *A Time to Heal.* New York: Harper and Row, 1979.

Goldwater, Barry M. *Goldwater.* New York: Doubleday and Company, 1988.

Harlow, Rex. *Oklahoma Leaders.* Oklahoma City: Harlow Publishing Company, 1928.

Lynch, Kevin. *Bryce Harlow.* Washington, D.C.: The Fund for American Studies, 1998.

Kissinger, Henry. *Years of Upheaval.* Boston: Little, Brown and Company, 1982.

Magruder, Jeb Stuart. *An American Life.* New York: Atheneum, 1974.

Milligan, James C. and L. David Norris. *Raymond Gary: The Man on the Second Floor.* Oklahoma City: Western Heritage Books, 1988.

Nixon, Richard. *In The Arena.* New York: Simon and Schuster, 1990.

_____. *The Memoirs of Richard Nixon.* New York: Grosset and Dunlap, 1978.

Price, Raymond K., Jr. *With Nixon.* New York: Viking Press, 1977.

Rather, Dan and Gary Paul Gates. *The Palace Guard.* New York: Harper and Row, 1974.

Safire, William. *Before the Fall.* Garden City, New York: Doubleday and Company, 1975.

Schisgall, Oscar. *Eyes on Tomorrow, The Evolution of Procter & Gamble.* New York: Doubleday and Company, 1981.

Smallwood, James M. *Urban Builder, The Life and Times of Stanley Draper.* Norman: University of Oklahoma Press, 1977.

Smith, Hedrick. *The Power Game.* New York: Ballantine Books, 1989.

Stewart, Roy P. with Pendleton Woods. *Born Grown.* Oklahoma City: Fidelity Bank, 1974.

Wicker, Tom. *One of Us.* New York: Random House, 1991.

Woodward, Bob and Carl Bernstein. *The Final Days.* New York: Touchstone, 1970.

MAGAZINES

American League of Lobbyists News. Washington, D.C.

New York Times Magazine. New York, New York.

The New Republic. Newsweek. New York, New York.

The Washingtonian. Washington, D.C.

U.S. News and World Report. New York, New York.

Interviews conducted by authors and on file in the Bryce Harlow Collection, Oklahoma Heritage Association, Oklahoma City, Oklahoma

Lamar Alexander. April 30, 1998.
Howard Baker. December 19, 1997.
David L. Boren. December 16, 1998.
Patrick Buchanan. January 23, 1999.
Charles W. Colson. February 3, 1998.
Trudy Harlow Dervan. November 5, 1998.
Robert Dole. January 21, 1999.
David J. Elliott. June 18, 1998.
Gerald R. Ford. December 12, 1997.
Bryce Larimore "Larry" Harlow. March 12, 1998.
Margery Gindling "Peggy" Harlow. December 14, 1998.
Sally Studebaker Harlow. June 19, 1998.
Emmett W. Hines, Jr. April 17, 1998.
Jane Fawcett-Hoover. June 4, 1998.
Melvin R. Laird. May 15, 1998.
Edward McCabe. May 6, 1998.
John Rhodes. June 30, 1998.
James D. McKevitt. April 14, 1998.
Donald Rumsfeld. June 8, 1998.
George P. Shultz. January 22, 1998.
Hugh Sidey. May 21, 1998.
Clyde A. Wheeler, Jr. December 12, 1998.

Documents provided to authors on file in the Bryce Harlow Collection of the Oklahoma Heritage Association, Oklahoma City, Oklahoma

William H. Darden. May 19, 1998.
Allan Cromley. January 21, 1999.
Edward McCabe. January 1, 1999.
Emmett W. Hines, Jr. January 1, 1999.
W. DeVier Pierson. July 27, 1998.
Lyn Nofziger. October 15, 1998.
Robert Bennett. January 30, 1999.
Jonathan C. Rose. February 10, 1999.
William H. Rehnquist. January 6, 1999.
Don V. Cogman. November 23, 1998.
Corinne Lindy Boggs. March 1, 1999.
James A. Baker, III. June 3, 1998.
Robert H. Michel. December 30, 1998.
Andrew J. Goodpaster. May 21, 1998.
President George Bush. May 26, 1998.
John S. D. Eisenhower. June 1, 1998.

A

D

E

F

J

K

L

M

MacArthur, Douglas 93
Machiavelli 13
Magruder, Jeb 203-204, 227
Manatos, Mike 260
Mandate for Change 55
Mansfield, Mike 107, 228, 243
Markley, Annabel 264
Markley, Rodney W., Jr., 152, 264
Marshall, George C. 13, 33-36, 45, 265
Martin, Jack 64, 82
Masters Golf Tournament 69
Mayflower Compact 117
McCabe, Edward A. 10, 43, 74, 77, 96, 118, 130, 138, 161, 208, 271, 278-279
McCaffrey, Mary Jane 57
McCann, Kevin 93, 108, 129
McCarthy, Eugene 169
McCarthy, Joseph 80-88
McClellan, John 119
McCormack, John 29, 107, 160
McElroy, Neil Hosler 132-134, 141, 143-146, 155
McGraw Hill 135
McKay, Douglas 48, 65
McKeon, Kay 147
McKevitt, James D. "Mike" 10, 121, 212, 221, 263, 265
McPhee, Henry Roemer 10
Meany, George 135
Meese, Ed 275
Meridian House Foundation 266
Merriam, Robert 130
Michel, Robert H. 10, 280, 282
Michener, Judith 10
Midwest Air Depot 33
Miller, Marilyn 10
Mills, Wilbur 178, 244
Minneapolis Tribune 159
Minnich, Arthur 107
Mississippi River 38
Mitchell, James P. 65
Mitchell, John 189, 198, 203, 213-214, 226, 245, 247
Mitchell, Martha 189

Mondale, Walter 256
Monroney, Mike 111, 193
Morgan, Gerald D. 50, 64, 87, 161
Morgens, Howard J. 143, 151
Mormons' Council of Twelve 77
Morris, J. R. 10
Morton, Rogers 208, 213, 218, 248, 250
Mosby, John Singleton 100
Mount Vernon 31
Moynihan, Daniel Patrick 180-181, 184, 197, 206-207, 211, 225-226, 280

N

Nasser, Gamel Abdel 106
National Archives 10, 214
National Association for the Advancement of Colored People (NAACP) 35
National Association of Manufacturers 222
National Federation of Independent Business 221
National Park Service 99
National Republican Congressional Campaign Committee 99
National Security Council 60, 109, 181
Naval Affairs Committee 38-39
New Republic, The 236
New York Herald Tribune 162
New York Times 21, 53, 90, 108, 170, 173-174, 179; *Magazine* 183-184
New York Yankees 112
Newsweek 198-199, 212
Nichols, Mary 76
Nixon in the White House: The Frustration of Power 199
Nixon, Pat 237
Nixon, Richard Milhous 13, 66, 70, 74-75, 91, 99, 107-108, 125, 132, 139, 145-146, 154, 157, 159, 163-173, 175-179, 181-189, 191-192, 194-205, 207-208, 210-220, 222-233, 235-236, 238-242, 244-249, 252, 260, 262-263, 266, 269, 273-

Sunray DX Oil Company—*see Sun Oil Company, Inc.*

T

Taft, Robert A. 215; Taft-Hartley Act 50; Institute of Government 266
Tennessee Valley Authority (TVA) 85, 88
Theroux, Gene 223
Thompson, Llewellyn 171
Thompson, Ralph G. 11
Thornton, Matthew 18,
Time Magazine 109
Timmons and Company 102, 208
Timmons, William E. "Bill" 186, 208, 217, 248, 254
Tinker Air Force Base 111; Tinker Field 33, 43
Tinker, Clarence 33
Tower, John 255
Toye, Gerry 152
Trohan, Walter 178
Truman, Harry 39, 44-45, 47-48, 52, 108

U

U. S. News and World Report 210, 281
Union Station 26
Unitarian Church 21-22,
United States Air Force 134, 273
United States Army 34-35, 81, 126; Air Corps 33; Reserve 32
United States Capitol Historical Society 265-266
United States Chamber of Commerce 266
United States Court of Claims 88
United States Customs 123
United States Department of Agriculture 79
United States Geological Survey 99
United States Navy 36, 39, 134, 169
United States Post Office 188
United States Public Health Service 123
United States Steel Corporation 152, 268
University Hospital 43
University of California at Los Angeles 180
University of Oklahoma 20, 22, 24-26, 30, 32, 75;124, 186, 189, 271, 281; College of Business Administration 266; College of Education 22
University of Pittsburgh 109
University of Tennessee 210
University of Texas 25

V

Van Hooser, Emma 18, 20,
Van Hooser, May—*see May Harlow*
Vandivier, Dave 127
Vietnam War 166, 170-171, 197, 199, 213, 227
Vinson, Carl 39-41, 46, 52-53, 132, 155-156, 194
Volpe, John 107, 195

W

Wall Street Journal, The 233
Wallace, DeWitt 135
Wallace, George 166, 170
Walter Reed Army Hospital 140, 167-168
War Department 13, 33-36, 42-43
Warren, Earl 202
Washington Monument 31
Washington Post 90, 224, 246
Washington Senators 112
Watergate 164, 188, 220, 224, 226-233, 236-240, 242, 244-248, 278
Watergate Hotel 224, 226
Ways and Means Committee 25, 27-28, 30, 32
Webb City College 18
Weeks, Sinclair 65
Weicker, Lowell P., Jr. 240
Weinberger, Casper 226
Welge, Bill 10
West Virginia University 22-24
West, Charles 20
Westmoreland Church 278

PERSONAL AND ~~CONFIDENTIAL~~

When
~~It was~~ eleven months ago, ~~when~~ last ~~I had the high honor to~~

~~appear before the assembled Houses of~~ the Congress ~~to present my~~ *my* views

on the State of the Union, ~~Then,~~ the conduct of government had just

been transferred, for the first time in two decades, from one of our

great political parties to the other. Thus my first message was, of

necessity, largely an expression of basic viewpoints and broad objectives

rather than the exposition of a detailed, comprehensive program.

Today, ~~therefore, I am especially happy that as I again come~~

~~before the Congress,~~ I am able ~~not only~~ to present a message relating

substantial progress ~~in the preceding twelve months but,~~ *Of* much greater

I bring
importance, a message of ~~good cheer~~ of justifiable hope -- of confidence
for
~~for~~ the year that lies ahead.

There has been heartening improvement in almost every area of

domestic and international concern during the past year. Bloodshed has

stopped in Korea. There, one aggression has been thwarted and others

made less likely. The forces of freedom in Korea, in Southeast Asia,

in Europe -- everywhere -- today are more vital, stronger, more assured.

Among scores of free nations, among hundreds of millions of troubled

peoples, the conviction is growing that mankind will not consume